ALSO BY JO-ELLAN DIMITRIUS

Guide to Jury Selection and Trial Dynamics

BY JO-ELLAN DIMITRIUS AND MARK MAZZARELLA

Reading People:
How to Understand People and Predict
Their Behavior: Anytime, Anyplace

Put Your Best Foot Forward

*Make a Great Impression
by Taking Control of How Others See You*

Jo-Ellan Dimitrius
and Mark Mazzarella

SCRIBNER
New York   London   Sydney   Singapore

SCRIBNER
1230 Avenue of the Americas
New York, NY 10020

SCRIBNER and design are trademarks of Macmillan Library Reference USA,
Inc., used under license by Simon & Schuster, the publisher of this work.

Set in Bembo

DESIGNED BY ERICH HOBBING

Manufactured in the United States of America

1   3   5   7   9   10   8   6   4   2

Library of Congress Cataloging-in-Publication Data
Dimitrius, Jo-Ellan.
Put your best foot foward : make a great impression by taking
control of how others see you / Jo-Ellan Dimitrius and Mark Mazzarella.
p. cm.
1. Impression formation (Psychology). 2. Social perception. I. Mazzarella, Mark. II. Title.
BF323.S63 D56 2000
302'.12—dc21   99-059604

ISBN 0-684-86406-1

*To those who have found their Compass,
and inspire us to search for ours.*

Acknowledgments

It is appropriate that we should begin this book with an acknowledgment of the contributions of those without whom it would not exist.

We want to start by thanking those who contributed the benefit of their years of study, experience and expertise: Paul Strand, Ph.D., Dean of Social Sciences at San Diego State University, who helped us design and administer many of our research surveys and questionnaires; Michael Herbelin, who applied his computer savvy to compile, sort and tabulate the results of those surveys and questionnaires; social psychologist Andrea Mosmann, Ph.D., and neuropsychologist Gilbert Calvillo, Ph.D., whose review of the manuscript was essential to assure its technical accuracy; and the many scholars, researchers and authors whose work has shed light on the mysteries of human behavior and inspired us in our efforts to understand the process of impression formation.

We also want to thank Susan Moldow, publisher of Scribner, for believing in us and in this project, and the many others at Scribner and Simon & Schuster whose talents and professionalism are remarkable: our editor, Jake Morrissey, who must have worn out a box of red pencils as he helped us focus and organize our thoughts and convey them more clearly; John Fontana and the members of the Scribner art department, who created the cover and graphics for the book; our copy editor, Charles Naylor, whose meticulous attention to detail has not gone unnoticed, or unappreciated; and Jennifer Swihart and Pat Eisemann of Scribner's publicity department.

We also are indebted to Michael Rudell, who believed enough in us and this book to include us among the authors he represents as agent and lawyer; and Michael Rondeau, a wonderful friend and colleague, whose clear perspective, writing skills and editorial talents contributed heavily to the structure of the book.

More than ten thousand pages of various drafts of this manuscript had to be typed and retyped, often under looming deadlines, before we settled upon the final version. We want to thank Melinda Lewis and Debórah Venuto for their assistance in converting our words to the written page. Our special gratitude goes out to Jamie Webb, who often burned the midnight oil deciphering handwritten edits and reorganizing text to keep the book on schedule, and to her husband, Harry DuMond, without whose good natured support neither Jamie, nor we, could have completed our tasks.

Put Your Best Foot Forward also could not have been written without the support of everyone at Mazzarella, Dunwoody & Caldarelli, and Dimitrius & Associates who picked up the slack at our offices as we devoted our time and energy to our research and writing. Sheena Odorico and Sue Williamson, who kept our schedules and our lives sane, deserve special recognition.

Mark is particularly grateful to Cheryl Mazzarella, whose generous contribution of time, insight and generous spirit throughout this process has been a blessing. Mark would also like to recognize three men who passed through his life, and he through theirs, more than twenty-five years ago. Don Eulert, Ph.D., Ken Richardson, Ph.D., and William Deseager, Ph.D., kindled in Mark a passion for literature, philosophy and religious studies that has not only survived, but flourished, through the years. Their talents as teachers, writers, poets and philosophers lit a flame that will burn always.

Jo-Ellan extends a special gratitude to the thousands of men and women, who over the course of almost two decades, gave of their time, energy and thought to participate in juries, focus groups, surveys and questionnaires. Each has laid an essential brick in the foundation upon which this book is built.

Most important, we want to thank our families who endured our dual roles as authors and speakers, and as legal and consulting professionals. Without their love, support, understanding and encouragement this book would not exist.

Contents

1. An Introduction to Impression Management   13

2. Impression Formation   19

3. The Compass Qualities   42

4. First and Lasting Impressions   76

5. Magic Pills   99

6. Toxic Traits   126

7. Physical Appearance   146

8. Body Language   180

9. Voice   203

10. Communication Style   219

11. Content of Communication   240

12. Actions   261

13. The Environment   289

14. Success   302

Afterword: Changing from the Outside-In   305

Put Your Best Foot Forward

CHAPTER 1

An Introduction
to Impression Management

Every day, every person you meet sizes you up within the first few seconds. They form impressions about who you are, what you think and how you are likely to act. And once those impressions are set in their minds, they are difficult to change.

The impressions others form of you are seldom based on rational thought or independent investigation. They are the product of hundreds of associations we all make between outwardly obvious characteristics and the invisible inner qualities we believe they reflect. These stereotypes and prejudices, some positive and some negative, are an intellectual and emotional shorthand. They arise from our past experiences, societal biases promoted or perpetuated in the media and the literature we read, and from the instinctive and emotional hardwiring within our brains.

When others form impressions of you, they follow the same process they use to reach conclusions about a package of taco seasoning on the shelf of their local market. They assume, without ever reading the list of actual ingredients, that it contains chili and other spices and preservatives. If it is a respected name brand, they take for granted that it is higher in both quality and price than the generic brand. If the package is attractive and inviting, they conclude the product inside must share those qualities. They make these assumptions because from past experience they believe such assumptions are warranted, and they don't have the time, energy or inclination to test their validity each time they reach for an item on the shelf.

Many of the stereotypical associations we make about others, like those we make about products on a supermarket shelf, are conscious, some are not. In seminars around the country we have challenged those who are reluctant to admit they judge others based on preexisting prejudices and stereotypes to answer a few simple questions about hypothetical people of whom they know nothing except one observable characteristic.

Who is more trustworthy: the salesman who fails to maintain good eye contact, or the one who does?

Who is more caring: the bank teller who smiles and says "Hello," or the one who doesn't bother to look up from her computer screen?

Who is more humble: the man who wears a ten-thousand-dollar gold Rolex, or the one who sports a Timex?

Who is more capable: the dentist who practices in a well-appointed office in a fancy medical office building, or the one with worn-out chairs in the reception area of his office in the corner of a neighborhood mall?

We're confident your answers will be the same as the hundreds of other people to whom we have posed these questions. And like them, you probably could articulate why you drew the conclusions you did. But many associations that are equally prevalent are triggered by subconscious or emotional reactions and are not so easily explained. Yet research has proven that they are just as influential to the formation of impressions.

Excellent examples of predominantly subconscious emotional responses are found in the extensive research that has been conducted on how colors affect everything from our moods, to the stimulation of our physical senses, to our impression of others. Children's hospital wards are often painted in pastel colors because they soothe patients' anxiety. Fire engines are painted bright red or yellow since our brains recognize and react more quickly to those colors. In research studies, individuals dressed in dark colors are consistently judged to be more competent, but less friendly, than those dressed in lighter colors or autumn hues.

The portion of our brain that processes cognitions, or rational thoughts—the cerebral cortex—accounts for only 10 percent of our brain's function. The balance of activity takes place in the brain stem, which is the region of the brain that controls such basic life functions as circulation, breathing and reflexes; the limbic system, which processes emotion and the hippocampus, which is responsible for memory function. Many of our strongest and most lasting impressions arise from within the limbic system, or "emotional brain." The genesis of these associations often cannot be explained. But through interviews, surveys and clinical research, what those associations are and what traits trigger them have been identified. With that knowledge you can effectively manage the impressions others form of you.

Put Your Best Foot Forward will teach you how people judge you, and why. It is based on information gleaned from more than ten thousand interviews, our review of the scientific and popular literature about how impressions are formed, and our analysis of thousands of questionnaire and survey responses. You will learn which qualities others find most important, and how each of the seven ways you paint a picture of your personality and values—appearance, body language, voice, communication style, the content of your speech, your actions and environment—can be honed to project the best possible impression of who you are and how you are likely to think and act. We will explain how you can accentuate your positive traits and eliminate (or effectively compensate for) those characteristics that create negative impressions. You will be given specific and detailed directions for what we call "Impression Management."

Like all recipes, the key to a great impression lies in its ingredients. There are four qualities at the foundation of every great impression:

- Trustworthiness
- Caring
- Humility
- Capability

We call these the "Compass Qualities," because they are like the four points of a compass that guide others to the conclusion that you can and will satisfy their most fundamental cravings: the desire to feel important and worthwhile, and to have their physical, emotional and professional needs fulfilled. The secret to forging positive impressions is to convey your trustworthiness, caring, humility and capability through a combination of traits and characteristics from which others will infer that you can and will fulfill these needs.

The techniques for successful Impression Management (which you will learn as you read on) are as simple in theory as they are in application. They are based on a few basic notions:

- Some outward traits enhance all four Compass Qualities.
- Some outward traits are toxic to all four Compass Qualities.
- Most traits are toxic to some Compass Qualities and enhance others— for example, a firm, powerful and confident voice enhances the impression of trustworthiness and capability, but diminishes the impression of caring and humility.
- For all but a few incurably toxic traits, there are other traits that function as antidotes.

Effective Impression Management requires only that you:

- Learn which traits have positive or negative effects on which Compass Qualities;
- Identify which traits you have;

- Accentuate the traits that enhance all four Compass Qualities;
- Eliminate those traits that are toxic to all four Compass Qualities; and
- Retain those traits that have both positive and negative elements, but "cure" their negative side effects with positive compensating traits.

If this doesn't strike you as simple, we assure you it is. A brief illustration will put the process into clear perspective.

One of our friends, John, is a huge man with a booming voice and hands like paddleball rackets.* He is extremely intelligent, assertive, blunt, energetic and confident. Though relaxed and outgoing, John is frequently impatient, and often confrontational. John recently formed a publishing company and hired several employees. Since John knows that we write and lecture about Impression Management, he asked us to help him create an effective "Impression Management Plan" to use with his employees. An abbreviated summary of our advice to John will serve to demonstrate the Impression Management technique:

- John's outgoing and energetic nature are pure positives. They enhance others' perceptions of all four Compass Qualities, and have no drawbacks. John should maintain them, even expand on them, as long as he doesn't go off the deep end.
- Obvious displays of impatience and confrontation are toxic, and have no redeeming value in any but the most exceptional circumstances. John should resolve to eliminate them, except as a last resort.
- John's size, powerful voice, assertiveness, direct communication style, and obvious confidence are all double-edged swords. They enhance others' impression of his trustworthiness and capability, but they are likely to create the impression that he is neither caring nor humble. They can make him appear intimidating, overpowering, unfriendly and arrogant. Because he wants his employees to know he is caring and humble, as well as trustworthy and competent, John should apply other traits as antidotes to remove the toxic side effects of these double-edged swords.

  Among many other ways to blunt his sharp edges, John can: lower his voice a bit; smile more; engage in warmer, more frequent eye contact; make a point to say "Good morning" and ask his employees about their lives and passions; wear warmer and more approachable colors and clothing styles; occasionally touch his employees' arms or hands in

---

*This anecdote is factual. But to protect others' privacy and confidentiality, we have changed the names or partially fictionalized many of the stories we tell throughout this book. All illustrations, however, are based on actual occurrences.

a nonsexual way; go to their offices when he wants to speak with them, rather than call them into his; remember their birthdays and their children's names and interests; listen intently as they talk; praise them more; and even bring in doughnuts on Friday mornings.

None of these suggestions will diminish his employees' positive impression of John's trustworthiness or capability. But collectively they will soften his otherwise intimidating persona in ways that will let his employees know he is also caring and humble.

Impression Management can be applied in this way by anyone in any relationship. It is equally effective in personal and professional interactions, regardless of gender, race, ethnicity, occupation, social or economic status, sexual preference, physical appearance or personality. It doesn't require that you compromise your integrity, abandon your individuality, or discard the traits you cherish most. It provides a process by which you can eliminate those traits you dislike anyway and enhance those that clearly improve your image. Impression Management leads to positive and lasting change because it brings out the best in each of us, not because it makes us all the same. It is one hundred percent effective because it empowers you to put *your* best foot forward.

HOW TO GET THE MOST FROM THIS BOOK

You will benefit most from this book if you create your personalized Impression Management Plan as you read it. Keep a note pad and pen handy. Draw two vertical lines from top to bottom of the pages of your notepad to divide them into three equal parts. Write "Dos" on the top of the left-hand column, "Antidotes" above the middle column and "Don'ts" above the right-hand column of each page. Here you will create your personal Impression Management Plan—a prescription for effective and lasting change that will transform the impression you make on others.

As you read on, each time you identify one of your traits that enhances all four Compass Qualities and diminishes none, write it down in the "Dos" column and whenever you spot a trait that diminishes all four Compass Qualities without enhancing any, write it down in the "Don'ts" column. If one of your traits enhances some of the four Compass Qualities and deemphasizes others, write it down in both columns. Next to it in the "Dos" column write down the Compass Quality or Qualities it enhances. Next to it in the "Don'ts" column write down the Compass Quality or Qualities it diminishes.

Now comes the critical part of creating your Impression Management Plan. As you read on, in the "Antidotes" column, write down the "remedies" for the toxic components of each trait you listed in both the "Dos" and "Don'ts" columns.

For example, as John realizes that his powerful voice is a double-edged Impression Management sword, he would make entries like these:

Dos	Antidotes	Don'ts
Powerful voice (increases trustworthiness/ capability)	Lower voice, smile, warmer eye contact, friendly greetings, warmer colors, touching, considerate actions, listening, praise, doughnuts	Powerful voice (decreases caring/humility)

If you make these entries as you read through this book, you will craft the same Impression Management Plan we would customize for you were we to spend days in an interactive workshop together. It will list the traits you should always stress, those you should eliminate, and how you can "manage" the rest to preserve their positive qualities and mitigate their negative ones. An occasional review of what you have created will be like a quick visit to the Impression Management doctor for prescriptions of magic pills to enhance positive impressions and antidotes for toxic traits. Do this and you will find it increasingly effortless to put your best foot forward—anytime, anyplace.

CHAPTER 2

Impression Formation

A "stereotype" is defined in *Merriam Webster's Dictionary* as a: "standardized mental picture that is held in common by members of a group and that represents an oversimplified opinion, prejudiced attitude, or uncritical judgment." The *Encyclopaedia Britannica* describes "prejudice" as, an "attitude, usually emotional, acquired without prior or adequate evidence or experiences." When we think of stereotypes and prejudices, we usually think of race, national origin or gender. But stereotypes and prejudices apply to almost every trait. Other people will harbor stereotypes and prejudices toward you if you wear black or pink, speak quickly or slowly, are rich or poor, tall or short, thin or fat, dowdy or fashionable, are a good or poor listener, articulate or inarticulate, courteous or rude, clean or dirty, organized or disorganized—the list is endless.

A single stereotyped trait, or several stereotyped traits taken together, may lead to wide-sweeping assumptions about you. People everywhere develop what psychologists call "schemas," or diagrams of what they expect from anyone who appears to fit their stereotypes. Primary associations lead to secondary and tertiary assumptions. The diagram may begin, for example, with the stereotype that a man who owns a pit bull is aggressive and violent. From there the diagram branches out. If he's aggressive and violent, he must be uncaring. If he's uncaring, he's probably not honest. Before long, a mighty oak has grown from a tiny acorn, all based on a succession of stereotypes.

In this chapter we examine how stereotypes and prejudices are formed, and how they influence impression formation. A clear understanding of this process is critical if you hope to present yourself in the best possible light by capitalizing on positive stereotypes and nullifying unflattering ones.

THE PRIMARY SOURCES
OF STEREOTYPES

We seldom have the time or inclination to make fully informed decisions about other people. So we rely on sources that do not require case-by-case analysis and often no rational thought whatsoever. Those sources are:

- Myth
- Personal experience
- Emotion-based stereotypes

MYTH

In the Middle Ages, many Christians were told that Jews had horns and tails like the Devil. As absurd as this is, some of those who never actually met a Jew believed it to be true. Today we like to think we are more enlightened, but we continue to accept a wide assortment of myths about members of certain groups. Some of these stereotypes are based on fact, but researchers find little support for many others.

People don't consciously distinguish between prejudices and stereotypes that stem from unfounded myth and those that are based on personal experience or emotional reactions. To a great extent, stereotypes that have no factual basis are swept into our social and individual consciousnesses along with those that do. As a consequence, you can't simply dismiss a stereotype that others might apply to you because you know it isn't warranted. Each trait you possess that is subject to any stereotype must be recognized, acknowledged and managed. Left unaddressed, some stereotypes will adhere to your advantage, still others will have no discernible impact, and many will work to your detriment.

PERSONAL EXPERIENCE

The most entrenched stereotypes and prejudices are those that are based on the actual experiences of the person who harbors them. During the jury selection process before each trial we have the opportunity to question jurors about their life experiences and biases. We have found that those who find it most difficult to set aside their biases are those whose prejudices were formed and reinforced by multiple similar personal experiences.

For example, in many criminal cases the jurors' attitude toward the police is a critical area of questioning during jury selection. Young African-American males who have had repeated negative experiences with the police find it almost impossible to set aside those memories when they are asked to evaluate the conduct of a police officer, particularly one who is white. Those African Americans who personally never had an unfavorable experience with a police officer still tend to harbor strong biases based upon the experiences of family or close friends; but those biases are less entrenched. Whites who have had bad experiences with police officers harbor biases against the police that are often as strong as those held by African Americans. The strength of the bias against the police, therefore, depends most consistently on personal experience, not skin color.

Almost everyone recognizes that all individuals who fall within a particular group do not embody the characteristics they attach generally to that group. Even the most abused young African-American male knows that all white cops aren't bad, and whites who have had consistently favorable exposure to the police recognize that there are some bad cops. But we all play the odds. If we have had consistent experiences with those who fit a particular stereotype, we conclude that others in that group are likely to think and act the same way. Our stereotypes and prejudices become more powerful as we see a stronger correlation between members of a particular group and their thought and behavior. This is true even among other members of the group against which the stereotypes are applied.

Jesse Jackson, for example, once said: "There is nothing more painful for me than to walk down the street and hear footsteps and start to think about robbery, and then see it's somebody white and feel relieved." African-American scholar Johnnetta Cole acknowledged that among black women, "one of the most painful admissions I hear is: 'I am afraid of my own people.' " William Oliver wrote: "In response to the prevalence of violence in their communities, many blacks manifest an overt fear of other blacks."

Since factually based stereotypes have been shown to be held most firmly by those who have the most extensive knowledge of their validity based upon personal experience, it is little wonder that those who are members of a stereotyped group often share the public's view of that group. Lawyers, for example, may recoil against the commonly held notion that as a group they are greedy and unethical. Yet that bias exists even within the legal profession. And assertive professional women are as likely as anyone else to believe that other assertive professional women are harsh and uncaring.

Studies also have demonstrated that those who are themselves victims of stereotyping and prejudice are no more charitable toward members of other groups than the rest of us. In a report from the National Conference of Christians and Jews, minority groups expressed stronger prejudices than those harbored by whites toward other minority groups, as reflected in this sampling from the report cited by Dinesh D'Souza in *The End of Racism,* 49 percent of the African Americans and 68 percent of the Asians surveyed thought Hispanics "tend to have bigger families than they can support;" 46 percent of the Hispanics and 42 percent of the African Americans viewed Asian Americans as "unscrupulous, crafty and devious in business"; and 53 percent of the Asians and 51 percent of the Hispanics thought African Americans "are more likely to commit crimes of violence."

Keep this in mind as you evaluate the probable stereotypes and prejudices that others might harbor toward you. Don't assume that other professional women won't harbor gender-based biases against you because you too are a professional woman, or that the smooth-talking salesman won't question your sincerity because you also fall into that category, or that the beautiful woman who obsesses about her appearance won't think you are shallow if you do likewise. Some won't. But many will. Until you have gathered enough information about a person to conclude reliably that he or she has not adopted generally prevalent stereotypes, assume that he or she has.

EMOTION-BASED STEREOTYPES

Many of the schemas we form of others are based neither on myth nor conscious recall of past experience. Often the impression we form is attributed to emotion or intuition. Intuition is often considered emotionally based; but it is actually based on experience, although it is accessed unconsciously.

Intuition arises when years of experience stored behind the curtain of our subconscious percolates from those deep recesses when our memory is triggered by similar experiences. All of us have stored an extraordinary amount of data in our brains about how others' behaviors relate to their beliefs and values. We know that those who smile sincerely are most often friendly; those who are great listeners are usually compassionate; and those who won't look us in the eye are frequently lying. When we see those behaviors, we seldom consciously think to ourselves: "She's smiling so she must be friendly," or "She's listening so she must be compassionate," or "She's looking away so she must be lying." We just "get a feeling," which is a message from our subconscious as it taps into our stored memory of prior experiences.

Intuition usually can be explained rationally. But we make many associations that cannot. For example, dozens of studies have equated the color of clothing with people's assumptions as to someone's professionalism or honesty. Navy blue consistently scores higher than bright flashy colors, and solids receive higher ratings than plaids or dramatic patterns. In part, this can be explained rationally. Through years of experience we have found that those who are more professional and honest tend to dress more conservatively, and those who dress in flashy clothes tend to be less professional and less honest. But the same rational process can't explain why we find pastel colors more soothing, black depressing, or bright colors more invigorating. Yet those reactions are so consistent that colors have often come to symbolize the emotions they represent. The Grim Reaper, executioners and morticians wear black. Easter and springtime, which represent renewal, are celebrated with pastels. And red is the color of choice to show sexuality, anger and other passions.

Even though emotional responses frequently cannot be explained, the associations between different traits and the character of those who display them can be established through clinical research. For example, we may not be able to say why pastels are more soothing than bright colors, but we can prove that almost everyone consistently reacts to them in that way when they are placed in rooms painted in either pastel or bright colors and asked which makes them feel more at ease.

Throughout this book we will explain why certain emotional reactions are triggered by particular traits. There will be occasions when the results of the research are clear—but defy rational explanation. As you read on, you may from time to time say to yourself, "That doesn't make sense." And you may be right. But remember, stereotypes and prejudices lie at the foundation of impression formation, whether based on myth, experience or emotional responses. They don't need to make sense to have an effect on how you are perceived.

The conclusions of the studies that cannot be explained rationally are no less valid—even if they appear counterintuitive. In some respects, such studies are the most important, since they provide data to be incorporated into your Impression Management Plan that can be derived from no other source.

As you assess potential stereotypes that someone may apply to you, consider their potential mythical, experiential and emotional foundations and evaluate the presence or absence of each of these factors:

- Whether a stereotype is commonly portrayed in the media or literature.
- The actual good or bad experiences, either personally or by family members or close friends of those who may judge you.

- The number of personal good or bad experiences they have had.
- The period of time over which those experiences have taken place.
- The reinforcement of bias or prejudice by the person's parents or others with significant influence on him or her.
- The extent to which the trait someone assumes you have will directly impact the personal or professional life of that person.
- How freely the person acknowledges the stereotype or prejudice.
- Whether the person consciously acts upon the stereotype or prejudice.
- Whether the stereotype affects one of our most basic emotions, such as fear, anger or insecurity.

THE INFLUENCE OF EMOTION ON IMPRESSION FORMATION

Dale Carnegie wrote succinctly in *How to Win Friends and Influence People*: "When dealing with people, let us remember we are not dealing with creatures of logic. We are dealing with creatures of emotion, creatures bristling with prejudices and motivated by pride and vanity." Nineteenth-century philosopher Alfred North Whitehead put it even more directly: "Ninety percent of our lives is governed by emotion." Whitehead has been proven to be correct both psychologically and physiologically. Only about 10 percent of the human brain's activity is conscious, rational and intellectual. The balance responds to stimuli at what psychologists call a subconscious, nonconscious or preconscious level.

For our purposes, the brain can be divided into three segments: the instinctive brain, the emotional brain and the rational brain. To appreciate how impressions are formed, it is important to understand how these three "brains within a brain" send, receive, sort, record and act upon messages. For purposes of illustration, the functions of these three components of the brain can be compared to how mail is processed in an imaginary company from the time it is first received on the loading dock until it is reviewed and acted upon by the executive upstairs.

How the Brain Functions

The brain consists of three basic components: the brain stem, the limbic system and the cerebrum or cerebral cortex.

The brain stem, or what we call the instinctive brain, evolved from the spinal cord and is sometimes called the reptilian brain since it includes the brain functions also present in fish and reptiles. The reticular activating system or RAS within the brain stem connects the major nerves in the body and the spinal cord to the brain, and processes the millions of impulses that are transmitted each second from our body's sensory systems to the brain. It regulates consciousness, sleep cycles, arousal, attention, heartbeat, respiration and other instinctive and autonomic functions of the body.

Think of the reticular activating system as Mr. Ras, the mail sorter, who unloads the bags of mail from the loading dock. He mindlessly throws out the junk mail, sends the routine bills to accounting, and routes the daily newspapers to the appropriate offices throughout the company. He then sends what's left of the incoming mail to the mailroom. Mr. Ras doesn't have to be bright. He just has to be efficient and consistent. His functions are routine, and require neither emotional responses nor rational thought.

The second component of the brain, the limbic system, lies between the brain stem and the cerebrum. The limbic system developed in mammals two to three hundred million years ago, and is the center of emotion within the brain. The limbic system consists of a number of different components, the most notable of which are the thalamus, hypothalamus, hippocampus and amygdala.

The thalamus lies in the center of the brain, and is the primary relay station from the sensory organs to the cerebrum. The hypothalamus lies just below the thalamus, and serves as a relay center for the autonomic nervous system. The hypothalamus helps regulate transmissions that are essential for survival, such as the "fight or flight reflex," eating and sex drive. It also helps regulate emotional responses. The hippocampus is the center for memory within the brain. It determines which of the millions of images that pass through the brain are retained for future reference, and which are acted upon and then discarded.

Finally, the amygdala works with the thalamus to assess the emotional significance of sensory input and provides emotional significance to the memories the hippocampus stores. The amygdala, which is more developed in humans than other mammals, is also the most developed of the brain's components at birth. It helps us suppress certain emotional and instinctive responses to which less developed mammalian brains react, which accounts for why we don't bite, scratch or strike others every time we feel fearful or threatened, as a dog or other animal might.

When we lose rational control, the amygdala has been overwhelmed. Even with extensive psychotherapy it is often impossible to determine why events may trigger emotional reactions that are so powerful our normal control systems fail. The explanation often lies beyond our capacity to know, because events may have occurred in our early childhood and been recorded emotionally by our amygdala long before our rational brains developed sufficiently to recognize them. They then lie dormant beneath our conscious minds until excited to revolt by future events.

To remember the function of the various components of the limbic system, think of them as the mail clerks in the mailroom on the first floor of the company office building. Mr. Thalamus, Mr. Hypothalamus and Mr. Amygdala make their decisions on what mail will be routed to whom, bundled with what other mail, marked urgent or set aside to be routed "whenever," based only on their emotional response to the mail that lands on their desks. Mail that is brightly packaged, or clearly stamped "rush" in red, or otherwise catches their attention, is carried enthusiastically upstairs. Other mail that arrives in plain manila envelopes or bores them is given low priority or ignored altogether. Before any piece of mail is sent upstairs, the guys in the mailroom wrap it in an emotional film of their making through which Ms. Cerebrum, the executive upstairs, must read it.

Mr. Hippocampus, who controls your memory, can be thought of as the file clerk in the mailroom. He works closely with Mr. Amygdala who tells him which parcels are particularly emotion laden and which aren't. Like Mr. Thalamus, Mr. Hypothalamus and Mr. Amygdala, Mr. Hippocampus acts only on emotion as he decides what to send to the warehouse, what to keep accessible on-site, and what to discard.

The third component of the brain, the cerebrum, is often referred to as "gray matter" because the neurocells in its surface are gray, in contrast to the white cells present in the balance of the brain. The cerebrum consists of six layers of neurons; four receive data and two send data. The cerebrum processes information, plans, thinks, coordinates thoughts and actions and formulates speech.

By the time the mail arrives at Ms. Cerebrum's desk, it has been sorted by Mr. Ras on the loading deck with neither thought nor emotion, and then sifted, prioritized, bundled and covered with an emotional film in the mailroom by Mr. Thalamus, Mr. Hypothalamus and Mr. Amygdala. Mr. Hippcampus adds his input by deciding if new mail should be sent upstairs along with any previously filed information.

Ms. Cerebrum may think that she receives complete, accurate and untainted information from which she can make the decisions that are critical to the well-being of the company. But she doesn't. Unfortunately for those who would prefer that all decisions were made logically, virtually every piece of data that arrives on Ms. Cerebrum's desk is imprinted with an emotional overlay.

Moreover, every decision that Ms. Cerebrum makes must be sent back through the mailroom before it is transmitted to the outside world. Ms.

Cerebrum may prefer to communicate with her key customers without the involvement of the gang in the mailroom, but she can't. She may want to stay calm, but if Mr. Amygdala is upset by her message, her face blushes, her speech rate accelerates and the volume of her voice increases. She may want to appear confident, but if the guys in the mailroom are nervous about her presentation, she gets a case of the jitters.

The human brain is obviously much more complex and difficult to understand than the process of handling the mail in this hypothetical company, but this analogy fairly represents the function of the brain, particularly if you consider that there is considerable overlap in the job descriptions of the mailroom employees. And it explains why we frequently act in ways that make no rational sense. Most important, it explains why you must communicate with emotion if you are to make the best possible impressions and why you won't be able to understand others if you don't recognize how their emotional brains communicate with you.

PHYSICAL REACTIONS AND "RATIONAL DECISIONS" THAT DON'T MAKE SENSE

The powerful influences of instinct and emotions on every aspect of our behavior, including impression formation, should come as no surprise if we consider how many common physical reactions and decisions occur with little or no conscious thought.

We blink when a friend pretends to throw something at our face even though we know rationally that he would never hurt us, but our instinctive brain acts in milliseconds (much quicker than our rational brain) to protect our eyes from damage. We open our mouths and inhale quickly when we are startled, as our instinctive brain prepares us to fight or flee by drawing a fresh supply of oxygen into our lungs. Our palms sweat, our throats become dry and our blood pressure, pulse and adrenaline rates increase when we watch a horror movie. Our rational brain knows that the bad guy with the mask and the bloody ax won't really cut off the baby-sitter's head, let alone ours. But our emotional brain doesn't distinguish between reality and realistic visual simulations and prepares us for action. Why are we afraid of harmless snakes, spiders and mice? Why do we fear enclosed spaces that pose no threat? Why do we grow faint when we look out a secure window to the street below? Why do certain smells make us hungry and other scents induce sexual arousal? Why does one song make us melancholy and another invigorated? Why does the touch of one object make us squirm and another calm us? The answers lie not with Ms. Cerebrum, but with those in the mailroom who have programmed us to respond without thought to many circumstances that present a perceived threat or opportunity.

Our emotional brain doesn't just influence our physical reactions. It also affects what we may believe is purely rational thought. The entire advertising industry is built on the premise that emotion, not logic, sells. Perhaps you've wondered why relatively few commercials provide any rational explanation for why you should purchase a product. Instead they favor catchy jingles and images of beautiful models, fast cars and serene landscapes. Advertisers know, as Elmer Wheeler wrote in *Principle No. 1 of Salesmanship* in 1936, "Don't sell the steak; sell the sizzle."

Most people make purchasing decisions on emotional grounds. They then seek to justify those decisions logically. You may find a piece of clothing that appeals to you, but is one size too small. Your rational brain, if acting alone, would say "lose the weight, then buy the dress." Your emotional brain, however, says: "I love it. I want it. I'll lose weight later." As eighteenth-century philosphy David Hume so aptly noted, "Reason is the slave of the passions."

Just as we buy on emotion and justify with logic, we enter into relationships motivated as often by emotion as by logic. You may fall in love with someone you know logically isn't "right for you." But you pursue the relationship anyway, driven by emotion that blinds your rational brain. Or you may quit your job in an emotional rage and try for weeks to justify the decision rationally.

Since the charismatic and energetic John F. Kennedy surprised the much more experienced Richard Nixon in the 1960 presidential election, political consultants have accepted the notion that those candidates who appeal most to the voters' emotional brains win. Most political historians believe that Nixon's demise was the result of the first televised presidential candidates' debates in which Nixon appeared nervous and anxious, his stage makeup running in rivers of sweat down his forehead and cheeks, while Kennedy was relaxed, energetic and friendly. The TV audience rated Kennedy the winner, while the radio audience, which didn't have the visual image of the nervous and tense Nixon to influence its emotional brains, thought Nixon won.

In a Gallup poll taken during each presidential election since 1960, voters have been asked to rate the candidates based upon three criteria: their stand on the issues; their party affiliation; and their likability. The candidate who scored highest in the likability category, a uniquely emotional brain criterion, has won every election. Higher ratings in either of the other two more logically oriented categories were not reliable indicators of success.

These are but a few of hundreds of examples of the control our instinctive and emotional brains hold over our rational brains. Unless you recognize this phenomenon, you will unwittingly make very poor impressions on others. On the other hand, if you understand the power of communication from emotional brain to emotional brain, you can use these natural reactions to create positive impressions.

YOUR EMOTIONS' INFLUENCE ON MEMORY

Remember Mr. Hippocampus, the irrational file clerk in the mailroom, who, with the assistance of Mr. Amygdala, decides what you will and will not remember? He's the one who tells the young child not to touch the stove because it causes pain, an emphatically unpleasant physical and emotional experience. He's also the one who makes you remember your first love's phone number even after you've forgotten the phone number in your own home during your youth and allows you to recall the names of those you like, or hate, long after you've forgotten the names of everyone else.

Every person you meet has his own Mr. Hippocampus, and will remember those aspects of your personality or behavior that make an emotional impact. They will be noticed first, considered most important and remembered the longest. If one of your traits opens the door to another's storehouse of memories, you will be swept into it, for better or worse.

THE IMPORTANCE
OF MEETING OTHERS' NEEDS

No bond is stronger than the one between child and parent. We enter the world entirely dependent upon our parents. During our infancy, our basic physical requirements are few: food, warmth, safety and an occasional diaper change. We crave love, attention and stimulation. As our parents dote on us, we learn to trust in our importance to them.

With age, our needs and desires mature. In childhood, we rely less on our parents to satisfy our physical needs. But on an emotional level, we continue to long for attention, encouragement and approval. Our trust in our parents and in our importance to them remain the cornerstones of our developing sense of security and self-worth.

Through adolescence and into adulthood most of our expectations that our needs will be fulfilled by our parents are transferred to others—our friends, lovers, coworkers. But our needs remain just as strong.

As adults we have the same basic cravings we have had since birth: the yearning to feel important and worthwhile, and the desire to have our physical and emotional needs met. Yet, unlike our parents, most of the people we encounter as adults are relatively indifferent to us. Where, then, do we turn?

We turn to those few who best meet our needs. We all sift through the multitudes to find those who will fill the void created when we left our parents' nest. If you are such a person, others will be drawn to you. If not, they will look for someone else who is.

The Need to Feel Important

Children don't just seek validation of their importance, they demand it. They cry when their needs aren't met; shamelessly fish for compliments when they have done something they believe is noteworthy and pout if they aren't supported in their efforts. As adults, most of us have learned to suppress obvious cries for attention and appreciation. But inside, the cravings run as deep as ever. As William James, known as the father of American psychology, noted, "The deepest principle in human nature is the craving to be appreciated." What follows are a few concepts you should keep in mind as you seek opportunities to fill this fundamental need.

- *Everyone Wants Strokes*

     Don't be fooled by someone's veneer of confidence, or assume that those who have achieved a healthy measure of success no longer crave the appreciation of others. The most needy among us are often the ones who are driven to the greatest accomplishments.

- *Don't Overlook Those Closest to You*

     We often neglect those we cherish most. Validation is particularly important in significant relationships; yet we are more likely to express our appreciation with a "thank you" to the clerk at the convenience store than to our spouses, friends and coworkers.

- *Timing Can Be Everything*

     Expressions of appreciation should not be reserved for just the good times. People need affirmation most when they feel most like failures. The man who has been laid off and fears he can't provide for his family, or the friend who has been dumped by her lover, or the salesman who has just lost a sale, are the ones who most need you to bolster their self-esteem.

- *Acknowledge Particularly Noteworthy Achievements*

     Few slights cut deeper than your failure to appreciate others for their unique contributions to your life. NFL Hall of Fame lineman Gene Upshaw said it well when he observed: "I've compared an offensive lineman to the story of Paul Revere. After Paul Revere rode through town everybody said what a great job he did. But no one ever talked about the horse. I know how Paul Revere's horse felt." Whatever you do, never make others feel like Paul Revere's horse after they have given their best shot to win your approval and admiration.

DISCOVER WHAT EACH PERSON NEEDS MOST FROM YOU

Over the years, we've done an informal poll about what people wish for when they toss a coin into a wishing well. We believe our wishing well test is a reliable way to find out what people most want in life. There are six big winners: happiness, money, fame, beauty, health and romance.

You might think that what someone craves most would be fairly predictable from their outward appearance. But it isn't. The driven and successful businessman may not yearn for greater profits as much as the friendship and admiration of his employees, and a handsome playboy may long more than anything else for a truly loving relationship.

If you expect to show others that you can meet their needs, you must first resolve to learn about them. In Chapter 10, "Communication Style," we emphasize the importance of incorporating excellent listening skills into your Impression Management Plan. Listening skills are critical since before you can evaluate which of your traits you should emphasize in any given relationship and which you should minimize, you need to know as much as possible about the persons you want to impress. Find out who and what they have been attracted to in the past, and why. What is unique about the employees they have promoted? Have they preferred intellectual types or artists? "Read" what their appearance, speech, actions and environment say about their values and what's important to them. Ask about their goals, dreams, hobbies and priorities. And listen.

Once you have determined what the other person wants, you will have acquired the knowledge needed to convey those traits that demonstrate you can meet those needs. Remember, in every relationship the other person asks, "What's in it for me?" If you aim to impress others, make sure you know what they hope your answer will be.

People Like People
Who Are Like Them

Somehow the phrase "opposites attract" has achieved a position of unwarranted legitimacy in our social lexicon. Sure, we are intrigued by others who are different from us. We seek friends, employees, partners and lovers who have qualities that complement ours. But research has shown time and again that the personal and professional relationships that are strongest, most fulfilling and longest lasting are those in which the people involved share basic values, life experiences, ideals, goals, mannerisms and even a common level of physical attractiveness. Our interviews with thousands of individuals over the years about their impressions of others have shown that there is a strong correlation between a person's impression of another and the measure of similarity or dissimilarity between the two individuals.

Many studies conducted over the years reinforce this conclusion. For example, in one, thirty-eight women and twenty-eight men were asked whether models dressed in three different styles of clothing, "alternative" (hippie/grunge/gothic), "casual" or "business," were more intelligent, wealthy, successful, attractive, extroverted, practical, able to fit in, likable, trustworthy, friendly and impulsive. While men were less influenced by the style of clothing than women, both men and women attributed more positive qualities to those who dressed in a style similar to their own. In another study that assessed patterns in speakers' nonverbal behavior, the researchers found that the audience was more persuaded by those whose nonverbal behaviors were similar to their own. In another study conducted in the sixties, researchers approached students on a college campus and asked for ten cents to make a phone call. When the researchers wore clothing that conformed to that worn by the person they approached, they were given the requested dime more than two-thirds of the time. When their clothing was different, they were successful less than one-half of the time. The influence of shared characteristics on impression formation has been found to be even more pronounced for those with lower self-esteem, and in relationships that involve an emotional commitment.

If everyone who has "made it" in your workplace, particularly the most senior executives, is a snappy, stylish dresser, you would be safe to assume that, in your company at least, you need to dress stylishly to be perceived as having "all the right stuff." If you dress like a university professor, you may never be given a key to the executive washroom. But if the decision makers in your company are all conservative, blue suit, white-blouse-with-skirts-to-their-knees types, your attempt to stand out with a lacy camisole and teal miniskirted suit probably will cry out "showboat," "not a team player," "flashy, but not centered." As Rudyard Kipling wrote, "All the people like us are We, and everyone else is They." It's difficult for a "They" to make a good impression on a "We."

Sometimes the best way to distinguish yourself is to fit in better than anyone else—to be the consummate conservative accountant, or the perfect construction foreman, or the prototypical salesclerk. If you work for a conservative, old-line company and you're concerned about the impression you make, distinguish yourself with the most classic, crisply pressed blue suit in the lot, not the latest Paris fashion.

Because we form more favorable perceptions of those who are like us, many writers have suggested that one of the most effective ways to appeal to others is to "mirror," or "echo" them. Duplicate their dress, their voice, their communication style, their actions, and even their environment the thought goes, and you'll win their approval. These techniques are indeed valuable, but they must be applied with an understanding of the difference between "mirroring" and "echoing," on the one hand, and "mimicking" on the other.

If someone dresses in a particular style, it reflects a look with which he or she feels comfortable and values. If you adopt a similar style of dress, it will create positive associations. On the other hand, if you duplicate others' wardrobe too closely—buy the same red blazer that you saw her wear the day before, or pick up the same polka dot tie your boss had on last week—you mimic them. While imitation can be flattering, you will seem unimaginative, not confident, and possibly even not too intelligent.

When you sit on a couch next to a person who lounges leisurely, if you also slump somewhat, you will convey the message that you are relaxed, comfortable and at ease. If you sit stiffly erect while she lounges, you may make her feel uncomfortable. And the reverse is true. If she sits up straight, back stiff, head erect, hands on her lap, legs pinned together, you can establish rapport with her if you mirror that posture. If you are too casual, you may make her feel awkward.

Speech, too, can be "echoed." If someone talks in a slow, calm voice, he'll be more relaxed if you also talk in a slow, calm voice. If the volume and pace of his speech increases with enthusiasm, you will affirm his feelings if you show enthusiasm in the volume and pace of your voice.

The same is true of the words you use. If someone speaks in simple terms and you respond with highbrow vocabulary, you send the message, "I'm smarter, better-educated, more professional and generally more worthwhile than you are." But when you effectively echo someone's language, you tell her that you share common interests, backgrounds and values.

On the broadest possible level, you can even mirror someone's general attitudes. If someone shows that he likes you, show him that you like him. If he treats you with respect, treat him with respect.

The difference between mirroring and mimicking is often a matter of degree. What is appropriate depends on the circumstances and the motives others might attribute to your behavior. If you appear condescending, patronizing, unimaginative or manipulative, your effort to mirror will backfire. But if the characteristics you adopt are viewed as an honest attempt to put the other person at ease, or to communicate more effectively, they will be welcomed.

In court we have seen many expert witnesses who have an impressive list of degrees and IQs in the stratosphere who use a simple vocabulary and adopt obviously simplistic ways to express their ideas. They echo the way they know the average juror speaks and thinks and purposely attempt to relate to them at that level. And the jurors know it. The jurors realize that the expert has purposefully avoided the use of terminology they won't understand in order to communicate with them more effectively. They appreciate the expert's efforts, and view her as sensitive and humble. The expert's image as intelligent and competent is not diminished in the process either. If anything, it's enhanced by demonstrating that she has the good judgment to know how to modify her presentation to make it meaningful to her audience.

On the other hand, we have seen both witnesses and lawyers adopt an overly casual demeanor or use slang in an attempt to identify with the jury. Many of the cases we handle are tried in the courts in downtown Los Angeles where a substantial number of jurors in any particular trial are African American. We have seen wealthy, well-educated and conservative white lawyers try to appeal to black jurors with the use of ghetto slang or repeated mentions of Martin Luther King or other African-American notables. On one occasion, a lawyer even told a jury during jury selection that Spike Lee was his favorite movie director. This was truly a misguided effort: Such obvious mimicking sounded condescending and manipulative and communicated that the lawyer had little respect for the jurors' intelligence.

To effectively mirror others you must look, speak and act in a manner that is not uncomfortable or unnatural. If you venture beyond your comfort zone and fashion a completely false veneer, you will be seen as hypocritical, dishonest or insecure. And, eventually, you will revert to behaviors that are more comfortable and natural, which will leave everyone who has absorbed your transformation disenchanted.

HOW TO MANAGE STEREOTYPES
AND EMOTIONAL REACTIONS

Management of others' involves a five-step process that allows you to identify and control reactions of others' stereotypical and emotional responses to you. The foundation of Impression Management is your awareness that the impressions you make on others are based on stereotypical associations, prejudices, emotional reactions and others' perceptions of your ability to meet their needs. Its success relies upon your ability to predict those reactions in others, and present your traits in a fashion that appeals to the individual or individuals you want to impress.

Step One: Recognize which traits have a positive or negative impact on impressions of trustworthiness, caring, humility and capability—the four Compass Qualities;

Step Two: Objectively evaluate what traits you have;

Step Three: Accentuate every trait that enhances all four Compass Qualities;

Step Four: Eliminate those traits that are toxic to all four Compass Qualities; and

Step Five: Retain those traits that have both positive and negative components, but "cure" their negative side effects with liberal application of compensating positive traits.

To do this effectively, you must learn to project a consistent and clear image of yourself with the aid of each of the "Seven Colors" that convey the Compass Qualities.

THE SEVEN-COLOR PRINTER

A few years ago we worked on a case that involved illustrated children's books. During the case we learned how a color printer creates the hundreds of subtle tones, hues and shades on the posters on your wall, the flyers you receive in the mail, and the pictures you print off your home computer. We discovered what causes some images to appear crisp, clear and almost three-dimensional, while others are flat, drab or out of focus.

Your home computer printer probably uses just four colors of ink—red (actually magenta), blue (actually cyan), yellow and black. Some commercial printers use just the same four colors. Others use many more. The ink is ejected in tiny dots onto the page. The various colors are combined to create a vivid and clear image in all the shades of the rainbow. The printers that produce the most striking images use a wider array of different colors, and apply them more precisely.

As we worked on the case, we were impressed by the similarity between how a color printer projects an image on the page, and how we paint the picture of ourselves that others see. We are, in essence, Seven-Color Printers who have at our disposal seven distinct "Colors" with which to create impressions. They are:

- Personal appearance
- Body language
- Voice
- Communication style
- Content of communication
- Actions
- Environment

The distinction between each of the Seven Colors can be seen if you consider how you form an impression about a character in a play.

Personal Appearance: Personal appearance is what you can see in a photograph of the actor in costume, set against a blank background with no motion, sound or scenery. You can see only his physical features and his clothing, jewelry and other accessories.

Body Language: Once on stage, you see the actor move, gesture and look around. You watch him interact with other actors and move about the stage. You still can't hear his voice and don't know what he says. But now who he is and how he thinks and feels are communicated through his body language and facial expressions.

Voice: Now, the speakers in the theater broadcast the actor's voice; but he speaks in a foreign language. You can't understand *what* he says; you can only understand *how* he says it. You can hear if his voice is fast or slow paced, loud or soft, hesitant or firm, shrill or calming. Even though you can't understand his words, you can sense if he is nervous, afraid, angry, confident, sexy, compassionate or harsh. As you hear his voice, you begin to form stronger impressions of his emotions and personality.

Communication Style: Suddenly the dialogue is in the language you speak. In addition to personal appearance, body language and voice, the actor reveals more of himself through the manner in which he communicates with others. Does he ask questions? Does he listen carefully to the responses?

Does he answer questions directly? Does he volunteer information? Is he blunt or evasive? Is he argumentative or compliant? Does he change the subject? Even without any thought about the content of what he says, you have a better sense of whether he is honest, confident, humble, egotistical, friendly, dignified or aloof, just from the manner in which he communicates.

Content of Communication: Now you focus on the actor's words. You can hear the stories he tells, the vocabulary he uses, how he expresses his thoughts, if what he says makes sense, and whether he talks just about himself or others. What he says adds even more information about his character.

Actions: With time, you notice how the actor's character is developed through what he does. Does he rush to be first in line, or politely open doors for others? Does he play golf or the violin? How does he act around strangers, coworkers, his lover?

Environment: Finally, you focus on the set in which this all unfolds. Where—surrounded by what, and with whom—do you find the actor? Where the actor lives, works and plays further create an impression of his character. The props—what he has brought into his life, and how he uses them—tell you even more. And his human environment—those he chooses, or allows, to surround him both at work and at play—add the last piece to the puzzle.

You are that actor. In every exchange you paint a picture of who you are with each of these Seven Colors. It is from that picture that others form their impressions of you.

For decades, researchers have questioned which of these Seven Colors has the greatest influence on impression formation. It seems that fashion experts usually conclude that the answer is appearance. Body language experts believe body movements and facial expressions are most important. Other studies, typically conducted by voice, communication or behavior experts, have determined that vocal qualities, the content or style of communication or our actions, have the greatest effect.

After reading hundreds of these studies, interviewing thousands of individuals, and evaluating thousands more surveys and questionnaires, we have an answer that reconciles the often inconsistent findings of other researchers. It is an answer that any printing expert knows well. The "Color" that gets the most attention is the one that stands out most dramatically. Black ink, if applied too abundantly or not aligned with the other colors, will distort and dominate the image. If yellow ink doesn't properly overlap blue, a vibrant green will appear chartreuse. If red and yellow are not perfectly overlaid, an orange hue emerges, trimmed in red on one side and yellow on the other.

A number of studies have been conducted over the years to establish what characteristics are most frequently noticed, retained longest and considered most important as people assess others' qualities. We will discuss many of those studies throughout this book and highlight associations made between specific traits and the qualities thought to be possessed by those who demonstrate them. A theme that runs through all of the studies, and is highlighted by many, is that anything that deviates from our normal expectations—stands out for any reason—will be noticed most frequently, remembered longest, and given the greatest weight. Sometimes one of a person's many traits will stand out in stark contrast against the others. For example, a conservative businesswoman may have a tattoo. On other occasions, the entire package of traits displayed by a person may be inconsistent with our expectations of how such a person should look, speak and act. For example, a professional whom we would expect to dress, speak and act conservatively might dress, speak and act very casually.

As you learn to convey the best possible image of yourself, bear in mind that any deviation from expected behavior will be given more significance than traits that conform to others' expectations. That is not to say that deviations are necessarily bad and should be avoided, since they may have either a positive or negative impact depending on the circumstances. But as you paint a picture of yourself with each of the Seven Colors, any inconsistency with others' expectations should be avoided unless the benefit it produces is clearly identified and understood.

PAINT WITH AS MANY OF THE SEVEN COLORS AS POSSIBLE

In most circumstances, you won't make a particularly loud statement about who you are from any single characteristic. Instead, that statement comes from a combination of all of the "little things" you do and say. To make the best possible impression you must use each of the Seven Colors as fully as possible. Some level of success in Impression Management can be achieved by enhancing something less than all characteristics; but like the image created by the printer, the best results depend upon careful application of each and every Color. Effective Impression Management is achieved only if you make contact with others face to face whenever possible.

As consultants, we constantly evaluate how best to communicate ideas and images. This same inquiry has been made by the media and others whose stock-in-trade is effective communication. The conclusions are always the same. We absorb much more information visually than we do aurally, just as we process more information emotionally than intellectually. Visual images are noticed more, make a greater impact, and are retained longer than aural impressions.

One study found that when information was communicated verbally alone, only 15 percent was retained after the exercise was concluded. However, when the same information was communicated verbally and supported by visual aids, 85 percent was retained after the same period elapsed. In the most frequently cited study on this topic, researcher Albert Mehrabian found that only 7 percent of the listeners' impression of another's presentation was derived from its content; while 38 percent arose from vocal characteristics such as tone, volume and pace; and the remaining 55 percent from the speaker's facial expressions and body movements.

Studies such as these must be viewed in perspective. They typically evaluate someone's initial response to a speaker who talks about something that is not of particular interest to the listener, or they explore the relative importance of the different Colors when there is an inconsistency between what is said and how it is said. When the subject matter of a communication is important to the listener, or when the content and nonverbal presentation are consistent, content becomes more important than other Colors. Also, as we discuss later, as relationships mature and we have more time to synthesize more nonvisual data, visual impressions become less significant. Once we have known someone for years, we no longer base our assessment of his character primarily on his appearance and body language, nor even on his voice, but on the quality of his work, friendship and deeds. But at every phase of every relationship impressions can be managed better if both visual and aural contact takes place.

In today's hectic world you may often communicate by e-mail or fax, which cannot project a visual image or reinforce that image through your vocal qualities. A telephone call is more effective, since at least the other person can hear your voice, and you hers. But there is still no visual input. To make the best impression, you must make contact. Make it a habit to speak face-to-face with those you most want to impress. If you can't meet face-to-face, at least speak over the telephone. Resort to communication by the written word only when you are compelled by practical necessity. And when you must be judged solely by the written word, give more, not less, attention to your vocabulary, grammar and the content of your communication.

Communication with less than all Seven Colors denies you not only the ability to transmit information, but also the opportunity to receive information from others, which is of equal importance. Throughout this book we generalize about the stereotypic associations and emotional reactions people have to particular traits and characteristics. Each of our generalizations is true for most people, but like all stereotypes, none applies equally to everyone. Each person brings into your relationship his or her unique personal experiences and values that will influence the impressions he or she forms of you.

Virtually everyone you encounter will value those traits we call "Magic Pills," and recoil from those characteristics we refer to as "Toxic Traits." But between these extremes, you will be able to make definitive judgments about how any one person will react to you only if you acquire as much information as possible about that person's past experiences, values, temperament and expectations. You will be able to gather that information more effectively only if you allow others to communicate their qualities to you with each of their Seven Colors.

DON'T WORRY:
YOU CAN CREATE THE DESIRED IMPRESSION

Many of those with whom we have discussed the principles of Impression Management have expressed concern that no matter how hard they try, they may not be able to consciously adopt traits that at first seem unnatural, or show emotion they might not feel at the time. They worry that if they must force behavior, it will be viewed with suspicion. Extensive research demonstrates that such concerns are unfounded.

Remember, everyone communicates first at an emotional level with little or no cognitive involvement. Studies show that our emotional brains tend to take what they see at face value. When someone attempts to project an emotion that he does not actually feel, he typically will adopt both verbal and nonverbal behaviors that are *more expressive* of that emotion than the verbal and nonverbal behaviors he displays when he really feels it. These more emphatic expressions of emotion are more obvious to others' emotional brains. As a result, those who feign emotions in the studies usually are considered by the judges to have a higher level of those emotions than the participants who are actually experiencing them.

This is particularly true of positive emotions. It is much more acceptable in our society to express positive feelings such as happiness, excitement and interest, than to express negative feelings, such as anger, envy and frustration. As a result, expressions of positive emotions, whether natural or forced, are easier to express and are more believable than false expressions of negative emotions. If you resolve to put on a happy face even when you are not happy, or show interest even when you are bored, you will effectively communicate those positive emotions because you have years of practice doing just that. It is more difficult for you to convey negative emotions realistically when you don't really feel them because you have had much less practice. But then, there are very few occasions when negative emotions enhance the impression others have of you.

There certainly will be times when it will be difficult to hide strong emotions or to convey feelings that you aren't actually experiencing. It's hard not to smile when you are elated, frown when you are sad, avoid gasping when you are frightened, or to stay still when you are nervous. If your emotional brain is consumed with these feelings, it signals your body to respond. In these situations, the most effective way to avoid undesired physical reactions is to override the underlying emotions by thinking of something that generates an opposite and compensating emotion.

Poker players are masters of this technique. One told us that whenever he has a winning hand, he thinks of an unpleasant moment from his past, such as the day his beloved dog died. He says he can literally feel the tension in the muscles in his face caused by the excitement of a winning hand drain away. When he has a bad hand but wants to bluff, he visualizes the day he first held his newborn son, which invariably brings a subtle twinkle to his eyes that he hopes his opponent's emotional brain will record as the sign of a winning hand.

These same visualization techniques will help you display pleasure, interest and other emotions in your everyday interactions. If your Impression Management Plan calls for you to smile at a meeting that you dread, think in advance of several happy moments in your life to replay mentally during the meeting. If the occasion calls for rapt attention, when you find yourself bored silly by someone's presentation, create an interest in him by focusing on the subtle changes in the intonation of his voice as he speaks, or think about the words he chooses to express his ideas. Let your rational brain outwit your emotional brain by injecting images consistent with the emotions you want to project. Remember, the emotional brain doesn't distinguish between realistic visualization and reality.

You will seldom create a conflict between your emotional and rational brains as you implement your Impression Management Plan. How you choose to dress, speak and act to make a favorable impression should feel good to you. But on those rare occasions when you find it difficult to force yourself to behave differently than you feel, have faith. You will be the only one in the room who is aware of your inner conflict.

CHAPTER 3

The Compass Qualities

"I can't understand why she got the promotion. I'm smarter."
"She seems to be the apple of his eye, but why? I'm better looking."
"I can't believe she doesn't trust me. I've never lied to her."

We've all wondered why people react to us and others as they do. We ask: "What did they do right?" or "What did I do wrong?" The answer is as simple as the reason the spaghetti sauce at a great Italian restaurant is so much better than what most of us make at home: A master chef understands the subtle properties of each ingredient he adds to a recipe. He knows that basil, oregano, thyme and parsley each has its unique flavor and potency and that the best ingredients must be blended carefully to achieve the desired result.

Impressions are made the same way. To make a great impression you need to understand the qualities that must be combined and how they compliment each other. In this chapter we will identify each of the ingredients that is essential to a great impression, describe how each of these qualities affects impression formation, and explain how they must be combined to create the best possible impression.

THE KEY INGREDIENTS
TO A GREAT IMPRESSION

Experience is the best teacher, and our experience is that trustworthiness, caring, humility and capability are the four qualities that most impress others. But even after two decades of experience, we know that it's always best to test our conclusions. So we did. First, we conducted our own study in which we asked 102 adults: "What is it about someone that makes a good impression on you?" We asked them to pick their top five choices from among twelve options, or to specify "other." The choices and the percentage of respondents who listed each choice among his or her top five were:

Quality	Percentage
Honest/Sincere	80.4
Caring/Compassionate/Kind/ Thoughtful/Considerate	68.5
Reliable/Comes through for you/ Performs as expected	65.2
Interested/Attentive to you and what you say	45.7
Intelligent/Bright	40.24
Competent/Good at what one does	39.1
Humble/Not egotistical/Not arrogant/ Not stuck on oneself	38.0
Outgoing/Friendly	35.7
Confident/Self-Assured	34.8
Good-Looking/Attractive	16.3
Classy/Dignified	10.9
Successful	8.2
Other	4.3

Even though our survey identified twelve different qualities, those that were rated among the top nine can be grouped within the four general categories of trustworthiness, caring, humility and capability—the Compass Qualities. The significance of this study lies not just in what qualities were rated highest, but also in those that were rated lowest.

Many people spend an enormous amount of time and energy trying to project qualities like attractiveness, classiness and success, even if they have to compromise other qualities in the process. Yet a very small percentage of those surveyed placed such qualities at the top of their lists. Even those who listed qualities such as good-looking, classy and successful among their top five choices tended to identify them as only their fourth or fifth choice. For example, only four people identified attractiveness as among the first three traits, compared to fifty-one who identified honesty and sincerity and fifty-two who identified caring, compassionate, kind, thoughtful and considerate as either the first, second or third most influential quality.

That is not to say that qualities such as attractiveness, classiness and success are not important. They are. But their contribution to a favorable impression is indirect. They are not valued in isolation, but only as they reflect the existence of the more cherished traits.

In addition to performing our own study, we also searched the literature for comparable research. Among the most thorough was a survey commissioned by Dr. Robert B. Pamplin, Jr. and Gary K. Eisler for their book *American Heroes*. The definition of a "hero" is a person who is admired for his achievements and qualities. While the question we asked in our survey, "What is it about someone that makes a good impression on you?" is couched differently than, "What makes a hero?" both questions elicit essentially the same information. As Rutgers University anthropologist Helen Fisher said of the Pamplin-Eisler study, "When the authors asked 950 American men, women, and teenagers what constituted a hero, they actually elicited from these informants contemporary American values."

In the Pamplin-Eisler survey, the respondents were asked to rate the importance of seventeen different traits on a scale of one to ten. As in our study, honesty and compassion were at the top of the list, and "being physically gifted," or "being famous," were given little importance. If this comes as no surprise to you, great. It means you will not have to adopt an entirely new perspective about what qualities lead to good impressions. If these results surprise you, perhaps they will make you appreciate that the traits you thought were most important for you to convey should be stressed only to the extent that they contribute to those traits that really are important—trustworthiness, caring, humility and capability.

TRUSTWORTHINESS

Words like "honesty," "sincerity," "believability" and "credibility" always seem to come to mind first when we ask what someone thinks "trustworthiness" means. These words are all synonymous with "truthfulness." But quite apart from the concept of "truthfulness," trustworthiness includes the concept of reliability.

If you flip back to the results of our survey, you will see that honesty and sincerity—the "truthfulness" components of trustworthiness—were listed by 80.4 percent of the respondents. But "reliability/comes through for you/performs as expected" was also listed by 65.2 percent of the respondents. This distinction is critical to keep in mind as you form your Impression Management Plan. For people to trust you, you must be *both* honest *and* reliable.

Honesty

People tend to define "honesty" differently depending upon whether they apply the concept to their own actions, or to others' behavior. Most people believe they act honestly as long as they don't affirmatively misstate a fact. But when they evaluate whether someone else is honest with them, they apply a higher standard. Traits that we expect from others but often excuse or ignore when we are the actor include:

- *Openness:* Do you really show others how you feel? Are you forthcoming, not only with facts, but with emotion? Or do you hide how you really feel?
- *Sincerity:* Do you truly believe what you say? Or do you just say it because it is expedient, socially acceptable or to avoid confrontation?
- *Integrity:* Do you have fundamental values and principles that guide your actions in a consistent and predictable fashion?
- *Manipulation:* Do you do or say things to achieve an objective that you do not acknowledge openly?
- *Exaggeration:* Whether the motive is good or evil, do you embellish in ways that make you untrustworthy?
- *Concealment:* Do you mislead others by omission, or justify an omission with statements like, "I didn't lie, you didn't ask me that"?
- *Half Truths:* Is what you say "technically" true, but misleading in context?

The best definition of dishonesty is "any act or omission that causes or allows another to be misled." This is the standard by which we measure others' honesty. Apply it as well to your own words and deeds. Don't engage in word games, subtle distinctions, misdirection, concealment or omission when someone expects you to be forthcoming. Intellectual justifications for your failure to be honest, open and truthful won't temper another's response when the facts become known. No one likes to play hide and seek with the truth. If you do, you may get away with it from time to time, but your victories will be short-lived.

Reliability

You may be as honest as the day is long, but you won't be viewed as "trustworthy" if you consistently fail to deliver because you don't plan ahead, are easily distracted, careless or make promises you can't keep. Reliability is the quality that leads others not just to believe you, but to believe *in* you;

to know that you will come through, that you will do whatever it is that you said you would do. Reliability gives the gift of peace of mind to those whose lives you impact—the peace of mind that comes from trust.

Many of us lack self-awareness and develop blind spots when we don't want to admit our own limitations. But whether you are willfully dishonest with others, or simply fool yourself, it won't matter much if others depend on you. If you unrealistically evaluate your proficiency with the computer and assure your boss that you can generate graphics to support his upcoming presentation, he will be upset when it becomes apparent that you exaggerated your abilities. If you promise your girlfriend that you will leave work in time to meet her for an 8:00 P.M. play, but don't show up until 8:30, you will lose trustworthiness, regardless of your good intentions.

If others can't depend on you, either because of frequent mistakes or a lack of self-awareness, they eventually will begin to question your honesty, not just your reliability. How many times can you tell your customer, "I'm sorry, there were unexpected delays," before he questions whether you lied to him when you said you had his order in stock? It won't take very many false assurances to your boss before she concludes that you intentionally overstate your abilities. And: "Honey, I'm sorry. I thought I'd be finished at work by seven, but it just took longer than expected," will wear thin fairly quickly.

Consistent Trustworthiness

To be perceived as trustworthy, you must be consistently reliable *and* honest. Reliability is quite easy to test. Either you cocsistently perform as promised, or you don't. But whether you are honest with others isn't always easy for them to determine. In many situations they can't prove or disprove what you say, and must rely on trust. Their trust in you arises out of consistently honest behavior—not just toward them, but toward others.

Your lover may not give it much thought at the moment if she hears you tell your boss without flinching that you won't be at work because you are ill, when you have just made plans to take a long weekend with her, or when she overhears you tell your mother that you weren't able to stop by to visit her as you promised because you were tied up at work, though she knows that the real reason you stood your mother up was that you took her out to dinner. But what will she think the next time you tell her you can't get together with *her* because you are sick, or you tell *her* you have to cancel your date because you must work late?

It may be tempting, even if you prize honesty, to occasionally sacrifice it when your back is against the wall, when you interact with those who themselves are not honest, when dishonesty is the only way to obtain some highly coveted prize, or when your dishonesty is directed toward someone whose opinion of you isn't valued anyway. But as St. Augustine cautioned fifteen hundred years ago, "When regard for the truth has been broken down or even slightly weakened, all things remain doubtful."

Regardless of your justification, when your dishonesty is witnessed by those whose opinions you value, you will lose trustworthiness in their eyes. Everyone knows that fundamentally honest character isn't turned on and off like a light switch. Once you've demonstrated that tendency, you may never recapture another's trust.

How Trust Is Developed

We live in an untrusting society and begin most relationships cautiously. Trust develops from a gradual give and take—a psychological "I'll show you mine if you show me yours." Each time our trust is validated, we increase our expectations, and show greater trust until, ideally, we learn to trust completely. This process evolves through three distinct stages:

- We identify predictable behavior;
- We infer character traits from that behavior;
- We acquire trust.

In the first phase we gather information. Each person notices how the other looks, speaks and acts in different circumstances. Each notices consistencies and inconsistencies in behavior: whether the other does as promised, what makes the other act calmly and what agitates him. Once we have gathered enough information to see patterns develop, we learn to predict one another's behavior.

In the second phase, we begin to infer character traits from the patterns of behaviors we have observed. We begin with the host of stereotypes we associate with trustworthiness. If someone's behavior is consistent with our stereotypes of a trustworthy person, it reinforces them. In time we begin to develop confidence that the other is trustworthy by nature.

Once our assessment of another's behavior has led us to infer that he or she is trustworthy, we enter the third phase—trust. At this point, we allow ourselves to believe that the person will act consistently with his or her past behavior and trustworthy nature. We no longer require specific validation or proof to predict the future.

Displaying consistently trustworthy behavior is the best way to encourage others to trust us. But trust is also created at an emotional level when either person in a relationship shows trust in the other.

Any inconsistency between our actions and beliefs creates what is known in psychological terms as "cognitive dissonance," or discomfort. We naturally try to eliminate this discomfort by reconciling our beliefs and our actions. For example, if a woman volunteered to work part-time for a charity, she would tend to form a belief in the charity's importance, independent of any rational analysis about the charity's true merit. If she devotes time and energy on behalf of the charity—that is, engages in behavior that makes sense only if the charity is worthwhile—she will have the psychological need to believe that the charity is worthwhile, and she will.

For the same reason, if someone engages in actions that reflect her trust of another, her trust in the other will increase. In fact, some research has shown that her own trusting actions toward another may have a greater effect on her level of trust in him than even his trustworthy actions toward her. Consequently, whenever we create situations in which another must trust us, we will enhance his or her trust of us.

Other research has shown that someone will trust us more if we trust him. There are several reasons why it is difficult to distrust someone who appears to trust us completely.

- First, we assume that trusting people are more trustworthy; and that those who distrust everyone else project their dishonest quality onto others.
- Second, those who are the beneficiaries of our trust tend to feel compelled to reciprocate by showing us trust, much like returning a favor.
- Third, we give someone power over us when we trust him. We have made ourselves vulnerable, and have vested him with a sense of importance. When empowered in this way, most people feel compelled to exercise that power charitably toward us—which means they will trust us more.
- Finally, our trust in another reflects our positive view of the relationship. We say, "We have the kind of relationship in which trust should flourish." This naturally encourages the other person to adopt that same impression of the relationship, and to act consistently with it.

As William Pitt observed, "Confidence is a plant of slow growth. . . ." Consistently trustworthy behavior, encouragement of others to trust us, and expressions of our trust in them, all contribute to the growth of trusting relationships. But we mustn't expect trust to evolve overnight.

CARING

Nicholas Green was seven years old when he was shot in the head and killed by highway robbers while visiting Italy with his family in 1994. It would have been understandable for Nicholas's parents to be outraged and bitter. But instead, to honor their son's life and assure that his death was not in vain, they donated his organs to Italian children. As shocked as the world was by the violent and tragic death of the young boy, his parents' compassion, generosity and forgiveness was even more overwhelming. The gesture brought praise from around the world.

In an increasingly impersonal world, those who show such compassion and concern for others are rare jewels. The Green family's caring gestures brought them international respect and admiration. Every day you, too, have the opportunity to touch others' lives in a multitude of ways by showing you care about them.

We use the word "caring" as the second point of the compass to embrace a variety of qualities that all have a concern for others at their core. Your expression of that concern toward others, as much as any other quality, feeds their craving to feel important and worthwhile, and to know that you can and will meet their needs.

There are cutthroat businesspeople who proudly proclaim that the key to their success is a ruthless assault on the world of business, and any who get in their way. They measure their achievement by the size of their bank accounts, not by the quality of their relationships. But these tales of ruthless professional conquest are rare. Very few of the hundreds of successful businesspeople described in the dozens of books that fall generally within the genre of "success literature," have achieved success, even if measured solely in dollars and cents, without a talent for building, rather than destroying relationships.

Matt, a successful businessman, told us a story that illustrates how important a caring nature can be. Matt was attending his second meeting as a recent addition to the board of directors of a small nutrition company at which the board was to decide which of several national accounting firms the company would use to audit its financial records. Each firm had sent representatives to make a presentation to the board's auditing committee. The auditing committee narrowed the field to two. The president of the company, William, who participated in all of the meetings, was asked to give his recommendations to the board.

William began by emphasizing that the senior member of the team sent by the first accounting firm, Dick, was extremely well qualified. His firm represented more publicly traded companies in the southwest United

States than any other, and had the best connections within the business and financial communities. William described Dick as extremely confident, perhaps to a fault. The impression Dick left was that his company would be doing William a favor if it agreed to let his accounting firm perform the audit, not that he truly cared about the company.

William then told the board that the senior representative of the team from the second accounting firm, John, was younger, and not as poised or confident. But he was friendly and paid close attention as William described his business, and the role he hoped the accounting firm would fulfill. John also was well qualified; but his qualifications and experience, and those of his company, didn't measure up to those of the first accounting firm.

After William's presentation to the board, Matt put the question directly to William, "Who do you recommend, and why?" William responded, "I think we should go with the second firm. John seems like the kind of guy who will think about us when he's shaving."

And that's who got the business—John, the guy who impressed William that he would think about William's company when he was shaving. That's who usually gets the business and forges the deepest and longest-lasting personal and business relationships; because he's the one whose concern for us makes us feel important.

Caring is shown in many ways. But no single means of displaying concern for others is as effective in isolation as it is in combination with the others. To convey the best possible impression of a caring nature, you should project:

- Love
- Compassion and kindness
- Friendliness
- Graciousness
- Interest and attentiveness

Love

You love your partner, and you love your dog—presumably in very different ways. That is the nature of love. It's almost indefinable in breadth and degree. Because love is equated frequently with only one of its many facets, romantic love, we chose the term "caring" to describe the second point of the Compass; but the broadest definition of love is synonymous with "caring."

No quality has so moved the great theologians, philosophers and poets as love. Buddha taught, "Cultivate a boundless heart toward all beings"; Buddha's Greek contemporary Plato said, "Love has the greatest power, and is the source of all our happiness and harmony"; the Apostle Paul wrote, "And now abide faith, hope and love, these three; but the greatest of these is love"; Gandhi believed, "Love . . . is the law of our Being" and Martin Luther King, Jr., said, "When I speak of love, I am speaking of that force which all the great religions have seen as the supreme principle of life."

It is little wonder that love, reflected in your caring and concern for others is so critical to the formation of their impressions of you.

Compassion and Kindness

Compassion and kindness so color the messages sent from others' emotional brains to their rational brains that few decisions about you will be untainted by their influence. Nice guys don't finish last. They're forgiven their mistakes more frequently, trusted more quickly, believed more readily, seen as more attractive, and consistently given the benefit of any doubt. Nothing predisposes others to form a favorable opinion of you more quickly and enduringly than when you show the guys in your mailroom that you're a kind and compassionate person. As Albert Schweitzer once said, "Constant kindness can accomplish much. As the sun makes ice melt, kindness causes misunderstanding, mistrust, and hostility to evaporate." In your attempt to forge favorable impressions, never ignore the power your compassion and kindness toward others has on their impression of you.

Friendliness

Most of us are attracted to outgoing, fun-loving people. They enjoy life and those around them; their happiness is contagious. They are the ones we hope show up at a party because parties are always more fun when they come. We don't mean the dance-on-the-table, lampshade-over-the-head type, but the few who are always in the middle of a lively, laughter-filled conversation. They don't all fit the same mold; but they all have a few traits in common.

They share. They share their jokes, their smiles, their eye contact, their touches, their conversation. They reach out visually, verbally and physically to connect. They're kind. Their humor isn't acidic. Their conversations aren't filled with gossip and sarcasm. They are positive and upbeat, supportive and encouraging. They are happy, trusting, and giving. And others respond.

We should all take to heart the Chinese proverb: "A man who does not smile should not open a shop." Maybe there are a few who believe that they are more effective managers or more devoted employees if they're all business, all the time. But they're wrong. Every relationship is enhanced by friendliness.

Graciousness

Graciousness is an elusive concept. When asked to envision a gracious person, one may think of a wealthy socialite, another of the perfect suburban housewife, a third of her elderly grandmother. But graciousness does not require a millionaire's mansion, June Cleaver's high heels and pearls, or the age and dignity of grandma. To impress others with your graciousness, just keep one basic rule in mind: *The most gracious people are those who make others feel most comfortable.*

Your actions can be viewed as gracious by one person, and pretentious or condescending by another. Their reaction will depend on how you make them feel about themselves. George Eliot once wrote: "Hostesses who entertain much must make up their parties as ministers make up their cabinets, on grounds other than personal liking." There are times when you should make up not only your dinner parties, but also your choice of clothing, vocabulary, conversation and behavior in ways that make others comfortable.

Off-color jokes, offensive remarks, rude behavior and other conduct we describe later as "Toxic Traits" show a distinct, and fairly obvious, lack of graciousness. But ungracious behavior needn't be so obvious. Any conduct that makes others feel awkward, embarrassed, nervous or unimportant will suffice.

As a society, we have lost many graces of days gone by. They have been replaced by the steely touch and electronic hum of efficiency. A warm smile and friendly "thank you," can't be delivered by e-mail. And no one can hug over the phone. You can't show your graciousness by opening a door, pulling out a chair, or helping someone carry a heavy package when you communicate only electronically.

To some extent, we are all victims; the reality of the twenty-first century. But you still have opportunities every day to extend courtesies, good manners and graciousness toward others. Those opportunities that arise must be nurtured to full bloom if you are to incorporate graciousness into your Impression Management Plan effectively.

Interest and Attentiveness

You are at a professional gathering when someone you know enters the room. You walk up, say "Hello" and extend your hand. She says "Hi," as she surveys the room over your shoulder. You are in an office meeting to discuss business issues with your staff, and one person seems more interested in the traffic outside than what you have to say. Or you are at dinner with your boyfriend. As you express your frustration with the computer system at work that crashed that afternoon, he can't take his eyes off the menu. What do these actions tell you? Do they say, "You're important, I care about you?" Do they show a willingness to meet your needs? Of course not. Such behavior cries out that neither you nor what you have to say matters.

As the seventeenth-century French philosopher François duc de La Rochefoucauld so aptly noted, "We frequently forgive those who bore us, but cannot forgive those whom we bore." Inattention and disinterest insert distance into a relationship and forge poor impressions. On one level you will insult and offend your partners when you fail to show them that they rate a few seconds or minutes of your undivided attention. On another, you convince them that no matter what abstract capability you may have to meet their needs, if you don't pay attention when they reveal those needs to you, that potential will never yield fruit. In the end, if you don't appear to be interested in them, they'll find someone who is.

Caring Is Also Marked by Consistency

A few years ago Tom worked at a company that lost its biggest customer. Everyone in the company was terrified that there would be layoffs. The owners called an all-hands meeting in an attempt to reassure the employees and to maintain morale and productivity. They announced that the loss of the customer was only a temporary setback, and assured everyone that their jobs were secure. Two weeks later, after some number crunching and handwringing, the owners laid off 15 percent of the workforce, including the woman who had the most years of service with the company.

The owners decided that short-term profitability was more important than long-term jobs and relationships. Their motive was obvious to everyone: Money was paramount, people were secondary. To compensate for the bloodbath, the owners tried to recapture the good will of their employees by sponsoring regular activities designed to show their friendship and support. They seized upon every opportunity to have baby showers, after-work drinks and hors d'oeuvres, and other company "celebrations." But they discovered that once they had surrendered their compassion, they couldn't buy it back with a few cocktail weenies and a couple of glasses of Chardonnay. Within a year, almost all of the employees who had survived the ax voluntarily left to take jobs elsewhere.

One cruel act will outweigh a dozen acts of compassion. Don't expect to be forgiven just because you were "having a bad day," or were under stress. Most of us share the sentiments expressed by Aesop, who wrote in "The Man and the Satyr," "I will have naught to do with a man who can blow hot and cold with the same breath."

HUMILITY

Humility, the third point of the Compass, is a unique quality. By its very nature it cannot be revealed directly. It magically disappears when some-one tries to display it. Humility must be inferred either from the absence of traits that are perceived as arrogant, self-centered or selfish, or from the existence of traits that show attention to others' needs—like compassion, kindness, graciousness and attentiveness. You cannot prove that you are humble. You can only prove that you are not.

Typically, humility is equated with "modesty," and is found lacking when signs of its opposite traits appear—arrogance, boastfulness, pride, pretension or vanity. But there is a second and even more powerful component to humility when applied to Impression Management—the concept of sacri-fice, team play, unselfishness and a proclivity not to consider oneself above others. It is the tendency to be unselfish in word, thought and deed.

Those who are modest are usually unselfish as well; and those who are arrogant are typically selfish. But that is not always the case. We've all seen professional athletes who are the consummate team players on the field, but flamboyant self-promoters off it; and others who quietly hog the ball at every opportunity; or actors who are shameless egomaniacs offstage, but never upstage anyone during a performance. The same is true in the workplace, social settings and at home. Someone can be horribly self-impressed, and still be willing to sacrifice her interests for others; and another may be as quiet and unpretentious as a church mouse, yet have no regard for anyone's interests other than his own.

Because we have all found that modesty and unselfishness, like arrogance and selfishness, are almost always seen in tandem, we make the same stereotypical assumptions from either or both of these separate elements of humility. It is, therefore, not enough to be modest and unassuming if you don't convey a willingness to sacrifice for others; nor will you be perceived as humble if you are unwilling to put others' needs before yours even if you are unassuming. To impress others with your humility, you must always project *both* modesty *and* unselfishness.

Modesty

Arrogance can destroy what might otherwise be a favorable impression as thoroughly as a nuclear blast. Have you ever wondered why the greatest Olympic swimmer of all time, Mark Spitz, was never able to parlay his Olympic success into a commercial one? He was handsome, articulate and comfortable in front of the camera. The problem was his arrogance. He was indeed great; and he was always quick to tell us all about it. Nancy Kerrigan, the silver medalist who suffered a controversial loss to Oksana Baiul in the 1994 Olympic women's skating finals, discovered that her pouty, distant and cold arrogance didn't sell either. Spitz and Kerrigan were both great athletes, but the public was blinded to their accomplishments by their arrogance.

On the other hand, Olympic athletes like decathlete Bruce Jenner, figure skater Scott Hamilton and gymnast Mary Lou Retton enjoyed great commercial success because they didn't act as if they were better than us because of their athletic accomplishments. They were "down to earth." They were humble. And we admired, respected and rooted for them, as we do for most people who have reason to be proud but remain humble.

Arrogance, vanity, conceit and self-importance trigger strong emotional reactions. When you expose others to that view of your personality they become angry, resentful and envious. When that occurs, their emotional brains so distort their rational brain's perception of you that you are destined to fight an uphill battle in your effort to make a good impression. No one wants to favor the arrogant with his or her friendship or respect.

Arrogance is such a powerful emotional stimulus that it even overcomes the basic rule that "people like people who are like them." Those who are honest are drawn to honest people; friendly people to others who are outgoing; the intelligent to other intellectuals; and professionals to professionals. But even the prideful respond negatively to others who are arrogant. As Benjamin Franklin said, "The proud hate pride—in others."

Unselfishness

In thousands of interviews, we have seen every combination of traits imaginable attributed to individuals—except one. We've never heard anyone say that a person was both selfish and caring. The two words just can't describe one individual.

We have a natural tendency to believe that those who are self-absorbed and selfish are not only likely to ignore our needs, but probably will sacrifice them for their own. As Sir Francis Bacon once said, "It is in the nature of extreme self-lovers, as they will set an house on fire, and it were but to roast their eggs." Egg roasters are everywhere: the woman who flirts with the love of your life, not because she's really interested, but because it feeds her ego, the coworker who is always first in line for the plum assignments that are likely to further his career but is nowhere to be found when it is time to do the thankless grunt work that ends up on your desk; the member of the PTA who rejects your ideas offhand if they differ from hers, for no better reason than to maintain control.

You don't need to be cocky and arrogant to lack humility. Even worse, you can be selfish and self-absorbed. Arrogance or cockiness is like the tip of an iceberg that warns ships to change course. But selfishness is the massive body of ice that lies beneath the surface and poses the greatest threat.

Balancing Humility and Confidence

Most people view humility like a seesaw. If you elevate yourself, you necessarily lower others. When you do, you make it clear that you neither consider them important nor have any intention of fulfilling their needs. You have focused on yourself. On the other hand, when you assume a supporting role in others' lives, you elevate them. You tell them that they are important, and that you will sacrifice your needs to fulfill theirs.

This doesn't mean you must always subordinate your needs to the needs of others. We have characterized humility as modesty and "unselfishness," rather than "selflessness," for a reason. "Selflessness" suggests the need to surrender your interests, goals, dreams and even your values, for the benefit of others. That will make you a martyr, but not necessarily a saint. As we speak of the importance of humility, we are not suggesting that you surrender your self-respect or dignity, that you allow others to take advantage of you, or that you refuse to stand up for what you believe, or what is right. No one respects a doormat.

Unselfishness does not require that you deny your own needs. When we tell a child not to be selfish, and to share her candy with her friends, we don't refuse her any candy for herself. You should have a healthy ego and a natural desire to be recognized for your abilities and achievements. Sometimes you want to be the star, not a member of the supporting cast. This is a noble objective. Without a measure of ego, self-doubt emerges, and with self-doubt comes failure.

Impression Management requires that you constantly balance one objective against another, and one trait against a second, third or fourth. You must find equilibrium between your natural desire and need to project confidence and capability on the one hand, and humility on the other, for without both you cannot make the best possible impression. That balance will come as you apply the Impression Management techniques you will learn in later chapters.

CAPABILITY

The first three points of the Compass—truthfulness, caring and humility—combine to create "character." In some casual relationships nothing more may be expected of you. But in all professional relationships, and in many personal relationships, others also expect you to be capable. They need to know that you can provide them with what they need, whether it is a secure job, a properly programmed VCR, or a well-prepared meal.

The traits that are most commonly associated with capability are intelligence, competence, confidence and professionalism. True leadership emerges when these traits exist in an individual who also shows the qualities required of "character."

Through our research and experience we have found that there are many common misconceptions about what lies at the core of people's perception of intelligence, competence, confidence and professionalism. Many people act in ways they think will advance their image of capability, but really don't. Instead, they produce toxic side effects. As you review our discussion of the principal components of capability, free your mind of whatever preconceptions may have driven your efforts to appear capable in the past, because if you're like most people, many of them are unwarranted.

Intelligence

Those without a remarkably high IQ shouldn't be discouraged. No one is likely to make you take an IQ test to measure your intelligence. Instead, the impression others form of your intellect will come from an assortment of traits you can control and enhance.

Our surveys reveal that intelligence is perceived primarily from one's knowledge, vocabulary, grammar, good judgment and common sense—none of which are within the exclusive province of those blessed with remarkable IQs. Knowledge can be gained by anyone, regardless of intellect. And anyone committed to improving his image can increase his vocabulary, and eliminate slang and bad grammar.

What most people value even more than raw intelligence is "good judgment," "common sense" or "street smarts." "Nothing astonishes men so much as common sense and plain dealing," as Ralph Waldo Emerson observed.

Many brilliant people lack common sense. Their deficiencies may be revealed by insensitivity to others, bad judgment, inappropriate behavior, an obsession with facts or topics that others find unimportant or irrelevant. If you are blessed with uncommon intelligence, make every effort not to fit the stereotype of the socially inept genius. Use the techniques you will learn later to convey your intelligence in socially attractive ways.

If you're not exceedingly intelligent, learn to trade on common sense and people skills. As Yale psychologist Robert Sternberg found in his study of what traits people associate with "the intelligent person," practical people skills are among the most important, and they don't require a high IQ.

Common Misconceptions About What Creates an Impression of Intelligence

As you formulate your Impression Management Plan keep the following misconceptions in mind. Many people fail to impress others because they adopt these traits. If you are guilty of any of them, mark them down in the "don'ts" column of your Impression Management Plan.

You Can't Rest on Your Academic Laurels

There's an old proverb, "Wisdom is not bought." And intelligence is not assumed simply from the existence of a college degree or lofty professional rank. Many people share Will Rogers's observation: "There is nothing as stupid as an educated man if you get him off the thing he was educated in."

In one of our surveys we asked what traits jurors believed were most important to the credibility of an expert witness. The manner in which the expert presented himself was almost twice as important as his experience, which in turn was almost twice as important as his credentials. Credentials and experience are factors that will be added to the mix as people assess your intelligence. But ultimately, your appearance, speech and actions carry much greater weight.

Don't Be Reluctant to Admit What You Don't Know

We don't suggest that you take every opportunity to acknowledge your ignorance. But many people believe that they will be considered less intelligent if they admit to anything less than omniscience.

We have interviewed hundreds of individuals about their reactions to witnesses who were unwilling to admit what they didn't know, or were critical of ideas or opinions of which they had no knowledge. Witnesses adopt this approach in an attempt to appear more intelligent. But it usually backfires. Jurors uniformly discredit their intelligence as a result. They think they're close-minded and opinionated. Even worse, they tend to believe that they have tried to "bluff" their way through their testimony rather than admit a lack of knowledge. This destroys their credibility, as surely as it will destroy yours. As Confucius said 2,500 years ago, "When you know a thing, to hold that you know it, and when you do not know a thing, to allow that you do not know it—this is knowledge."

Don't Compromise Accuracy for Speed

We wish we had a dollar for every time we've seen a witness destroy his credibility because he was under the impression that the jury would think he was less knowledgeable and intelligent if he took a moment to think about a question before he answered it. Instead, a witness will fire back a quick response that proves to be incorrect, and spend the next half-hour backpedaling. On the other hand, we have seen many witnesses who paused and carefully contemplated their responses. Jurors uniformly respond well. They perceive the witness's pause as a sign of honest and intelligent reflection, especially if accompanied by consistent body language.

Don't be afraid to say "Let me think about it," or "I'll have to look into that and get you an answer tomorrow." Precision is associated with intelligence. Statements that are made so quickly that they couldn't possibly have been well thought out diminish the impression of the capability of even the most intelligent person.

If You Don't Have Anything Intelligent to Say, Don't Say Anything at All

Like those who are always quick with an answer, those who believe that they must constantly interject their thoughts into a conversation to appear intelligent risk failure. Your intelligence will be judged by the *quality*, not the *quantity*, of what you say.

As important as it is to display your intelligence when the opportunity arises, bear in mind the wisdom of Mark Twain: "It's better to keep your mouth shut and appear stupid than to open it and remove all doubt." Or, as more recently expressed by Chris Matthews in his book *Hardball*, "Only talk when it improves the silence."

Useless Knowledge Isn't Impressive

Ralph Waldo Emerson once wrote, "An Indian has his knowledge for use, and it only appears in use. Most white men that we know have theirs for talking purposes." Some people seem resolved to impress us with their intelligence by displaying their knowledge of words or facts— which so far as we can tell, have no useful purpose—or by sprinkling their conversations with obscure vocabulary and trivia. Most of us carry neither dictionaries nor encyclopedias to interpret others' obscure references; nor do we want to.

Those who communicate their thoughts most clearly and effectively are most highly respected. Knowledge of facts or words that helps you accomplish this objective is valuable. But any attempt to trot out obscure words or facts to show how smart you are usually backfires. It makes others feel inadequate, which in turn makes them resent you.

Clever Is Not Necessarily Good

Those who are crafty usually believe their cleverness is admired. They are able to outwit, take advantage of or embarrass others with their clever tongue, mind and actions. But for intelligence to be revered, it must be of a sort that fulfills, not threatens, our needs. Cleverness, craftiness and shrewdness are much more frequently feared than revered. This is not the quality of intelligence that leads to favorable impressions. It will cause others to be suspicious of you, and devalue your intelligence; since they will assume you get by on trickery or craftiness, not raw intellect.

Competence

Recently a repairman came to Jo-Ellan's house to fix a broken microwave. She quickly formed a negative impression of his competence. He seemed like a nice enough guy, moderately articulate and appropriately dressed. But as Jo-Ellan watched and listened, she identified a number of characteristics that combined to form her poor impression of him.

It seemed an effort for him to shuffle from one side of the kitchen to the other. He looked down at the floor almost apologetically as he spoke. Instead of saying what he thought was wrong with her microwave, he was quick to say that he had no way to know for sure. When Jo-Ellan asked him to call the appliance store to see if one of the parts that might be needed was in stock, he asked her to make the call.

Not surprisingly, this microwave repairman never did get his act together. Jo-Ellan ended up calling another company. When the second repairman showed up, he was friendly and extremely positive. As he walked into the kitchen he commented, "I've serviced this microwave before." In fact, Jo-Ellan did have the microwave serviced years earlier. When she checked her records, she found that it was the same repair company, and obviously the same repairman.

In just a few minutes, the second repairman identified what part was broken and was able to tell Jo-Ellan the exact cost of the repair from reference to his loose-leaf notebook that specified the cost of the part and the labor charge. His knowledge and preparation were impressive. But what impressed Jo-Ellan most was his "can do" attitude. His behavior in every respect illustrated the core of competence: the ability to get things done correctly, promptly and efficiently.

The only way for others to know for certain that you are competent is for them to give you a chance to prove yourself. But you will be given that chance only if you project traits that cause others to believe you can get the job done. Competence is inferred from intelligence and confidence. Intelligent people are assumed to be competent because they have the intellectual power to perform. Confident people are thought to be more competent because they are presumed to have reason for their confidence.

Any trait that reveals intelligence and confidence will help establish an impression of competence. In addition, we have found that competence is directly inferred from these four traits:

- Attention to detail
- Initiative
- Preparation and planning
- Careful thought

Attention to Detail

Unfortunately, we rarely encounter someone who is particularly good at what he or she does. A person who understands what we call the "95/5 rule" is an even greater rarity. The "95/5 rule" is: "The last 5 percent of any effort creates 95 percent of a lasting good impression."

If a painter spends 95 hours painting a house, but leaves before he spends the last five hours needed to carefully assure that everything is cleaned up and no spots have been missed, the owner will focus on the last 5 percent, no matter how well the painter performed the first 95 percent of the task. If an employee spends 10 hours preparing a thorough report, but doesn't spend the last 30 minutes proofreading it, and typographical and grammatical errors abound, the boss will focus on the employee's lack of attention to detail, which in turn will raise questions about the reliability of the information contained in the report.

After the fact, it's easy for someone to tell whether you are a rarity who actually tends to every detail. But before you get the opportunity to prove yourself, people will have to draw that conclusion from the way you look, speak and act. If your hair isn't combed, your clothes aren't neat, your shoes aren't shined and you don't speak in a logical and orderly fashion, why should they assume your work will reflect any greater care? But if you're well dressed, immaculately groomed, and appear on time for an interview with several copies of your resume neatly tucked inside a carefully labeled folder, you will appear to be attentive to detail and someone who understands the "95/5 rule."

Initiative

Employee performance reviews are an invaluable source of information about the traits that are considered important by those who must judge others' qualities. We have reviewed more than a thousand performance evaluations that rate employee competence and have found that initiative, or more frequently the lack of initiative, is mentioned more often than any other trait apart from "attention to detail/lack of attention to detail." Management consultants and career counselors have written volumes that stress how important initiative is for anyone who hopes to get ahead in the workplace. We completely agree.

Nothing will frustrate your bosses, coworkers or customers more than when they see the ball that they thought they placed in your court come bouncing back to them without resolution. When that happens, you leave them with the impression that if they want it done right, they'll either have to do it themselves, or find someone else to take care of it. On the other hand, one sure way to impress everyone in your life is to be that one in ten who looks for solutions, and doesn't rest until he finds them.

It may be difficult to show initiative at a first meeting or interview. But opportunities usually arise early, and frequently, in every relationship. You may be able to communicate that you are the type of person who takes initiative from something as simple as volunteering to prepare and route minutes of a meeting; or calling ahead to make reservations at the restaurant where your friends plan to meet for dinner.

Preparation and Planning

The most effective way to convey competence in a job interview is to prepare for it. Learn everything you can about the company and even the person who will interview you. Be prepared to ask intelligent questions that reveal your preparation. Your questions also will help you better evaluate your audience, which will make you perform better. The interviewer then will assume a greater degree of competence not only from your advance preparation, but also from your enhanced performance in the interview.

Preparation and planning are directly associated with an increased probability of competence in every exchange, not just interviews. The fact that you thought enough to prepare says much; the extent to which preparation improves your performance says even more.

Careful Thought

Our emotional brains get very nervous when someone to whom we entrust an important task seems to act too quickly. We wonder: Has he really thought this through? Has he considered all of his options?

People want to know that you are willing to take the time required to get to the right answer. If you appear to make decisions hastily and without careful evaluation of your options and their consequences, you won't instill trust in others. Don't interrupt others as they try to explain a task, promise them completion in record time or announce after a millisecond's thought that you know exactly how to solve a problem with which they have struggled for weeks. It is possible that they'll think you are significantly more gifted and competent than they are. But more likely they'll think you're careless.

Confidence

Norman Vincent Peale's 1952 book *The Power of Positive Thinking* popularized the notion that confidence gives us the courage and resolve necessary to achieve our full potential. But when confidence is displayed outwardly, it does more than empower you; it motivates others to believe in you, which gives you the opportunity to prove that your confidence is warranted.

When asked to describe what makes someone appear confident, those we surveyed rarely based their belief upon what someone *said about himself*. Boastfulness, self-promotion, cockiness, arrogance, pride and conceit, however, are high on the list of traits that create a negative impression. These traits are extremely toxic, and unnecessarily detract from others' impressions of your trustworthiness, caring and humility. Many people have such a fundamental misunderstanding of how confidence is conveyed that they damage their image when they try to display it. You will convey confidence without tarnishing your image in other respects only if you project confidence with traits that are consistently well received, and avoid those that are not.

Traits Which Do and Don't Communicate Confidence

When we asked 125 adults what most impressed them that a person was confident, the person's body language was mentioned more than twice as frequently as any other category. Within the category of body language, posture was the hands-down winner. "How they carry themselves," "The way they stand," "They hold their heads up" and similar comments were repeated frequently. Other more general references to body language were also common, such as "calm," "relaxed" and "demeanor."

A number of other traits that are overlooked by those who attempt to project an air of confidence are also quite safe and effective. They include:

- *Candor:* When you freely and unapologetically express your ideas, opinions and values you show your confidence. If you qualify your opinions constantly or, worse yet, appear reluctant to express them at all, you create the impression that you are unsure of yourself. But remember, if you express your opinions so adamantly that you appear close-minded or controlling, you will diminish other qualities.
- *Consistency:* We respect those who have confidence in their beliefs. If you are wishy-washy and change your beliefs, opinions or priorities with the wind you will do more than simply project the impression that you have no firm convictions. Your constant vacillation will be associated with a lack of belief in yourself.
- *Enthusiasm:* Your level of enthusiasm is directly equated with your confidence, as long as it amounts to more than nervous energy.
- *Initiative:* When you are proactive and take initiative, you reveal courage and faith in your ability to accomplish tasks.
- *Strength:* Physically fit individuals with excellent posture are assumed to be confident, even if they have adopted these characteristics to overcome basic insecurities.
- *Vocal Quality:* "How someone speaks" came in second to posture in our survey that asked what traits lead to the conclusion that someone is confident. A strong, unhesitant voice exudes confidence.

Each of these traits can be managed in ways that will produce no toxic side effects. Yet those traits most frequently adopted in an effort to appear confident—hornblowing, the know-it-all approach, domination and criticism—not only fail to project confidence effectively, they are replete with often incurable negative associations.

Hornblowing

There will always be the Muhammad Alis of the world who say with conviction, "I'm the greatest," and have the ability to back up their claims. The boastfulness of these few may be seen as complete confidence. But more frequently, those we have interviewed interpret self-promotion by others as an effort to talk not only their audience, but themselves, into believing their own press. Even if you are able to effectively communicate your self-confidence through self-promotion, your confidence will be seen as cockiness. People will assume that you are so self-centered that you won't apply whatever knowledge or skill you possess for their benefit. By any measure, boastfulness is the least effective and desirable way to communicate confidence. Instead, follow Will Rogers's admonition, "Get someone else to blow your horn and the sound will carry twice as far."

The Know-It-All

Confidence, like competence, doesn't require that you are right all the time or think you are. If you waver constantly, apologize for your thoughts, and are unsure of yourself, you will be doubted. After all, if you don't believe in yourself, why should anyone else? But if you profess to have all of the answers all of the time, it will have the same effect on others' perceptions of your confidence as it does on their perceptions of your competence. The approach will wear so thin so quickly that others' responses will be to decide that you are either insecure or arrogant. Either way, you lose.

Domination

Another common misconception is that you can show confidence by controlling others. If you attempt to dominate every conversation, head every committee, choose every restaurant, and win every argument, astute observers may think you're insecure. Those who don't believe you are insecure will be so put off by your behavior that any association between your conduct and the confidence you want to convey will be overwhelmed by the more emotional reaction that you are pushy and overbearing. Conquest runs afoul of every rule of good Impression Management, including those that create a positive impression of confidence.

Criticism

You will diminish your impression of confidence if you are critical. You won't enhance it. To borrow a biblical coinage, most people sense that those who are highly critical of others think their light shines brighter when they hide another's under a bushel basket. We ask ourselves, "Why?" What we are likely to conclude is that those who are critical feel the need to tear others down to build themselves up. That doesn't display confidence. Most people share Kahlil Gibran's sentiment, "Deliver me from . . . people who acquire self-esteem by finding faults with others."

Professionalism

You don't need to hold a graduate degree to be "professional"; nor are you "professional" just because you do. The bank teller who greets each customer with a friendly, "Hello, may I help you?" is professional. The telephone operator who tells the caller: "Hold your horses, I'll get to you when I can" isn't. The cab driver who keeps his car clean and neat, and seatbelts readily accessible, is professional. The housekeeper who leaves the windows streaky isn't. The policeman who asks politely, "May I see your license, please?" is professional. The doctor's receptionist who asks in front of a crowded waiting room, "Are you here to see the doctor about that discharge again?" absolutely, positively isn't.

In our most recent survey we asked the respondents to identify what traits most influenced their impression of someone's professionalism. The way someone "dressed" was identified by 29.1 percent of the respondents as the first trait they considered. Another 6.4 percent listed "appearance" or "grooming." More than 35 percent of the respondents, therefore, identified appearance-related traits first. By comparison, body language and vocal traits tied for second place, each accounting for 14.6 percent of the total responses. Only 8.2 percent of the respondents identified someone's job or educational level as the first characteristic they considered as they evaluated whether someone is "professional."

In the narrative portion of the participants' responses to our questionaires, we found three themes arose most frequently as people discussed what impresses them as professional.

- *Appearance:* The first criterion is whether you are neat, clean and appropriately dressed for your position. Whether you are a schoolteacher, postal worker, appliance repairman or jet pilot; whether you wear a required uniform or have complete discretion in your choice of wardrobe, don't take your decision about grooming or what to wear lightly.
- *Graciousness:* If you are loud, pushy or discourteous, or if you embarrass, interrupt, ignore or are otherwise insensitive to other's needs, you will not be viewed as professional, regardless of your academic qualifications or job status. On the other hand, if you display dignity, good manners, courtesy, respect for privacy and graciousness, you will be well on your way.
- *Dedication:* Julius Irving described what it means to be professional as, "Doing all the things you love to do on the days when you don't feel like doing them." If you have a nine-to-five attitude and just go

through the motions, you won't be seen as professional. If you skip your breaks to get your job done well, and come in before nine or stay after five if that is what is required, you will. Professionalism means letting your boss, coworkers, and customers know that they can count on you to get the job done right, no matter what. It requires an outward display of commitment, responsibility and dedication.

LEADERSHIP

What makes us turn to certain men and women for direction and inspiration? Leadership. We did not include "leadership" among the four points of the Compass because it is not truly a separate quality. It is what emerges when a single individual possesses all of the qualities represented by the Compass. The *character* reflected by trustworthiness, caring and humility alone cannot create leadership; nor can the *capability* embodied by intelligence, competence, confidence and professionalism. It takes both remarkable character and capability to be an inspirational and powerful leader.

By "leadership" we do not mean "authority." We have all known those in positions of authority who do not possess the Compass Qualities. They may be high achievers, but they aren't *leaders* in the true sense of the word, they're just *bosses*. When we speak of leaders, we also are not referring to politicians or CEOs alone, but also to the millions of parents, teachers, Little League coaches, small business owners and partners of all types who have found their Compass.

In our research, we discovered the same characteristics of true leadership were identified repeatedly, whether by respondents in our surveys or experts on business management. As you read through them you will see how each trait reflects on one or more of the four Compass Qualities.

- *Leaders are doers:* Leaders take charge. They are proactive. They are outspoken. They volunteer. They don't wait for things to happen. They make them happen. They are willing to take risks *and* responsibility. They contemplate, but they don't obsess.
- *Leaders are confident:* Leadership requires confidence, not swaggering cockiness, but a calm, natural, effortless control.
- *Leaders lead, they don't push:* True leaders don't force anyone to follow them; they make others want to follow them. They don't abuse their authority for ego gratification, but exercise it purposely, to benefit not just themselves but those they lead.

- *Leaders watch over their flock:* Leaders make others feel important and cared for. They are sensitive to their needs and desires. They do not expect their followers to respond to their own needs, but are sensitive to the needs of those who follow them.
- *Leaders are open-minded:* Opinionated, headstrong know-it-alls are seldom successful leaders. Effective leaders recognize that the knowledge required for leadership is enhanced by a willing ear and an open mind.
- *Leaders support and empower others:* Leaders bring out the best in their followers with their support and encouragement.
- *Leaders appreciate others:* Leaders give praise and credit freely. They are not stingy with accolades, and do not steal others' thunder.
- *Leaders trust others to succeed:* Leaders know when and whom to trust, and with what to trust them. They encourage others' success, and give them the incentive to strive for it.
- *Leaders show respect for others:* Leaders don't act superior to those they lead. They recognize it is human nature to like those who like us, trust those who trust us, and respect those who respect us.
- *Leaders show true personal character:* True leadership is not acquired by authority, but by influence. Such influence is obtained by trust in the fundamental character of a leader.
- *Leaders are enthusiastic:* Enthusiasm energizes those who follow a leader, and injects them with the leader's commitment and dedication to his or her cause.
- *Leaders inspire:* Leaders inspire others with their vision, creativity, innovation and imagination. They engender a belief in a positive future, which their followers hope to achieve for their benefit, not just the leader's.
- *Leaders are capable:* Successful leadership requires performance. Capability, in the form of intelligence, competence, confidence and professionalism, is required to instill trust that a leader will be able to create order from chaos and to guide his or her followers through both calm and tumultuous times.
- *Leaders lead by example:* Leaders ask no more from their followers than they are willing to give themselves.
- *Leaders build partnerships:* Leaders do not sit atop the wagon pulled by others, but join them side by side to pull together toward a common goal.

If you strive to become a leader by incorporating each of these fifteen characteristics into your Impression Management Plan, you will have captured the essence of the Compass.

THE COMPASS AS
A SINGLE INSTRUMENT

The four Compass Qualities are interdependent, like the four points of the compass we have used to symbolize them. The absence of any one quality adversely affects each of the others, just as strength in one or more areas helps shore up weaknesses in others.

We are frequently asked, "I understand that all four Compass Qualities are important, but which is *most* important?" It seems that human nature cries out for a contingency plan in the event one or more of the Compass Qualities must be scuttled. We liken the choice that must be made when one of the Compass Qualities must be compromised to achieve another to the dilemma that faces shipwreck survivors adrift in a lifeboat. Water, food and shelter from the elements are all indispensable. Which one should be sacrificed depends upon how much benefit each will provide if it is retained, and how much will be lost if it is jettisoned.

TRADEOFFS

Invariably, there will be occasions in your life when seemingly irreconcilable conflicts arise between the qualities we all hold dear. We wrestle with this daily as we work to help lawyers and witnesses present themselves in the best possible light. If an expert witness talks too much about his credentials, will he adversely impact the jurors' view of his humility? If a lawyer is brutally candid about the opposing party's foibles, will she be seen as cold, critical and harsh, maybe even unprofessional? If a judge bends over backward to be fair, will he be perceived as weak?

After years of weighing and balancing the four Compass Qualities to arrive at the best Impression Management Plan for each person and circumstance, we have found that a few general rules will help guide you to the best result.

> *Rule Number 1:* No trait can be compromised without affecting every other trait.
>
> *Rule Number 2:* Never compromise trustworthiness.
>
> *Rule Number 3:* In social environments, don't compromise caring or humility for capability.
>
> *Rule Number 4:* There are no clear-cut rules that govern which Compass Qualities you should emphasize in professional relationships. You must evaluate each relationship separately.

No Trait Can Be Compromised
Without Affecting Every Other Trait

The four essential ingredients in the recipe for a great impression must be added to the mix with a steady eye on how each impacts the others. Because of the interrelation among each of the Compass Qualities, you cannot focus on any one to the exclusion of the others without repercussions. There are times when you will need to make tradeoffs; but if you understand how a touch more of this ingredient or a pinch less of that will impact the recipe, you will find that the creation of an effective Impression Management Plan is not difficult.

Never Compromise Trustworthiness

Most of us really don't care if our dentist is egotistical or humble. We want her to be caring and capable. And we also want her to be trustworthy. We don't want to question whether she has recommended dental work simply because her son's college tuition check is due next week. We would like our mechanic to be friendly and humble also. But if he is honest and does a good job, we can live with a mechanic who is a grouchy egomaniac. And our friends don't have to be rocket scientists, but we want them to be caring, humble—and trustworthy.

You may be able to achieve some measure of success in many relationships, even many long-term relationships, though you lack caring, humility or capability. But if people don't trust you, you won't, and can't, make a good impression. In every relationship, begin with the uncompromising objective to convey trustworthiness.

That is not to say that there will never be occasions when even the most honest among us will be less than candid. In fact, brutal honesty is often unnecessary and counterproductive. We don't suggest that you sacrifice caring, humility and capability unnecessarily in favor of an uncompromisingly rigid standard that requires you never to speak a falsehood, sugarcoat the truth or keep your honest feelings to yourself. Anyone who does is like a bull in an emotional china shop.

You don't feel compelled to tell your toddler that Santa Claus, the Easter Bunny and the Tooth Fairy are just make believe. When your favorite uncle comes to visit with his overbearing, opinionated and rude second wife, hopefully you don't meet them at the door with, "It's wonderful to see you Uncle Harry, but why did you have to bring *her* along?" And how far will you climb up the corporate ladder if you feel obligated out of a commitment to complete candor to point out just how stupid you think your boss is every time he makes a mistake.

No one will blame you if you compromise truthfulness on appropriate occasions. In fact, they will expect and demand it of you. The impact of a lie almost always depends on your motive. Perhaps the rule "never compromise truthfulness," should be qualified. A better way to state the rule might be "never compromise truthfulness for selfish gain, or when the lack of candor will hurt someone else."

At first blush, this may seem to be a very difficult line to draw. But it isn't if you just put yourself in the shoes of the person with whom you have not been completely candid, and ask how he probably would have responded if you had been candid. Then ask how he would likely respond if he discovered you were not completely honest. Uncle Harry won't think any less of you because you kept your thoughts about his new wife to yourself; but he probably would be quite offended if you didn't.

Whatever you do, don't fool yourself into believing, or expecting others to believe, that your motives are something that they aren't. An attempt to justify deceit on the basis that "what they don't know won't hurt them," doesn't further a noble purpose. If you don't tell your spouse about an affair because you "don't want to hurt him," no one will accept that your deception was justified. And if you lie to your employees about the prospect of a year-end bonus to enhance morale, you really aren't acting with altruistic motives. Your behavior is a deceptive effort to maintain morale and productivity by misleading your employees to believe there is a pot of gold at the end of the rainbow if they just work hard. When they discover that you lied, they won't thank you for sparing them anxiety about how they are to pay for those extra holiday expenses.

In any situation in which your lack of truthfulness cannot be justified charitably, don't compromise trustworthiness. It must be considered the first among equals as you develop and project the four Compass Qualities. Have faith that any relationship worth maintaining will withstand a healthy dose of honesty. As Oliver Wendell Holmes wrote, "Truth is tough. It will not break like a bubble, at a touch. Nay, you may kick it about all day, and it will be round and full at the evening." The same can't be said of deception.

In Social Environments,
Don't Compromise Caring or Humility for Capability

Others respond to your trustworthiness, caring and humility primarily at an emotional level. Their assessment of your capability, on the other hand, is influenced more by their rational brains. If you do or say something that they find foolish, or if you make an honest mistake or drop the ball, they may be frustrated or disappointed if they relied on your capability to fulfill their needs. But it is unlikely that anyone will become enraged because you prove to be less capable than expected. If you are untruthful, uncaring or egotistical, however, others will take it personally; and their emotional brains are likely to respond violently. We can't recall ever thinking to ourselves, "I really dislike that person, because he or she isn't very bright." But, like most people, we certainly have taken an immediate dislike to others who we thought were dishonest, cold or cocky.

In professional interactions it is often necessary for you to emphasize your capability. If asked to provide input during your annual performance review so that the decision makers in your company can determine your year-end bonus, you are expected, and in fact required, to tout your accomplishments. When you interview for a job you need to point out your strengths. When you attempt to convince a client or customer to follow your recommendations, you must stress your past experiences and successes to enhance your credibility.

But the balance between humility and capability that is appropriate in professional interactions typically will be viewed as conceit in social environments. If you interview for a job and are asked, "Tell me a little bit about yourself," you might begin, "I received my undergraduate degree with honors from Duke University, and a Masters and Ph.D. from Columbia, where I was selected for a Fulbright Scholarship." This would be perfectly appropriate, particularly if not delivered in an overtly arrogant or self-impressed fashion. But imagine how you would react if you met a man at a party, asked him to tell you a little bit about himself, and he started off, "I received my undergraduate degree with honors from Duke University. . . ." You'd probably gag.

The impression others form of you in purely social environments will be influenced much more by their assessment of your character than your capability. Save your confident self-promotion and blatant displays of intelligence for appropriate occasions in the workplace. Your friends and family are much more interested in knowing that you are trustworthy, caring and humble.

There Are No Clear-Cut Rules
That Govern Which Compass Qualities
You Should Emphasize in Professional Relationships

Rachel just turned fifty when she decided that she wanted a face-lift. The waiting room of the first doctor she saw brought back memories of the last time she visited the Department of Motor Vehicles. The chairs were inexpensive and worn. A scratched and stained coffee table offered an assortment of old *National Geographic* and *People* magazines. The receptionist wore a casual cotton dress and no makeup. Even before she saw the doctor, Rachel decided that she didn't want to entrust him with her face. Her expectations were that a plastic surgeon, and his staff, would be fastidious, well-groomed, and very appearance-conscious. After all, that's their business.

The next plastic surgeon she interviewed had an office in an upscale medical building with a beautifully decorated waiting room. Contemporary paintings hung on walls that were covered with a fabric that accented the pillows carefully positioned on baby-soft leather couches. A glass sculptured coffee table housed the latest editions of an assortment of fashion magazines and an exquisite crystal statue. The receptionist was a beautiful woman in her mid-thirties, who was dressed in a business suit and looked as if she just walked off the cover of one of the fashion magazines on the waiting room table.

Everything about the office met Rachel's expectations. It was clean, tasteful, elegant, new and stylish—exactly as she envisioned her new face. While the skill of the two surgeons may have been comparable, Rachel's decision to entrust the only face she had with the second surgeon was easy. It had nothing to do with the surgeons' relative trustworthiness, caring or humility, and everything to do with her assessment of their probable capability.

In some cases, more than one Compass Quality may be important when someone selects a professional. Day care providers furnish an excellent example. The most important quality for a day care provider is usually a warm and caring nature. For eight hours a day our young children will look to him or her for comfort, affection and warmth. But we also expect day care providers to be capable. A loving and friendly day care provider who doesn't instill confidence that he or she will keep our child out of harm's way or stimulate her intellectually doesn't have "all the right stuff." A day care provider, therefore, must project both caring *and* capability.

In professional situations, once you recognize how various aspects of your outward appearance impact others' impressions of the qualities you possess, follow the same three-step process that we consider each time we prepare a witness to testify at trial:

- Consider what qualities people value most in someone in your profession;
- Ask yourself how others expect someone in your profession to display those qualities; and
- Meet those expectations.

THE POWER OF THE COMPASS

When we ask ourselves whom we admire most in life, it is not the president of the United States, the most powerful man in the world, or Bill Gates, the most wealthy, or beautiful models or talented actors and singers. It is those people who have truly found their Compass and are guided by it each moment of their lives. It's Stan, a sign electrician who works in a blue-collar job, and lives in a middle-class neighborhood. He is not handsome, wealthy, famous or blessed with some unique talent. But he is a man who is constitutionally incapable of deceit and lives a life at peace with himself and those who surround him. He is a loving father and husband, a dedicated and loyal friend and a hard-working employee. He doesn't speak ill of others, and has a smile and kind words for the clerk at the grocery store, his daughter's teacher and even the police officer who stops him to give him a speeding ticket. He is a man who, as Confucius would have said, is "a superior man." Not because he thinks he is, but because he knows that he isn't.

CHAPTER 4

First and Lasting Impressions

Any successful real estate agent will tell you that "curb appeal" is critical to a quick sale. However wonderful your house may be on the inside, no one will call the number on the sign out front if the house doesn't make a good impression from the street. Much the same can be said about the impressions others form about you.

WHY FIRST IMPRESSIONS
ARE SO IMPORTANT

To anyone who says, "I don't need to worry about first impressions, once they get to know me, they'll love me," we say, "good luck!" Unless you get your foot in the door with a good first impression, you'll seldom have a chance to prove yourself. Bad first impressions can be corrected. But to do so, you have to overcome human nature; and that's not easy.

First impressions tend to last because:

- Others immediately form stereotypical associations about you that are frequently entirely emotionally based;
- Once emotional impressions are formed, they color later rational analysis;
- Others assume their first impressions are correct; and
- Once impressions are formed about you, others' rational and emotional brains seek to validate those impressions.

STEREOTYPES REGISTER IN OUR EMOTIONAL BRAINS ALMOST INSTANTLY

Our emotional brains evolved at a time when quick reactions made the difference between eating or being eaten. Rational thought takes much more time to process than stereotypes or emotions.

As a result, emotional biases and stereotypes lie at the foundation of most first impressions. Any later assessment of your character will be colored by this initial impression. Test this hypothesis yourself. Isn't it true that you typically form the impression of someone like, "She's really nice," and *then* think about what he or she did or said that led you to that belief? You don't first evaluate someone's behavior and then say to yourself, "In view of that behavior, I think it's fair to conclude that she is really nice."

EMOTIONAL IMPRESSIONS COLOR LATER RATIONAL ANALYSIS

Any decision is only as reliable as the information on which it is based. Once someone has formed a first impression based on an emotional or stereotypical reaction to you, her rational analysis will be affected, whether or not she realizes it. The decisions Ms. Cerebrum makes are always colored by the emotional spin the guys in the mailroom have put on whatever traits you display. She will believe that she has reached a correct and logical conclusion about you, even though it is based on emotionally laden and perhaps distorted information. That may work to your advantage, or it may be devastating, depending upon how well you manage that first impression.

EXPERIENCE TELLS US THAT OUR FIRST IMPRESSIONS ARE USUALLY CORRECT

With the passage of time, those who have formed an opinion of you may question whether that opinion is justified. But they will begin with the belief that their first impression is correct. Almost everyone we interview tells us they trust in their first impressions because they have found that for every one person about whom they have said, after the fact, "I guess I misjudged him," they pegged ten accurately from the start.

Research validates our confidence in the accuracy of our first impressions. In a recent study, students were introduced to one another and asked to assess the others' characters based upon their brief exposure. Later, the students' initial impressions of one another were tested against each participant's assessment of his or her own character, and input from individuals who knew each of the participants well. The research found that in slightly more than two-thirds of the cases, the group's prediction of the qualities of the members of the test group was confirmed by the individuals and their closest friends and family members. In another study, the group's initial assessment of one another was found to be correct approximately 80 percent of the time.

These research results are borne out by our experience as well. In many cases we spend years working closely with lawyers and witnesses. We see them in a variety of situations and form strong impressions of their characters. When the lawyers and witnesses ultimately are exposed to jurors, and we interview the jurors afterward about their impressions of the witnesses and lawyers, we find that the jurors' initial assessments of them is almost always accurate.

When others form first impressions of you, their experience tells them they are probably correct, which means you have the burden to persuade them that they are wrong. This would be an uphill battle even if others were truly open to the possibility that they misjudged you. But, in reality, others tend to resist even persuasive evidence if it contradicts their first impressions.

WE SEEK TO VALIDATE OUR FIRST IMPRESSIONS

To create positive impressions you must identify any stereotypes someone might apply to you early in your relationship and manage them from the inception. Once someone applies a stereotype to you, he will seek to confirm it. As Daniel Goleman notes in *Emotional Intelligence,* "People remember more readily instances that support the stereotype while tending to discount instances that challenge it." Because you will be subjected to a greater degree of critical examination once a stereotype has arisen, the slightest notion that you fit the stereotype will cause him to think, "Aha, I knew it." As a result, someone will believe that his stereotype-prompted judgment of you is valid, even though an objective assessment of your appearance, speech and behavior would contradict it.

The psychological term "cognitive consistency" explains why first impressions are often lasting impressions. Cognitive consistency is the theory that we seek consistency between reality, and what we believe reality to be. Once we form a belief in the existence of something, we are reluctant to see things differently. We want to believe we are right, and find it disturbing to accept the possibility that we're wrong. This tendency not only leads us to accept our initial impressions without question in most cases, it also prods us to see others in whatever light fulfills our existing expectations—even when that isn't justified.

In our research we came across an article that discussed the frequency with which married, middle-aged men and women have affairs with their high school sweethearts decades later. The study dramatizes the strength of our tendency to distort reality to conform to impressions implanted in our emotional brains. It seems that even twenty or more years later men and women still see their high school idols as they were then, the captain of the football team or the head cheerleader—vibrant, fit, attractive eighteen-year-olds—not as they are now—balding, overweight, stuck in a nine-to-five rut. Their high school impressions are still embedded in their middle-aged emotional brains, which resist seeing their dream girl or boy in a realistic light. Their rational brains not only don't challenge the impressions implanted by their emotional brains, they adopt them.

In another study that demonstrates how our initial impressions cause us to seek to confirm them, researchers observed seventy-nine interviews of prospective employees by three different interviewers. When they had favorable first impressions of prospective employees, the interviewers asked fewer "tough" questions and gathered less information about the interviewees. Instead, they spent much more time "selling" themselves and their company. As a result, they created a relaxed and friendly environment to which the applicants responded more favorably.

When the interviewers formed initially unfavorable impressions of the interviewees, they asked more specific and pointed questions targeted to confirm their initial negative impression. The interviewers' nonverbal behavior toward these applicants also changed. Their body language, vocal tone and communication style were less friendly and solicitous, which resulted in greater discomfort and correspondingly poorer performances by the applicants.

We expect that the experienced interviewers were able to size up the interviewees fairly quickly and make an accurate preliminary assessment of their potential in most cases. But in those cases in which the interviewers may have misjudged the applicants initially, their behavior toward the applicants reinforced their first impressions. Their positive or negative behavior created a self-fulfilling prophecy by inducing either favorable or unfavorable performance in response.

The same process is repeated constantly in both professional and personal relationships. If you are rude and abrupt with your new employee, that employee is likely to form an impression that you are uncaring and egotistical. Every future encounter will be colored by that initial impression and by the employee's natural reluctance to change his opinion of you. Even later acts of kindness will be ignored or minimized. The employee also will behave less positively toward you, which makes it less likely that you will warm up to the employee. The employee will then believe his initial impression of you was accurate. Likewise, if you show up for your first date with dandruff on your shoulders, you will immediately create the impression that you have poor grooming habits; and your date will tend to pick up on mild bad breath or wrinkled clothes that might otherwise have gone unnoticed.

As a result of this tendency, someone will be convinced that he has given you a fair opportunity to prove that his initial impression of you was wrong. But he really won't have been open-minded. We have confirmed this phenomenon many times in post-trial interviews. Jurors almost always form their impression of the lawyers and witnesses very early during a trial, and seldom change that impression. Those jurors who form a favorable initial impression of a witness or lawyer will give a positive spin to the very same testimony or behavior that is seen in a negative light by those who have formed a negative first impression. They all believe that they view the witnesses and lawyers accurately and with open minds. But the fact is, each sees or hears something different depending upon the bias created by his or her initial impression.

If a person's initial emotional response to you is poor, any further "analytical" assessment of you will be so tainted that it is unlikely to change his or her impression. Faith in the accuracy of a first impression, and the psychological need to reaffirm it, will build an often insurmountable barrier to a change of heart—or mind. But the opposite is also true. A good first impression puts you on a track to success from which it is much more difficult to be derailed.

FIRST AND LASTING IMPRESSIONS ARE BASED ON THE SAME QUALITIES, BUT ARE REVEALED BY SOMEWHAT DIFFERENT TRAITS

As we discussed earlier, surveys of those qualities that people find most important to impression formation show that trustworthiness, caring, humility and capability, not good looks or success, are what form lasting good impressions. To determine whether the same qualities would be identified if the focus were on *first* impressions, we asked 135 adults to identify the most important and second most important characteristic that caused them to form a positive *first* impression, or a negative *first* impression. The respondents were not given a list of characteristics from which to choose, but could specify whatever they felt was most important.

The results are shown in the table below. The number of times a positive quality was mentioned as a first or second choice is reflected in the first two columns. The total number of times it was identified as either the first or second most important positive quality is set out in the third column. The number of times the negative side of a characteristic was mentioned is set out in the fourth, fifth and sixth columns. The seventh column, "Grand Total," reflects the number of times each characteristic was mentioned in either a positive *or* negative context.

CHARACTERISTICS THAT LEAD TO A POSITIVE/NEGATIVE IMPRESSION UPON FIRST MEETING SOMEONE							
	Positive			Negative			
	First Choice	Second Choice	Total	First Choice	Second Choice	Total	Grand Total
Trustworthiness/Lack of Trustworthiness	53	30	83	13	16	29	112
Caring/Lack of Caring	30	26	56	29	19	48	104
Good/Bad Dress or Appearance	12	15	27	13	11	24	51
Humility/Arrogance	0	0	0	17	14	31	31
Positive/Negative Attitude	4	2	6	13	9	22	28
Good Manners/Rude	1	2	3	17	2	19	22
Intelligence/Lack of Intelligence	2	12	14	2	5	7	21
Good/Bad Hygiene	1	2	3	4	9	13	16
Calm/Angry or Hostile	0	0	0	3	10	13	13
Competence/Incompetence	5	3	8	2	3	5	13
Confidence/Lack of Confidence	3	4	7	0	0	0	7

If you turn back to the results of our survey on page 43 of what characteristics lead to a favorable impression generally and compare them to the results of our survey of what creates a favorable *first* impression, you will see that the criteria for positive first *and* lasting impressions are remarkably similar. There is, however, one significant difference—dress and appearance—which is relatively insignificant to the formation of *lasting* impressions, but shot past all but trustworthiness and caring on the list of characteristics that formed *first* impressions. The explanation for this is as simple as it is important.

Personal appearance, body language and voice have greater influence on initial impression formation than other colors, since they provide us with information that can be processed instantly. As relationships mature, however, we begin to acquire information from sources such as communication style, content, actions and environment that usually require more time and thought to communicate and evaluate.

In a job interview, for example, the interviewer will rely heavily upon your personal appearance, body language and voice as she forms her first impression of you. If your clothing is neat, clean and appropriate and you are well groomed, the interviewer will infer that you are meticulous and socially adept. She will have to rely on these appearance-related traits initially to reach that conclusion, because she will have very little information from other sources. As the interview progresses, she will acquire more information about you from your communication style and the content of what you say. As a practical matter, she probably will learn little about your actions or environment, unless you are hired.

Qualities like friendliness or arrogance are easier to assess from initial visual and oral input than other qualities like trustworthiness. We make assumptions about others' trustworthiness based in part on personal appearance, body language and voice, but in most cases what someone says and does ultimately carries more weight. But it takes time and exposure to validate trustworthiness based on someone's actions.

As we describe how each of the Seven Colors can be applied to create great impressions, bear in mind that early in a relationship, appearance, body language and voice must be given particular attention to assure others will form a favorable first impression of you. As your relationships mature, the other four Colors will assume greater significance. They may not be the key to great first impressions, but they are essential to creating good lasting impressions.

PASSIVE AND ACTIVE TRAITS

You may have noticed when you reviewed the chart listing the character-istics that lead to a positive or negative first impression that a number of characteristics were identified frequently as negative traits but seldom as positive ones. These include a lack of humility, negative attitude, rudeness, bad hygiene and anger. For example, humility was not mentioned once as a positive trait, but arrogance was mentioned as a negative trait thirty-one times. We refer to such traits as "passive traits" because their positive side has much less impact on impression formation than their negative side. Other traits, like intelligence and confidence, are more frequently described as positive traits, and their opposites, a lack of intelligence or a lack of confi-dence, are mentioned much less frequently. Confidence, for example, was mentioned seven times as a positive trait, but lack of confidence was never mentioned as a negative trait. We call these "active traits" because they are shown affirmatively. Most traits, like truthfulness and caring, are both active and passive, which means that both their positive and negative aspects contribute to impression formation.

The distinction between active and passive traits can be seen if you con-sider the impression you form of those you meet for the first time. As you drive home with your companion from a gathering where you have met a number of people for the first time, you're likely to comment, "Joe sure was friendly," or "Janice seemed very bright." These characteristics play a role in your initial impression formation because they are noticed when they are displayed actively. On the other hand, you probably have never said, "Joe sure was clean," or "Janice didn't do anything rude all night." Good hygiene and common courtesies contribute much less to impression formation. But if Joe or Janice had been arrogant, rude or filthy, the negative side of these pas-sive traits would have made a powerful impression. The positive side of pas-sive traits are not particularly noteworthy because we expect everyone to display them. But we don't expect people to be grumpy, harshly critical, short-tempered, dirty, rude or smug. When they are, we notice.

Keep the distinction between passive and active traits in mind as you create your Impression Management Plan. To make a good impression, you must make an effort to display active traits such as trustworthiness, caring, intelligence and confidence. But don't expect to make any great headway just because you display the positive side of passive traits. No one will be impressed that you wash behind your ears, use deodorant and are dandruff-free, or that you don't belch or slam doors in people's faces. This just meets minimum expectations; it doesn't score many points. But if you display the negative side of any passive traits, such as arrogance, rudeness, bad hygiene or quick anger, you will make a very poor impression. The best impressions, therefore, are made when you display active traits and scrupulously avoid any hint of the negative side of any passive traits.

PREPARE TO MAKE A GREAT FIRST AND LASTING IMPRESSION

Ninety-five percent of all lawsuits are settled before the judge's gavel falls on a single day of trial. Lawyers spend months, even years, preparing for trial even though they know their carefully scripted opening statements and masterful witness examinations probably never will be put on public display. But every good trial lawyer knows she has to be ready when opportunity knocks. There's even an old adage among trial lawyers, "The case you don't prepare for trial is the one that will go to trial."

Life is no different outside the courtroom. You anticipate that Mr. or Ms. Right might be at a party and dress up in anticipation of the chance to bowl someone over with your beauty, charm and grace, only to be disappointed. You hope that each sales call will be the one that will bring in the big account and you prepare a flawless presentation, even though you realize that disappointment is more probable than success. It's easy to adopt the attitude, "What's the use?" But when you do, you create a self-fulfilling prophecy of failure. As Confucius said, "In all things, success depends upon preparation, and without such preparation, there is sure to be failure."

A thirtyish, single mother and radio talk show host in San Francisco shared a story with us that highlights the importance of always preparing to make a great impression. Becky had taken her young son to the playground at the local park on a cool Northern California morning. She threw on some old sweats and a pair of tennis shoes and headed out the door without giving any thought to her appearance. She admitted that whenever she went to the park she fantasized that she would meet a single father there with his child and she would strike up a conversation that would lead to a meaningful romance.

As she pushed her son in the swing, a woman perhaps five or ten years her senior approached her. "Do you speak English?" the older woman asked.

"Yes," Becky answered.

"Do you have any friends or family who might be interested in a position as a nanny?" the older woman continued.

Becky saw firsthand the power of stereotyping. Becky has a dark complexion, brown eyes and dark brown hair. In her community there are many Hispanic nannies who frequently take children to the park during the day. The older woman had concluded from Becky's dark complexion, hair, eyes, dress and presence at the playground with a young child during the middle of the day, that she: (1) was Hispanic or some other foreign nationality; (2) might not speak English; and (3) was a nanny.

Becky wasn't offended by the woman's assumptions but she realized that her dream of meeting a young, professional, well-educated man at the park was not likely if her potential Prince Charming drew the same conclusions the older woman did.

As Oprah Winfrey said, "Luck is a matter of preparation meeting opportunity." Positioning yourself to make a great impression is a matter of playing the odds. If you prepare to make a great impression on only isolated occasions, the chances are you'll miss many opportunities. But if you're always prepared, you'll make the most of opportunities when they do arise.

SIX STEPS TO MAKING A GREAT IMPRESSION

Everyone you meet *will* form an immediate impression of you. With advance planning you can manage that impression. This is equally true whether your contact is face-to-face, over the telephone, or solely through the written word transmitted by letter, fax or e-mail. Even though personal communication has the power to create stronger impressions, don't ignore the impressions that you make by other means. The same concepts apply in any type of communication. You can't always use all Seven Colors to paint the best possible image of yourself, but you should always make the best use of those Colors that are available.

Preparing to make a great impression is a five-step process.

Step one: Learn to see yourself as others see you.
Step two: Be clear about your objective.
Step three: Know your audience.
Step four: Create an individualized Impression Management Plan for each important encounter.
Step five: Roll with the punches.

Learn to See Yourself as Others See You

Even though psychologists and psychiatrists may disagree in theory, no one should know you better than you know yourself. You know how you think, how you feel, what you value, what you hate, your strengths and weaknesses, whether you're nervous or confident, honest or deceitful. Even if you accept the notion that you know more about yourself than anyone else, research regarding self-perception suggests that you probably don't accurately assess how *others* perceive you, particularly with regard to your nonverbal behavior. In one respect or another (and usually in many), most of us are not viewed by others as we view ourselves. Sometimes we have a more charitable view of ourselves than others do; but research demonstrates that more often we are actually more critical of ourselves than others are of us.

A good example of how important it is to see yourself as others do comes from an employee review conducted by Paula of a young attorney in her law firm several years ago. The employee was reviewed by Paula and several of the firm's other partners. A common theme in each of the reviews was the concern that the employee, Larry, was arrogant and not a team player.

Larry was shocked when Paula relayed this concern to him. He thought of himself as humble, and always willing to do whatever was in the firm's best interest. The problem was that he was a very good-looking man, a former model whose perfect grooming and posture, confident air and outspoken nature led others to believe that he was stuck on himself. To some degree he was simply the victim of his extraordinary good looks and the stereotypical associations that arose from them. But to a larger degree the impression resulted from a combination of traits that accentuated those negative stereotypes. Many of those traits were within Larry's control; others were an indelible part of his nature.

Larry was assertive and outspoken. Paula counseled him to back off a bit and tone things down. In informal settings in particular he needed to relax and quit acting as if he were in front of a camera. In public, he should avoid mirrors like rattlesnakes—better that a hair should be out of place than anyone should see him glance sideways as he walked by his reflection. He also needed to disclose more about himself and to be more conversational. Larry was a private person and didn't ask much about others' personal lives, just as he preferred that others not probe into his. But one of the best ways to overcome a perception of egotism is to ask others about themselves. They love it, and naturally assume anyone interested in them must be okay.

Larry didn't realize that the image he thought he projected was dramatically different from what others saw. This is not an isolated example. People seldom see their own facial expressions or body motions as others do. When you look in the mirror you don't duplicate the subtle expressions that you transmit to others' emotional brains in your real-life encounters. You also have a distorted sense of the quality of your voice, as was no doubt reflected in your reaction when you first heard your voice on tape. You may litter your speech with filler words and sounds like "um," or "okay" or "ah," and be genuinely surprised when someone points out this characteristic to you. Or you may interrupt constantly and be oblivious to this bad habit.

Many individuals' lack of self-awareness isn't limited to subtle nuances. For example, even remarkable facial tics can go totally unnoticed, as Mark discovered in a trial several years ago. Mark's client, Roy, was a successful businessman who had a noticeable facial tic, particularly when he was nervous or upset. The left corner of his mouth and left cheek would jerk violently downward and the sudden tension in his neck muscles would pull his chin toward his left shoulder. The tic was dramatic, obvious and frequent.

During jury selection, Mark wanted to make sure that the jurors understood that this was a neurological condition, and not a sign that Roy was lying whenever it happened. He asked the jurors if they would be able to keep an open mind about the truthfulness of Roy's testimony even though he might occasionally flinch. Mark did not speak with Roy about this issue before trial, as he did not want Roy to become any more self-conscious than Mark presumed he already was; and Mark knew there was nothing either of them could do to stop it. It never occurred to Mark that Roy might be unaware of such an obvious trait. So he was shocked when Roy bent over as he sat down after he finished questioning the jury and asked, "What facial tic?" At first Mark thought Roy was joking. But he wasn't. He had never noticed it. Apparently no one had called it to his attention, or if they did, Roy had ignored their comments.

If you're serious about making a great impression, you must become aware of both your strengths and your weaknesses. That degree of personal objectivity is difficult to achieve unless you invest the time and energy required to learn how others see you from every source possible.

Videotape

Videotape will allow you to view your appearance and body language and hear your voice as others do. If you have never videotaped yourself and watched, you'll be amazed, perhaps shocked. If you don't own a video recorder, buy one or borrow a friend's and videotape yourself in as many different situations as possible. Pretend to give a speech to imaginary occupants around your dinner table. Set up the recorder on a tripod in the corner of the room and sit on the couch and have a conversation with a friend. Videotape yourself as you enter a room, walk across it, and take a seat.

Videotape yourself frequently enough that you become relaxed in front of the camera, and not so self-conscious that your normal behaviors are affected. Then watch and listen to the tapes. Identify what characteristics you have and those you lack. Are you energetic or passive? Open or closed? Dominant or submissive? Outgoing or shy? Is your voice melodic or monotonous? Loud or soft? Distinct or nasal? Are you a good listener or do you interrupt frequently? Do you ask others questions, or do you just talk about yourself? Do you make good eye contact? Do you smile? You may think you know the answers to these questions, but we can assure you that if you try this exercise you'll find that your view of yourself is inaccurate in many significant respects.

Look in the Mirror

Though less effective than videotape, looking into the mirror—*objectively*—can be an eye opener. Look at your hair, makeup, clothes, posture. Watch yourself walk and talk. As you do, pretend you are someone else who is looking at you. Try to imagine someone you know who has the traits that you identify in yourself and ask how you react to him or her.

Ask Others How They See You

Your closest friends and family are probably more objective about you than you are. The challenge is finding friends and family members who will honestly express their views, both positive and negative. Assure them that you want candid feedback and that you won't be offended or defensive if they give it. Practice a warm smile and "Thank you, I really appreciate the feedback," to encourage their candor when they favor you with it. If you appear shocked and offended at the first hint of constructive criticism, you're not likely to receive much more.

Watch Others

During the day notice people who make a particularly good or particularly poor impression. Identify what makes them stand out. Then ask yourself how you measure up. Don't limit yourself to just coworkers and family members. Turn on the TV and watch "professionals." Motivational speakers whose livelihoods depend upon their ability to make great impressions often tout their wares on the cable channels; and there are always newsmen and women, as well as talk show hosts and the actors and actresses in TV shows and movies.

Keep Your Eyes and Ears Open

Most people don't like to point out others' flaws, at least not to their face. But sometimes they will hint at them, often behind a thin veil of humor. "Sleep in your clothes last night?" really means, "You should take more pride in your appearance." "Will you please speak up, I can't hear you," might be a nice way to say, "Your mumbling is really annoying." And, "I'm surprised you spend so much time with *her*," may translate, "The company you keep doesn't speak very highly of you." An isolated remark shouldn't trigger the panic alarm. But if you hear repetitive comments about a particular aspect of your appearance, speech or behavior, examine it closely, even if the remarks are made in passing or in jest.

Also keep your eyes open for telltale signs that something you do has a positive or negative effect on others. The most effective way to judge the impact of your behavior on others, particularly your nonverbal behavior, is to watch others' nonverbal behavior in response. If you tend to move your hands expressively as you speak, watch how others react to you when you're most animated. If their eyes are fixed on your hands, the motion distracts them. If they only occasionally glance at your hands then back at your face, and otherwise remain attentive, your animation may help you deliver a powerful and memorable message. When you tell jokes, do people laugh and smile naturally, or do they favor you with only a courtesy response? If you bore others, they won't be able to hide their boredom. If you antagonize them, they will show offense. Keep your eyes and ears open.

Watch Out for the "Emperor's Clothes" Syndrome

Don't be fooled by what we call the "emperor's clothes" syndrome. Or, as Ann Landers put it, "Don't rely too heavily on your dog's admiration." You may be in a position of such authority or dominance in a particular environment or relationship that you will receive positive reinforcement no matter how you look, speak or act. The CEO's executive secretary is likely to rave about his new Ferrari, even though she privately thinks, "No wonder I didn't get a decent bonus this year, the selfish creep spent all his money on a flashy car." And it's unlikely that your new girlfriend will volunteer that your tight-fitting jeans make you look silly. More likely, in an effort to please you, she'll tell you how great you look.

Don't Assume Others
See You Through Your Eyes

Jo-Ellan was in Starbucks one morning when a man in his late twenties walked in. He wore an appliance service company's uniform shirt and shorts that revealed tattoos flowing down the outside of both of his calves from his knees to his ankles.

"Your tattoos are very interesting. Do they have any particular meaning?" she asked.

He seemed thrilled that someone had noticed, and responded proudly, "The one on my right leg symbolizes the natural forces of earth, wind and fire. The other one is an original creation by my friend who's a professional tattoo artist."

"They're fascinating." Jo-Ellan added, "They must have hurt."

As he puffed out his chest, he said, "They took over four hours each; and you can't believe how much it hurt. But then, if they weren't painful and expensive, everyone would have them." He was completely serious.

Jo-Ellan couldn't help but think how interesting it was that he had projected his own beliefs and values onto everyone else. Very few of us would want to have a significant portion of our bodies covered by huge, brightly colored tattoos. But he truly believed that since he did, everyone else must also, and that the only reason we didn't all line up at the tattoo parlor was because we wanted to avoid the pain and expense.

You may hang out with a group that finds tattoos expressive, long hair cool, and extensive body piercings trendy. Or your peers may think the chic, glamorous look is always appropriate. But the question is whether the people whose opinion of you will influence your success and happiness share those beliefs. If your objective is to be well received, your focus must be not on what you think about yourself or the people who share your values and characteristics, but on what others will think about you.

Be Clear About Your Objective

What you hope to achieve in an encounter should dictate how you prepare for it. The goal is always to project the four Compass Qualities. But there are times when it is more important that you emphasize certain qualities, even at the expense of others.

A woman who dresses in a sexy and revealing gown to attend a professional cocktail party will show that she's attractive and outgoing, but at what expense to her professional image? A middle manager who touts his successes at the monthly sales meeting may reveal his confidence and capability, but what does he say about his caring and humility? A woman who boasts of her ability to unload soon-to-be-obsolete product on an unwitting buyer shows she's clever. But is she honest?

Before any important encounter, always ask yourself what impression you hope to make. You can't hit a target if you don't have it clearly in sight.

Know Your Audience

Positive impression formation always requires a transmitter and a receiver that are in sync. What may impress one audience may be unimpressive to another. Think of yourself as a radio station that must clearly identify its target market before it decides on the content and format of its broadcasts. If it wants to appeal to a talk show audience, it emphasizes lively chat. If it hopes to reach listeners at work, it adopts an easy listening music format. If its audience consists of eighteen- to twenty-five-year-olds, it plays the contemporary top forty.

Unlike radio stations, you don't have just a single audience. You have many. One moment you may want to appeal to a conservative business-man, the next to your coworkers, and a few hours later to your friends or family. To be successful in each relationship, you can't always present the same content and format. You should project the Compass Qualities in every encounter, but how best to achieve that objective will vary from situation to situation.

The first step to knowing your audience is to identify their expectations and probable stereotypical associations. If you were to meet a client for a business lunch, you could anticipate that he would expect that you would dress and act professionally. He might also expect that you would take him to an upscale restaurant, pick up the bill and be solicitous if you were trying to curry his favor. If you dressed or acted too casually you would disappoint those expectations, which would tend to create a negative impression.

On the other hand, if you were to make a lunch date with a high school classmate, her expectations would be very different. She would not expect you to take her to an expensive restaurant, or pick up the check. She would expect a more casual, free-flowing conversation, and less formal dress and behavior. If you showed up in your new Brioni suit and kept it buttoned at the waist throughout lunch, designer tie cinched tight, and posture as erect and formal as your speech, you would disappoint her expectations. She would probably think you were full of yourself, nervous, unfriendly or boring.

There are many ways to gather information about the person or people you want to impress. Whenever possible, this information-gathering process should begin in advance of your first meeting and continue as the relationship grows.

Before a job interview, for example, you should learn as much as possible about the company. Company brochures, newspapers and the Internet provide invaluable information. If you know someone at the company, take her out to lunch and pick her brain. You may discover that a distinctive corporate environment exists in which emphasis is placed more on one quality in its employees than on others. Stop by and visit the company before the interview. See how it's furnished. Is it stark and efficient, or luxurious and opulent? Watch the employees. Are they all business, or is there a friendly patter that reflects a casual environment? Notice the working conditions. Are people crammed in small cubicles, or do they have large, private offices? Is there a staff room with plenty of space for employees to relax during breaks and at lunch, or does everyone grab a quick bite at his or her desk? The corporate environment is usually a reliable reflection of the values of its decision makers. Your awareness of those values will help determine how you can appeal to them if you choose to.

Even in casual relationships, advance preparation is invaluable. If you're invited to a party and you're not sure of the proper dress, call ahead and ask. You don't want to show up in a suit when everyone else is casual. Before you meet your future in-laws, find out everything you can about them. Where do they work? What do they do for fun? Do they go to church? Do they have any hobbies? What have they liked or disliked about your partner's previous romantic interests? What are their political leanings? Do they have any quirks? Forewarned is forearmed. The last thing you want to do is unwittingly offend them, or trigger any unique negative stereotypes they may have. Instead, you want to emphasize those aspects of your personality, background, and beliefs with which they will make positive stereotypical associations.

The information-gathering process shouldn't stop when your encounter starts—it should be just beginning. As you evaluate your audience, keep in mind: How do they dress and speak? Are they animated or reserved? Are they open or guarded? Chances are they'll be most comfortable, and most impressed by you, if you do not display characteristics that are in stark contrast to their own. Don't just mirror the way they act; mirror the way they think. The better you understand what is important to them, the greater your ability to deliver it.

We are routinely invited to what are known as "beauty contests." The prospective client contacts several firms and arranges for interviews before deciding whom to hire. The interviews usually follow a similar pattern. After an exchange of pleasantries, the client describes the case and asks for our thoughts. We're then expected to discuss what we think the most important issues are, what research and pretrial investigation can be done to determine how best to present the case and how that research and investigation can be incorporated into the trial theme. The business goes to whoever makes the best impression. The challenge is to identify what is most important to the prospective client's decision-making process, and demonstrate that we're the ones to make it happen.

We've found that the first step to success in "beauty contests" is to identify the ultimate decision maker, and to evaluate his or her primary goals and priorities. For example, some clients favor a "scorched earth" approach to litigation. Money is no object, as long as they win. These clients are most impressed by an aggressive, no-holds-barred approach. Other clients may prefer a more practical, cost-effective solution. They form a more favorable impression of those who propose a quick, creative and inexpensive plan.

Before we launch blindly into an analysis of the case along with our recommendations, we need to know whom to convince and what is important to him or her. We can't possibly do this if we start our presentation too soon. So we ask questions that encourage the decision makers to talk, and we listen. We find out about their attitude toward litigation and the opposing parties, their previous experience with litigation in general and lawyers and consultants in particular. We ask about the importance of the litigation to their company, and whether their objective is to reach a quick settlement, or hunker down for a long siege. We can't present ourselves or our ideas in ways that will meet their expectations until we gather this information.

These same techniques are as applicable for a salesman as he makes his first sales call on a new prospect or a man and woman at lunch for the first time. They're effective because they accomplish the objectives you must always keep in mind as you try to create good impressions—to make others feel important and to show them that you can fulfill their needs. If you ask questions you will learn what those needs are; and in the process you also will demonstrate that others' concerns, beliefs and objectives are important to you.

A friend of ours, an avid fly fisherman, put it best: "If you want to catch a trout, the first thing you have to do is find out what they're biting. Sit on the river bank and watch. If they're eating mosquitoes, use a fly that looks like a mosquito. If they're eating wasps, use a fly that looks like a wasp. The important thing is to use whatever bait is attractive to them. You have to think like a fish, not a fisherman."

Create an Individualized Impression Management Plan for Each Important Encounter

Once you have honestly evaluated your strengths and weaknesses, are clear in your own mind about the impression you hope to create and have learned as much as possible about the people you want to impress, it's time to put together a specialized game plan for any important encounter. It doesn't have to be a major overhaul of your general Impression Management Plan. In fact, it shouldn't be. If monumental change is required, either your general Impression Management Plan needs to be rethought, or you are about to venture dangerously outside your comfort zone in your attempt to make a favorable impression in a particular instance.

Consistency is important to a lasting good impression. If you try to play the role of the conservative businessman from nine to five, and then attempt to be the life of the party at every office social gathering, your coworkers will wonder which is the real you. People don't compartmentalize that easily. They may question whether you are really as professional as you try to appear at work, or whether you are really as friendly and outgoing as you appear to be after hours. They will wonder if you can be trusted to reveal the real you in either environment. The comment, "I've never seen that side of you before," is not always a compliment. If the "new side" you have revealed complements others' perceptions of your core values, great. But whenever the "new side" is inconsistent with the "old side," watch out.

Your general Impression Management Plan should be the foundation of your individualized Impression Management Plans. Changes should be subtle and consistent. Preparation of an individualized Impression Management Plan is essentially the same as that required for your general Impression Management Plan.

- *First:* Keep your eye on the Compass. Every first and lasting impression requires trustworthiness, caring, humility and capability—usually in that order. Deviate from your general Impression Management Plan only if you identify a specific need.
- *Second:* Ask yourself whether in this particular situation, with this audience, one or more of the Compass Qualities should be emphasized more than the others.
- *Third:* Ask what traits should be emphasized to enhance the Compass Quality or Qualities that are particularly important.
- *Fourth:* Consider how emphasis of those traits may impact other Compass Qualities.
- *Fifth:* If emphasis of particular traits in furtherance of your individual-

ized Impression Management Plan will be toxic to certain Compass Qualities, determine what traits you can add to the mix as antidotes.

For example, if you are to make a presentation at work in which you believe you must aggressively promote your experience and successful track record to be most persuasive, you should modify your general Impression Management Plan to emphasize capability. Your general Impression Management Plan shouldn't include large measures of self-promotion; but in this instance, you know that is required if others are to accept your proposal.

You should therefore incorporate statements about your experience and past successes. But you should recognize that such statements will tend to make you appear less humble. To compensate, you should apply healthy doses of traits that reflect humility. You should make a point to keep your body movements relaxed and open to avoid appearing cocky. You should smile and engage in warm eye contact. Your voice should be soft and conciliatory, not strident or overconfident. You should use words like "we" and "our" frequently, and share credit for your past successes with others. You should thank everyone for their consideration of your suggestions. You should even make a point to get coffee for others at the meeting as you pour your own. None of these techniques will diminish the image of capability you want to project when you tell the group, in essence, "I have the experience, expertise and track record to back up my proposal." But these compensating traits will keep the group from concluding that you are arrogant.

As you read through the remaining chapters, you will see that there are many traits that act as antidotes for any toxic side effects that might result from emphasis of any one Compass Quality. Once you have mastered the techniques of Impression Management, you will find it easy to make adjustments to your general Impression Management Plan when called for on special occasions.

Roll with the Punches

The corollary of the axiom "If it ain't broke don't fix it," is "If it's broke, fix it." That is not to say that you should abandon your general Impression Management Plan at the first bump in the road. You may find it awkward to smile at first if you're not accustomed to smiling; and it may take a while to feel comfortable when you engage in prolonged eye contact. Don't stop just because it's difficult at first. And don't abandon your general Impression Management Plan when you discover that you didn't anticipate everything—modify it.

There are always exceptions to the rules. Throughout this book we describe what we have found to be typical or expected responses to particular behaviors. But you may encounter those—no, you *will* encounter those—who do not react in typical or expected ways. For example, what might be seen by most as a friendly inquiry may be viewed by a particularly private person as a rude intrusion into her privacy. If you watch carefully, you'll see that reaction in her facial expressions, body language, voice, or speech. If you ignore these signs, your efforts to appear friendly will backfire, and you will seem uncaring. But if you recognize them, you can back off to the level of contact that she associates with friendliness.

You will need to be flexible and adaptable from time to time. Think of your approach to Impression Management as a dance class for life. Learn the basic steps, and when the music calls for a unique flair you'll be prepared to improvise.

OVERCOMING BAD IMPRESSIONS

Adversity is the ultimate test of character. Unfortunately many of us don't test well. Many bad first impressions are made when you reveal traits that you would normally suppress because encounters take place when you are not at your best due to stress, physical or emotional difficulties, fatigue or distraction.

Effort and focus will overcome many short-term challenges, but when your best efforts can't mask the symptoms of short-term physical or emotional conditions, such as when you are ill or are so overwhelmed emotionally that you can't put your feelings aside, it is often best to explain your situation so that others can factor the circumstances into their evaluation of you. We frequently suggest just that to lawyers who must call witnesses to the stand to testify when they are not at their best. They are often well-advised to begin their examination with the question, "How are you today," knowing the answer will be, "I'm doing fine, if I could just shed this awful cold." Juries are consistently sympathetic. No one wants to begin a meeting with a comment like, "Please forgive me if I'm not as articulate as I might otherwise be as I discuss my proposal. Our four-month-old kept us up all last night with the colic." But a statement like this is usually well received. Of course, if you ramble on for the next hour and your message can't be understood, no apology will compensate effectively for the poor impression you will make.

Sometimes it is inappropriate to share the reasons why you aren't at your best. You can't start off a meeting, "I'm sorry if I'm a little disorganized this morning; I was at a friend's bachelor party last night until 4:00 A.M. and have a horrible hangover." And unless you want to make your audience extremely uncomfortable, you can't volunteer, "Please excuse me if I'm somewhat distracted, I just found out my wife is leaving me for the cable guy."

There will be times when your physical or mental condition is such that you can neither: (1) overcome it with extra effort or "temporary fixes" like a splash of cold water, an aspirin or a cup of coffee; or (2) justify your diminished capacity with a socially acceptable explanation like, "I was up all night with a colicky baby." When that occurs, do everything you can to avoid encounters in which you will make an unfavorable first impression. Reschedule your meeting. Ask someone else to cover it. Don't allow a less than favorable impression to be formed if you can avoid it gracefully.

On those occasions when you simply must interact with others at something less than your best, correct any possible misimpressions as soon as possible. Mark suffered a bout of laryngitis shortly after he started his law firm. He never completely lost his voice; but all that was left was a squeak that sounded like a novice playing the violin—hardly a voice that would leave a positive impression with a prospective client. Sure, it wasn't Mark's fault, and it wasn't his natural voice. It didn't have the power, resonance or tone that conveyed competence, professionalism and success. His voice was just plain irritating.

Mark had several phone calls to make that he knew could be delayed a day or two until his voice returned. That's exactly what he did. He didn't want to have to explain away a bad first impression. But there were also a few phone calls that Mark simply couldn't postpone. During those phone calls he was quick to apologize for his voice, and tried to keep the conversations as short and to the point as possible, since the longer he spoke, the more vividly the impression of his voice would be implanted in the listeners' emotional brains, even though rationally they would understand that the voice they heard was not his true voice.

Mark also made a point as soon as he recovered to call each person he spoke with while his voice was raw. He wanted to replace whatever lingering memories might have been recorded in their emotional brains with the impression of his normal voice as quickly as possible.

Unfortunately, there will always be occasions in life when you are caught flat-footed, or commit one of those unspeakable faux pas that make you feel like diving under the closest furniture for cover. You've made a bad impression.

- Mary's at the grocery store when she runs into the cute guy from the marketing department at work whom she's been dying to meet. She's wearing an old pair of jeans and a T-shirt, no makeup, and her hair's a mess.
- Jerry's racing from the parking lot across the street to the building where he is late for a very important meeting with a prospective new client. As he crosses the street a man driving a blue Mercedes, also obviously in a hurry, screeches to a halt just a few feet in front of him and honks. Jerry, already stressed because he is late, mutters an obscenity and gestures at the man behind the wheel. Unfortunately, no more than two minutes after Jerry rushes into the office for the meeting, the man behind the wheel of the blue Mercedes walks in. As luck would have it, he *is* the prospective new client.
- Rachel has wanted to be assigned to the International Widget account for two years. She finally gets the nod. Her first project is a disaster because she makes all of her calculations based on four-sprocketed widgets instead of six-sprocketed widgets.

When you commit such a faux pas, don't hide from it. Acknowledge it. Apologize for it. Explain it. Correct it. Do something to implant a new and better image in the emotional brains of those who have seen you at your worst—and do it quickly. Mary might make a point to drop by the marketing department the next day, looking her best, to say "Hello." Jerry should apologize profusely and explain that the meeting with his new client was extremely important and he didn't want to be late. Rachel should immediately revise all of her projections and resubmit the project with her sincere apologies for any inconvenience.

After over four hundred trials, we could fill a book with stories about those who either successfully or unsuccessfully rebounded from bad first impressions. With very few exceptions, the stories of those who quickly and candidly addressed their indiscretions and took immediate action to correct the bad impressions they made have happier endings than the tales of those who buried their heads in the sand and pretended nothing ever happened. People can be much more understanding and forgiving than you might think. But you have to take the initiative immediately to change that bad impression. If you ignore it, it will harden like quick-setting cement.

CHAPTER 5

Magic Pills

Man has always searched for miraculous cures. Penicillin, the polio vaccine and Viagra were heralded as wonder drugs because of their phenomenal power to cure illness without toxic side effects. There are also "magic pills" that can be used to create great impressions. Although each has unique properties and works in different ways, they all have a number of characteristics in common:

- They can be applied in every encounter;
- Most of us are physically, mentally and emotionally able to use all of them;
- They don't cost anything and don't require dry cleaning or a fitness trainer;
- Each of them tells everyone you meet that you care about them and are ready to meet their needs;
- Unless taken in massive quantities, they have no toxic side effects; and
- Each, by itself, enhances the impression you make. In combination, the impact is remarkable.

Doug, in many respects, is a model for how to make a great impression. The traits that make great impressions always came naturally to him. As a young man fresh out of college, he quickly became the number one salesman for one of the largest life insurance companies in the world. By the time he was in his early thirties he had become a successful real estate developer who could instill the trust and confidence in investors that was required to persuade them to venture millions of dollars in his projects.

While in the midst of writing this chapter, Mark met Doug in the lobby of one of the hotels Doug owns. From the time Mark first saw Doug across the lobby until they entered the elevator for the ride up to Doug's office for their meeting, Doug demonstrated each of the Magic Pills we describe in this chapter.

As Doug turned the corner and saw Mark across the lobby, he immediately caught Mark's eye, and a smile spread across his face. As he closed the gap between them, Doug picked up his pace and sustained both his initial eye contact and smile. His relaxed but excited appearance and slight forward lean said, "I'm glad to see you, old friend."

As Doug came closer, he reached his hand out and clasped Mark's firmly but comfortably. As he shook Mark's hand, Doug momentarily cupped Mark's right hand in both of his, and raised and lowered their hands slowly two or three times. While still shaking Mark's hand, Doug took his left hand and placed it on Mark's right shoulder and turned him toward the elevator. As he did, he gave Mark a light tap on the shoulder, released their clasped right hands, and walked beside him toward the elevator.

Throughout the exchange, Doug didn't lose eye contact and his smile never faded. His greeting, "It's great to see you, how have you been?" was spoken with an enthusiasm that couldn't help but make Mark feel special.

No doubt you noticed the Impression Management techniques that come naturally to Doug:

- Eye contact
- Smiling
- Handshake and greeting
- Posture
- Enthusiasm

We have encouraged hundreds of people to use these Magic Pills liberally, and we have never seen an overdose when they have been applied with a measure of common sense. If you are not in the habit of using these Magic Pills at full strength, at first it's normal to think that you are exaggerating them. But that is not how they will appear to others. Eye contact that to you seems unnaturally long because you're not accustomed to it will not be too intense. A smile that seems overblown will appear perfectly appropriate. Posture that feels stiff if you tend to slouch is probably still not erect enough. And energetic motions and enthusiastic vocal qualities that may seem extreme to you are seldom considered unnatural by others.

As you learn to incorporate these traits into your regular routine, don't worry about overdoing them. Be concerned that you use them *enough*.

EYE CONTACT

From the time we are small children, we see the eyes of cartoon characters pop out of their heads. Dollar signs are seen in the eyes of cartoon characters when they think of money. Smoke and fire appear when they are angry; and their eyes expand to cover half of their face when they are fearful. The expressiveness of the eyes of cartoon characters is only one of dozens of ways that we have been told from childhood that the eyes are the windows to the soul. It is little wonder that our eyes are often the first place others look as they form impressions of us. And other's reliance on them to reveal clues about us isn't misplaced.

Our eyes have a unique capacity to perceive and transmit emotional messages. Impulses transmitted between our eyes and our brains travel through a conduit of nerves that is twenty-five times larger than those that run from the brain to the ears. These messages transferred between our eyes and our brain produce measurable physiological responses. For example, our pupils enlarge perceptibly when we are sexually excited, angry or lying; and the deep, soft appearance of someone's eyes as she gazes into the eyes of her lover, sometimes called "bedroom eyes," is not a myth. It's a physiological response designed to allow us to receive and send emotional messages better. Strong eye contact also releases a variety of chemicals in our brains, which act as temporary stimulants. The physical "rush" you feel at the heart-stopping moment when you catch the eyes of a beautiful man or woman, or when you are confronted with aggression or fear, is a physiological reaction triggered by the messages sent from your eyes to your brain.

Eye contact creates a powerful conduit between you and others. It helps build rapport that not only makes others more receptive to your communication, but also increases their level of self-disclosure to you in most instances. In one study, the length of job candidates' responses, and the amount of information they imparted, was found to increase based on the level of the interviewer's eye contact. Other studies have established that teachers who maintain good eye contact with their students impart more information that is understood better and retained longer. In another study those subjects who were paired with someone who did not engage in eye contact were reluctant to initiate any form of communication with the other person, thus depriving them of the benefit of communication exchanged not just by mutual gaze, but in any manner whatsoever.

We have found only two exceptions to the rule that good eye contact enhances communication. First, both men and women tend to disclose more intimate or highly personal information without direct eye contact. Even moderate eye contact creates a greater degree of discomfort under these circumstances. This is why people will typically avert their gaze when they relay embarrassing or highly personal information. The second exception is that men, more than women, will disclose less if eye contact is too intense. Overly intense eye contact can create a defensive response that results in withdrawal.

The topic of eye contact arises frequently in our post-trial interviews. In most instances, jurors associate good eye contact with honesty and bad eye contact with deceit. In our experience this is one of the most common stereotypical associations—if not *the* most common. Many studies show how prevalent these associations are. Witnesses in courtrooms are thought to be more credible when they do not avert their gaze. Airline travelers are considered more suspicious and are more frequently searched when they avoid eye contact as they are questioned by customs inspectors. And salespeople are more believable if they look their customers in the eye.

It may seem ironic that research studies have shown that when some people lie they actually overgaze—that is, engage in *more* eye contact than normal. But on reflection, this confirms the near-universal perception that good eye contact reflects honesty and bad eye contact reveals dishonesty. Experienced liars know the importance of good eye contact. Intent on *appearing* honest, they make good eye contact, just as they often avoid nervous gestures that people also associate with dishonesty.

If you maintain good eye contact, you will project that you are trustworthy. If you avoid eye contact, you will raise doubts about your credibility. The only exception documented in both scientific research and our practical experience is when strong eye contact is accompanied by other characteristics that people interpret as "phony," such as what we call the "sincere furrowed brow look," or inappropriately familiar touches such as the politician's handshake, exaggerated smiles, or the invasion of someone's "personal space." When other verbal and nonverbal behavior points toward insincerity, good eye contact is often swept into the same category.

Eye contact is also on top of the list of traits that reveal interest, attention and attraction. In a 1985 study, researcher Monica Moore monitored more than two hundred women at a party to determine how they successfully captured the attention of men. Smiling and eye contact were the most effective tools. We all like friendly people, and we associate good eye contact with interest, friendliness and attraction. The attention and interest that is communicated by good eye contact makes others feel important, and encourages them to believe that you stand ready to meet their needs. This doesn't just attract the guy or gal across the bar. It draws customers, friends and those with whom you interact in the workplace. It shows that you are open, friendly and interested, which makes you more likable.

Research also has found a positive correlation between a listener's assessment of a speaker's level of eye contact and his intelligence, competence, confidence, social skills, professionalism and sophistication. In one study, students participated in a series of exercises designed to test their social interaction skills. At the end of the exercises the other members of their group evaluated their level of eye contact, and equated it with their self-confidence. Even those individuals who did not consider themselves self-confident were thought to be self-confident by their peers if they engaged in strong mutual eye contact. The finding that even those who are not confident appear to be confident if they maintain good eye contact, once again demonstrates that your conscious efforts to convey qualities usually are successful, whether or not you actually possess those qualities.

Good eye contact doesn't just make you appear more confident and capable, it actually improves your effectiveness, both in business and social settings. Studies show that good eye contact instills trust and confidence in you by others, and substantially increases persuasiveness. It also reflects a positive attitude toward others, which in turn facilitates cooperation in both workplace and social settings.

THE ELEMENTS OF EYE CONTACT

"Where do I look?" is one of the questions asked most frequently by witnesses as we prepare them to testify at trial. There is no clear-cut answer, but there are some general rules: more eye contact is better than less; eye contact should be consistent with your overall demeanor and facial expressions; eye contact does not require that you stare directly into another person's pupils; and your eyes should move slowly as they capture another's gaze and as they leave it. Beyond these few generalizations, effective eye contact depends on the circumstances, and requires a basic understanding of the individual components of effective eye contact.

- Gaze intensity
- Where to look
- Eye movement
- Duration

Gaze Intensity

As we refer to different types of eye contact, keep our definitions in mind.

> *Intense:* Intense eye contact is focused, of long duration and not accompanied by casual or friendly body movements or facial expressions. It is usually perceived as hostile, angry, controlling, threatening or doubting.

Attentive: Attentive eye contact may be more or less prolonged and direct as intense eye contact. It becomes attentive, rather than intense, when it is accompanied by softer facial expressions and more relaxed and friendly body motions. It shows interest, friendliness and curiosity.

Soft: Soft eye contact is less prolonged. It also is accompanied by relaxed and friendly facial expressions and body language. Soft eye contact is perceived as casual, friendly, approachable, warm and less focused.

Distracted: Eye contact is distracted when it tends to connect, disconnect and reconnect quickly and frequently. Typically the moments of contact are brief and the periods of disconnect longer. Distracted eye contact reflects boredom, preoccupation, aloofness or disagreement.

Avoidant: Those who purposely avoid eye contact will not allow another's eyes to catch theirs. Any eye contact is fleeting and infrequent. Avoidant eye contact typically reflects fear, shame, anger, embarrassment, extreme discomfort, disgust or dishonesty.

As you evaluate what level of intensity is appropriate for different encounters, bear in mind that how eye contact is perceived by participants in a conversation often depends upon the nature of their relationship and whether both of the partners in the interaction engage in similar eye contact. Two partners who are romantically linked may "gaze into one another's eyes" with an intensity that would be uncomfortable or even threatening if they weren't intimately involved. A student might "stare" intently at his teacher as the teacher explains the answer to a problem, yet the teacher would not interpret the gaze as an attempt to intimidate or dominate.

If you have trouble visualizing the difference between these levels of eye contact, take a moment and look in the mirror. Stare at yourself as if you were another person. Look directly into your pupils and show no facial expression. Now grit your jaw and the muscles around the corners of your eyes and purse your lips. You will look intense, intimidating, unapproachable. This is intense eye contact.

Now look in the mirror again and look directly into your eyes. But this time relax your facial muscles as you look for variations in the color of your eyes. Does the color change slightly from location to location? Are there any flecks of different colors? Freeze, and notice how the sternness has left your face but the attentive look hasn't. This is attentive eye contact.

Finally, look in the mirror and allow your eyes to wander slowly to the bridge of your nose, then the outside corner of one eye, then the outside corner of the other, up to the bottom of the eyebrow, and then back to the pupils. As you do this, relax your facial muscles and think of something humorous. Let a faint smile appear not just on your mouth, but also in your eyes. This is soft eye contact.

We haven't yet found a way for you to display distracted or avoidant eye contact in a mirror. To do that, you'll need a video camera. Turn on the video camera and think of the lens as the eyes of another person. Look into the lens for a second or two, then glance away briefly. Then look back, and glance in the other direction for a few more seconds. As you do, show no emotion on your face. Now play back the videotape. That is how distracted eye contact looks.

Finally, turn the video camera on again. This time, envision a laser coming directly out of the camera toward your eyes. Act as if you would be blinded if you looked directly into the laser, but try to look at the base of the camera the top of the camera, and the sides of the camera for brief moments, and then look away. Replay the videotape, and you'll see what avoidant eye contact looks like.

Where to Look

When we refer to eye contact, we don't necessarily mean a pupil to pupil connection. Ask a friend to stand five feet away from you and stare straight into your eyes. Now ask him or her to look just below one eyebrow, then at the bridge of your nose, then to the corner of one eye. You will be able to detect the subtle difference if you watch for it. Yet in actual conversation you will have the impression of good eye contact when your friend looks in each of these three locations. Eye contact will seem much more intense if it is always focused on the pupil, and much less intense if it wanders throughout the area within one half to one inch from the pupil.

Eyeball to eyeball gaze is typical in a business exchange when the emphasis is on transferring and retaining information. In that environment it's generally a good idea for you to gaze directly at the other person's eyes, unless for some reason you consciously choose to soften the gaze. Even in this environment, however, it's a good idea to take the pressure off every once in a while by glancing briefly at the eyelid, corner of the eye, or bridge of the nose. When you drop your gaze below the level of another person's eyes it can be seen as a sign of subservience or self-doubt. Unless you want to project that image, make sure your eyes wander slightly upward or laterally.

In casual or social settings avoid pupil to pupil contact for prolonged periods unless you want to communicate intimacy. Let your eyes wander within that one-half-inch to one-inch radius from the center of the other person's eyes. This will produce all the benefits of good eye contact without risking too much intensity. If your eyes wander as far down as the other person's mouth, neck, or body, it may be taken as a sign of sexual interest.

Eye Movement

How you establish and terminate eye contact also sends messages to others. You should establish and terminate eye contact slowly. Don't jerk your eyes to meet theirs, nor quickly withdraw them when you choose to break off eye contact, nor blink frequently. Instead, your eyes should move slowly to theirs, stay in contact, and after an appropriate period of time, slowly move away.

Eye contact that is initiated with a sudden motion accentuates its intensity. It can be disconcerting and threatening. However, if eye contact is made by slowly moving your eyes toward another's until you achieve a mutual gaze you will establish the benefits of good eye contact yet minimize the potential adverse effects of overly intense eye contact.

Likewise, if you break off your gaze suddenly, it is more likely to be seen a sign of submissiveness or a lack of confidence or friendliness. Even if someone stares you down until you feel compelled to look away, don't yield suddenly. Slowly move your eyes away from his as if you're in complete control. If you move them away too quickly you will send him the message that he has succeeded in his effort to dominate you.

Duration

In a typical conversation, people engage in direct eye contact about half the time. Eye contact between 40 and 70 percent of the time generally will produce neither a strong impression of disinterest or avoidance, nor trigger a defensive response. But eye contact at the low end of this range won't maximize its potential positive impact. You will have the greatest positive impact if you attempt to maintain eye contact about 60 to 70 percent of the time.

In professional situations, more prolonged eye contact is appropriate, particularly when important information is exchanged that needs to be communicated and retained effectively, or when you want to assert more control. When you speak one on one with someone in this type of exchange, you can maintain eye contact for 70 to 80 percent of the time without appearing too intense. When you speak to larger groups, you should maintain eye contact with someone in the group almost all of the time. You may choose several individuals who seem to be the most receptive and spread your eye contact among them, or you may give all of the members of the group equal time. However, if you maintain eye contact with any one member of a large group for a prolonged period, you will make that person uncomfortable.

Some individuals are more or less sensitive to eye contact than others as a result of their background, personality or mood. Someone who is particularly shy, or influenced by a culture in which eye contact is used sparingly, may interpret what most of us consider to be a normal level of eye contact as a sign of aggression or discourtesy. Those who welcome and expect more intimacy will expect longer periods of eye contact.

If someone appears reluctant to engage in direct eye contact, be sensitive to the possibility that she may find even moderate eye contact threatening and uncomfortable. Don't force your gaze upon her. Whatever positive associations most people may make with prolonged eye contact will not apply to her. Instead, you'll come across as pushy, unfriendly and overbearing. On the other hand, if a person has a tendency to maintain constant eye contact, she won't be offended if you do likewise. However, she may interpret even normal breaks in eye contact as inattention or unfriendliness. If she uses intense eye contact as a means of control, she may also interpret your evasive gaze as submissiveness.

To avoid the risk that others will think that you use eye contact to dominate them, occasionally break off eye contact first. If you consistently maintain eye contact until the other person looks away, it may seem that you are staring him down. Remember, people want to feel important. If you force them to react to you in a submissive manner, you violate that fundamental rule. Unless you have a legitimate and overriding need to establish dominance, as for example in a hostile employee review or adversarial meeting, you will find that you lose more points than you gain when you show that you are the king of the eye contact hill. That's not good Impression Management.

Among the most interesting research on the impact of the duration of eye contact on impression formation is that which explores how your physical position relative to another can affect his reaction to your eye contact. If you are seated facing another, he'll expect you to look at him at least occasionally. If you don't, you will seem rude, shy, unfriendly or aloof. If you are seated next to him and have to turn to capture his gaze, he will expect less eye contact and will feel uncomfortable if you engage in frequent sideways glances at him. Research also indicates that the closer strangers are to one another, the less they welcome eye contact. For example, an attempt to maintain eye contact from just a few feet away from someone in an elevator may seem rude, or even threatening.

SMILING

Smiles run the gamut from a broad toothy grin, to a threatening, or lecherous sneer. In between there are nervous, anxious and smug smiles, forced and awkward smiles, smiles of embarrassment, comforting and encouraging smiles and the faint smile of a pleasant moment remembered. The most elegant and expensive wardrobe, lavish jewelry and flawless hairstyle cannot overcome the negative emotional impact of a scowl. Yet a smile that says "I'm happy to see you" will double the luster of any wardrobe and the beauty of the most ordinary face.

There is something inside each of us that responds powerfully to a natural, uninhibited and sincere expression of pleasure. The uncontrollable wagging of a dog's tail, the spontaneous smile of a baby, the light that shines from the face of an old friend when your eyes meet from across the room—they're electric. They energize us. They can pull us from the depths of depression or despair, or create a bond between them and us that even the most eloquent words cannot.

The magic quality of smiling has been reported frequently in studies that demonstrate its infectious nature. One study, for example, examined the public's emotional response to President Reagan's tendency to intersperse his communication with pleasant and reassuring smiles. The study found that viewers, including those who were not Reagan fans, tended to smile in return as they watched him on video. Another study found that during the 1984 presidential campaign viewers who watched a network broadcaster who smiled more frequently when he talked about Ronald Reagan than Walter Mondale were more likely to vote for Reagan than Mondale. The same voting pattern did not occur among viewers of the other two network broadcasters who did not smile perceptibly more when they spoke of one or the other of the two candidates.

Strong stereotypes attach to those who smile freely. When we see someone flash a sincere, happy smile, our emotional brain predisposes us to believe that he is sociable, competent, likable, caring and trustworthy. The impact of these associations on our assessment of an individual's character is well illustrated by a number of studies in the courtroom that have shown that smiling defendants are considered more trustworthy, good, honest, genuine, obedient, blameless and sincere than nonsmiling defendants, and are treated more leniently as a result.

When your smile is sincere and natural, the muscles around your mouth, jaw, and eyes all actively participate. Watch a young baby who smiles and you'll see what we mean. His entire face, and often even his whole body, is involved. This truly spontaneous and sincere smile can be difficult for many of us to generate at will. Men, more than women, tend to be self-conscious when they smile; and it shows.

Physiologically, the natural full-face smile requires the involvement of two facial muscles: the zygomatic major, which lifts the corners of the lips and cheeks, and the orbicularis oculi, which circles the eye and pulls the skin from the cheeks and forehead toward the eyeball. The muscles around the mouth can be consciously contracted by most of us in a manner that appears relatively natural. The muscles around the eye which must be involved to project the most natural and spontaneous smile are not as easy to manipulate. But you can learn to incorporate them into your smile as well. All of the models and actors who flash those beautifully engaging smiles weren't born with special abilities. They have simply learned to smile with their entire face.

Try it. Look in a mirror. Smile first with just your mouth as you watch your eyes. Now squint, which calls upon the muscles that surround your eyes. Then relax your eyes and repeat the exercise several times. Don't worry if you look a little goofy at first.

Now smile and use those same muscles that caused you to squint, but contract them ever so slightly. Relax your face and think of something funny or pleasurable. Your eyes should be smiling. Repeat this as you brush your teeth, wash your face, or put on makeup. Make it a habit. With practice, even those of us who are self-conscious or not instinctive smilers can learn to adopt a pleasant and natural-looking full-face smile. We may never be Tom Cruise or Christie Brinkley, but we can improve, and improve significantly.

Take comfort as you learn to smile more naturally that almost any but the most sleazy or phony smile is better than no smile at all. For example, in one study 151 students participated in an exercise in which two women displayed four different facial expressions: a natural smile, a false smile, a miserable smile, and a neutral face. The student judges were told that the two women had committed some transgression and were asked to assess their trustworthiness and genuineness. The student judges who viewed photographs of the women rated them more trustworthy and genuine as long as they smiled, or tried to.

A smile communicates positive qualities all by itself. It also adds meaning to other traits that might otherwise be unnoticed or misinterpreted. Most verbal and nonverbal cues carry many potentially ambiguous meanings. We can best determine which of several possible meanings to attribute to a trait only if other consistent characteristics help create a clear pattern. For example, if you engaged in expressive arm motion and rapid speech others might think you were agitated or nervous. But if you accompanied those traits with a broad smile, those negative interpretations would not fit the pattern. Instead, the conclusion that would make sense to others based on your arm movement, rapid speech *and* smile, would be that you were animated, enthusiastic and happy. Without the smile, no one could be sure what to make of your arm movement and rapid speech, and could well misinterpret them.

This was demonstrated in a study in which each of 320 subjects viewed one of thirty-two different videos that depicted actors who displayed different eye contact, posture and distance combinations. No one in the videos ever smiled. Without this critical piece of the puzzle, the subjects found it difficult to interpret the meaning of the actors' behavior. Like the actors in this study, you won't be able to communicate pleasure, friendliness, interest, confidence, appreciation and most other positive emotions effectively if you don't smile.

THE HANDSHAKE

If you're like most people, you haven't given much thought to when or how you should shake hands. But before you settle in with the attitude that handshakes don't really matter much, consider the results of the following study.

A sales training company conducted an experiment to test how something as simple as a handshake might influence the honesty of complete strangers. The researcher placed a quarter in plain view in a phone booth and watched as seventy-five strangers used the phone. As they left, he approached them and told them that he left a quarter in the phone booth, and asked if they found it. Over one-half of them lied.

He then repeated the experiment. This time, as the strangers left the phone booth he approached, *first shook their hands,* and then told them that he left a quarter in the phone booth and asked if they found it. This time only fourteen lied. He didn't change his routine, other than to add a brief handshake. Yet dishonest responses were reduced by *two-thirds.* The results of this experiment dramatically underscore the importance of a handshake. If you're thinking "I'd better start shaking hands, and shaking them well," good. You should, if you want to connect with others and make the best possible impression.

The handshake is thought to have originated as a sign of friendship and peace, represented by an open, weapon-free hand. Over the millennia the handshake has taken on much greater significance. A good handshake shows a person to be open, confident, sincere and friendly. Overpowering handshakes project dominance, control, egotism and often a lack of trust-worthiness. Weak handshakes prompt stereotypes of insecurity, disinterest, secretiveness, shyness, aloofness or timidity. Awkward handshakes, in which the grip is haphazard or the motion jerky, indicate nervousness or a lack of social skill and sophistication, which in turn reflects poorly on a person's capability.

In our society the handshake represents a unique opportunity because it is the only time we universally accept physical contact by total strangers, casual friends and intimate acquaintances alike. It is also the one occasion when we freely allow, and in fact expect, others to approach within our most intimate personal space, which is generally the distance of your out-stretched arm. (More on this later.) It's not the gesture itself that holds the magic; it's the emotional bond that results from even a few moments of physical contact and the intimacy created by close physical proximity.

Depending upon the situation—a formal encounter, a greeting between casual friends, or an exchange between intimate acquaintances—we all have different expectations of what amounts to appropriate and inappropriate physical contact. Men and women also have different expectations when they greet those of the same or different gender. What might be appropriate and well received in one situation may spawn a neg-ative reaction in another. Our response is, as is often the case, a function of our expectations.

We expect, and welcome, mutuality. If we engage in any behavior toward another—including a particular type of handshake—we feel most comfortable when the other person reciprocates. If he shows less familiar-ity, we feel shunned. If he is more familiar, we may feel threatened or uncomfortable. We're most comfortable when our expectations, desires and actions are mirrored by others.

Keep the concepts of expectations and mirroring in mind as we discuss each of the components of a great handshake.

- Initiation
- Grasp
- Grip
- Posturing

- Motion
- Duration
- The second handshake
- Secondary physical contact
- Verbal and nonverbal accompaniment

INITIATION

Older etiquette books contain extensive rules for whom, when and under what circumstances you should initiate a handshake with another. Men should wait for women to extend their hand. Subordinates should wait for superiors. Those who are new members of a group should wait until they are introduced by an established member, and so on. Forget it. Those rules have no sway in today's culture unless you plan to meet the queen of England.

In almost all cases, the question is not *whether* you shake someone's hand, but *when*. You can either reach out your arm and hand early, while some distance away from someone, or wait until you are close. The sooner you initiate the handshake, the more anxious you will appear to exchange the greeting. If you begin to initiate the handshake too early you can appear overeager, awkward or artificial. If you wait until you have stood next to someone for even a few seconds before you reach out your hand, you run the risk that the gesture will appear to be an afterthought, or made reluctantly.

If you approach a person from some distance, time the handshake so that your hand has moved up to waist level when you arrive within easy reach of the other person's hand. If you are within hand grasp distance from someone as you are first introduced, or first decide to initiate a handshake, try to be the first one to do so. If you stand next to someone for too long under circumstances in which an introductory handshake would be in order and wait until she makes the first move, she may think you are unfriendly or distant.

GRASP

The second ingredient of a handshake is the grasp, as distinguished from the grip, which we discuss next. We've all experienced those awkward fingertip clutching handshakes that occur either when someone grasps your hand before it is firmly in his, or when he withdraws his hand just as you begin to close your grasp. Either way, one person feels silly and uncomfortable, and the other appears reluctant to participate.

Whether by a man or a woman, the ideal handshake is fully engaged. Your palm should rest flat against the other person's palm, and the web between your thumb and index finger should be in gentle contact with the web between his. If you have inserted your hand firmly in his, your ring and pinkie fingers should be able to curl comfortably under the bottom of his hand, to hold and lift it as you shake.

GRIP

We've also all experienced a broad range of grips, from the dead fish, limp handshake of a rag doll, to the bone-crushing clench of someone who seems to have mistaken you for one of those grip-testing machines at the arcade. The limp handshake conveys a feeling of insecurity, aloofness, weakness or distraction. The vice grip is normally perceived as a sign of attempted domination or control.

Your grip should be firm but comfortable. Generally, hold the other person's hand about as firmly as you would hold a large tumbler full of water. Your grip may vary depending upon whether you are a man or a woman, and whether you shake the hand of a man or a woman. Two men will typically grip one another's hands more firmly than a man will grip a woman's; and two women will typically grip one another's hands more delicately than they grip a man's. Your grip may vary as you mirror the strength of others' clasps; but it should not vary too much.

POSTURING

Posturing during the handshake also sends distinct messages. The most common techniques involve pushing or pulling the other person's hand toward or away from his body, or turning his hand either palm up or palm down. Each gesture conveys distinct messages.

You can push another's hand away from yourself and toward the other person either during the handshake, or as you break off the handshake. In either event, you send the message that the handshake was not welcome. You figuratively and literally reject the other person's hand. Or you can grab another's hand and pull it toward you. This is a dominant behavior. It's a way to control the exchange, and may send a message that similar attempts to control are likely to occur in other aspects of your relationship.

When you offer your hand palm up, you make a friendly, but submissive gesture. The impression the other person is likely to receive is that you are friendly, but lack confidence, and if you lack confidence, you may lack capability. If you turn the other person's palm up, and assert a dominant, palm down position for your own hand, you show control. If you have a tendency to grab another's hand and rotate yours so that it is on top, bear in mind that your action may go unnoticed consciously, but it may be recorded by the other person's emotional brain as a sign of a domineering personality.

MOTION

A vigorous, rapid up-and-down movement when you shake hands can be distracting and uncomfortable. When you exchange your initial greetings, you don't want distractions. You want to bond. A jerky motion also can be interpreted as a sign that you are nervous or feel awkward—emotions that you do not want to reveal, even if you feel them. Two to three smooth cycles of up-down, up-down, is plenty. More than that gets tiresome and seems overeager.

The range of motion of each cycle also should not be extreme. More than two to four inches from the bottom of the stroke to the top can make you appear nervous, overeager or awkward. Little or no motion in the handshake may leave an impression of distance, passivity, arrogance and noninvolvement.

DURATION

Handshakes can last for only a moment, or they can linger for several seconds. Long, lingering handshakes tend to feel like "hand holding." You wouldn't hold hands with a stranger, or with someone with whom you have only a professional relationship, and they won't tend to welcome it. Others' "permission" for you to touch them and enter into their "personal space" during a handshake is not without limits. The more formal or brief your relationship, the shorter the handshake should be—up to a point. A very short, quick handshake will seem perfunctory, and insincere. A two-second handshake is the bare minimum. For close friends, or any relationship in which a greater degree of physical contact would be appropriate, a handshake of several seconds, but generally not more than four or five, is in order.

To appear welcome to the interaction, attempt to be the last person to release the grip. As you conclude the last handshake "pumps," pause momentarily and slightly lessen the pressure of your grip until the other person has released hers completely. When you linger a moment you demonstrate that you have welcomed and enjoyed the exchange.

THE SECOND HANDSHAKE

The handshake may be your only opportunity to make physical contact with another. Don't pass up the opportunity to do it twice in every exchange—once coming and once going. Most of us shake hands when we first meet someone, but miss the opportunity to reinforce, and in fact significantly enhance, our impression by shaking hands again as we say good-bye. The "good-bye" handshake can be even more effective than the "hello" handshake. Sometimes both handshakes will be very similar; on other occasions it may be appropriate to add components to the "good-bye" handshake which would not have been appropriate for the "hello" handshake.

If, after a brief and formal "hello" handshake in a business or social setting, you have spent enough time with someone, and the conversation has been warm and friendly, it might be perfectly appropriate, and in fact desirable, to make your "good-bye" handshake more intimate. As you say good-bye, a longer handshake, possibly accompanied by a touch on the arm or your clasped hands with your free hand, usually will be well received. It is a way to say, "Now that I know you better I've come to like and respect you even more." Even if the conversation has been awkward or confrontational, the second handshake can send an important message. It says, "I still like you," or "I want to resolve whatever differences we may have." Leave the exchange on this positive note.

SECONDARY PHYSICAL CONTACT

As we described Doug's handshake earlier, we mentioned how Doug cupped Mark's hand in both of his and later placed his left hand on Mark's shoulder and gave him a pat. This type of secondary physical contact during a handshake can be extremely effective, or it can backfire miserably. A two-handed handshake, or a handshake accompanied by a touch on the forearm, shoulder, or back, is more intimate than a traditional one-handed handshake. That's great if that level of intimacy is consistent with your relationship. But watch out. Too much physical contact in view of the nature of the relationship can be toxic. It can make others nervous and suspicious, and can make you appear overly aggressive and familiar, and untrustworthy. The two-handed handshake, sometimes known as the "politician's handshake," generally should not be used in a first meeting, or in a purely professional greeting.

The addition of a hug or kiss to your greeting is like adding habanero chili pepper to a recipe. It will have an effect; the question is how much. You can't go wrong with a warm handshake, a big smile, and an "It's great to see you again." But go the extra step with extreme caution.

Hugs reflect a level of intimacy that should not be forced on an unwilling subject, male or female, particularly in a professional setting. If you have a close friendship, a light hug is generally well received and may in fact be expected. If it is welcomed, the physical intimacy of a hug will tend to add to the emotional bond created by a handshake alone.

Keep in mind that male/male, female/female, and male/female physical contacts carry different charges. It makes most men uncomfortable to be hugged by another man. Women are generally much more receptive to hugs by other women. Male/female hugs, like kisses (even pecks on the cheek), potentially damage your impression. Whoever initiates the hug or kiss creates a sexual dimension to the relationship. Unless the boundaries of your relationship are well established, don't go there without your eyes wide open. That's not to say that if you hug someone of the opposite sex you will necessarily be perceived as unprofessional, flirtatious or sexually aggressive. But you will risk raising those questions in the other person's mind, as well as in the minds of any spectators.

VERBAL AND NONVERBAL ACCOMPANIMENT

Handshakes aren't exchanged in isolation. They are part of a package that includes your body language, facial expressions, eye contact, voice and the content of what you say. To be most effective, the handshake must be in sync with all of your verbal and nonverbal behaviors. We have found that a few simple techniques will enhance the positive impact of your handshake.

Maintain Constant Eye Contact

This is not the time to let your gaze wander. You may need to glance quickly to your hands as they meet to avoid an awkward miss; but the glance should be fleeting, and your gaze should return immediately to the other person's eyes.

Begin to Speak as You Shake Hands

If you don't exchange greetings as you shake hands, the handshake will appear perfunctory. You do not want to give the impression that the handshake was a formality you just wanted to get out of the way before you got down to business. Take advantage of the opportunity to connect verbally while you are still connected physically.

Call Others by Name

Something almost magical happens when others call us by name. Any sales trainer will tell you that this helps build a bond between people. It is personal validation, because someone's name is personal. But don't overdo it or you will appear insincere. Once at the beginning, once at the end, and every few minutes during the conversation is plenty. Unless the other person is considerably older or in a position of distinct authority, the use of first names is usually appropriate. If in doubt, refer to others as Mr., Mrs. or Ms., until they invite you to do otherwise.

Introduce Others

Take the opportunity to introduce people to one another. Everyone loves friendship brokers. Many people are too reserved or inhibited to introduce themselves to strangers. Yet most shy people love when someone else breaks the ice for them.

Give Thought to Your Greetings

"Primacy" and "recency" theory tells us that the first and last words you speak usually will be remembered longest. As the first words out of your mouth during an encounter, your greeting deserves forethought.

There is a significant difference between, "Howdy," "Hi ya," "Hi," "Hello," "Good afternoon" and other brief salutations. Some greetings are very informal, some much more formal. Your greeting should match the occasion and the relationship in which it is used. Additionally, greetings are more memorable if they aren't simply one- or two-word "hellos" or "good mornings," which are so commonplace that they usually aren't even noticed. Add, "Hi, it's good to see you again"; or, "Hello, I've heard wonderful things about you from Bob, and have been looking forward to meeting you." Even a few personalized words will make your greeting more than a perfunctory exchange of words that probably will go unnoticed.

Avoid the Post-Handshake Silence

That potentially awkward few seconds when you have both said "Hello" and look at one another wondering what to say next is an opportunity to show how friendly, relaxed and in control you are. Fill the void with a comment that jump-starts further conversation. It can be as simple as asking someone you just met at a convention what company he is with, or someone you have met at a wedding if she is a friend of the bride or the groom.

Remember Something Personal

Another effective way to demonstrate your interest in someone is to remember details of his personal life. Opportunities arise in every setting to inject a personal note, but are particularly easy and natural to incorporate into your "hello" and "goodbye" handshakes.

During a sales call a customer may casually mention that he plans to leave work early to watch his son's Little League game. If you are alert to the opportunity to show your interest in the man personally, not just professionally, you can ask, "What's your son's name? How old is he?" or "What position does he play?" Your customer will hear, "I like you, I'm interested in you, and what goes on in your life is important to me." When you part company, as you shake hands, say "good luck at the game," and he'll feel even better about you.

POSTURE

Performers call it "presence." Politicians call it "charisma." The rest of us mostly just call it "bearing." It's that something about the way someone walks, stands and sits that shows class, dignity, confidence and control. We see it when someone walks into a room, as she stands and talks with others, even when she relaxes in a chair.

It doesn't much matter how people dress—sweats or an evening gown, jeans or a tuxedo. They don't even need to be good-looking. Sometimes they're large, sometimes they're small. They just have "it"; and "it" almost always includes good posture. Think of someone you know who has "it." Think about how he walks. Or better yet, next time you see him, watch how he moves, stands and sits. It's a safe bet that he has great posture. You probably never even consciously considered how his posture influenced your positive impression of him—because the impact was noticed only by your emotional brain.

Good or bad posture can be seen from across the room, and is recorded by our emotional brains with even a quick glance. Posture makes a particularly strong impression because, unlike more subtle nonverbal clues generated by tiny muscles, posture involves your entire body.

In one study, a hundred people viewed photographs of models with slumped body posture (heads bowed, shoulders relaxed and forward, stomachs relaxed) and other photographs of people with upright body posture (heads upright, chest out, shoulders back). Based on their body posture, the "judges" assumed those with poor standing and sitting posture were less popular, exciting, ambitious, friendly and even less intelligent than those with good posture. In another study, sixty participants assessed the emotional states of twenty-one sketched figures. Positive evaluations of the figures' happiness, anger, caring, security, fear, depression and self-esteem increased in relation to their improved posture.

Our own experience, drawn from hundreds of interviews that have addressed the stereotypes associated with posture, confirms that people believe that those who have good posture have the capacity to lead, are self-confident, interested and honest. Slumped, casual or loose body posture is associated not only with a lack of self-confidence, leadership ability, and interest, but also with a lack of attention to detail, and hence reflects poorly on reliability and capability.

Great posture is a Magic Pill for everyone but is a particularly valuable antitoxin for those who display other traits that are associated with a lack of confidence, leadership, interest and intelligence. Men or women who are shorter than average, have weak or tentative voices, have less impressive wardrobes and are generally less physically attractive should be particularly mindful to incorporate good posture as a fundamental component of their Impression Management Plans.

As we discuss how to improve your posture, expect that good posture at first will feel exaggerated and uncomfortable if you have stood, sat and walked with bad posture your entire life. Take a few minutes to videotape yourself before and after you do each of the exercises we're about to suggest. Perform each of the exercises in what you feel to be an exaggerated manner. Then watch yourself on tape. You'll see that you look perfectly natural; and more important, you look great.

Since our torsos are the largest portion of our anatomies, they play the most significant role in good or bad posture. Begin to improve your posture by straightening your back and pulling in your stomach. Stand in the middle of the room with your feet directly under your shoulders. Pretend you're a young child trying to meet the minimum height requirement for the roller coaster. Keep your heels on the ground, but stretch your legs, back and neck skyward. Now relax and assume your normal standing position, and repeat the exercise several times.

Many people will increase their height during this exercise by as much as an inch. They also dramatically improve their posture in the process. Periodically during the day, remember this exercise, and repeat it until you find that you no longer increase your height perceptibly.

The next most frequent posture "no-no" is slumped shoulders. Most of us are unaware of how much we slump our shoulders, particularly when we sit. Even those who have excellent standing posture are often shocked the first time they view a videotape of themselves in a seated position. They look like vultures perched on a tree limb.

To test your degree of shoulder slump, stand against a bare wall. Assume your normal posture. If you're like most people, your buttocks and your lower or middle back will touch the wall. Straighten your upper body until you feel the ridges of your shoulder blades strike the wall. Now, push your shoulders toward the wall until your shoulder blades flatten out, and your entire upper back touches the wall. The distance you have to push your shoulders toward the wall before your entire upper back comes into contact with it indicates the degree of your shoulder slump.

Repeat the exercise several times. Stop when your upper back is pressed against the wall and step away from it. Get that camcorder out and videotape yourself. You'll probably feel like you're pushing your chest out; but when you see the videotape, you'll realize that you're not.

Once again, during the course of the day stop periodically and rotate your shoulders back as if you were up against that wall. Do this frequently until you find little change in your shoulder position before and after you perform this exercise.

Most people who have learned to stand up straight and hold their shoulders back will find that their head follows suit. But sometimes, even after posture is improved in other respects, people will continue to relax the muscles in the back of their neck and allow their head to drop. Even if you have otherwise good posture, if you tend to walk, stand or sit with your head lowered, you will trigger many of the negative impressions associated with poor posture generally.

To test your degree of head bowing, stand in front of a mirror with your eyes closed, your back straight and your shoulders back, but with your head in the position that is normal for you. Now, as you open your eyes and look into the mirror, lift your head. Don't pull it back so far that you look down your nose at yourself or expose the bottom of your chin. But pull it back far enough that your eyes needn't look up or down at all to directly catch your gaze in the mirror. Repeat the exercise again. This time notice how far your chin moves upward during the process. Practice this exercise every morning as you brush your teeth, shave or put on your makeup, and every evening before you go to bed until you find your head no longer moves whatsoever.

This is the head position you should assume when you walk, stand or sit. When you speak with or look at others, raise or lower your head as necessary to look them directly in their eyes. You will appear aloof or egotistical if you look down your nose at someone. If you must raise your eyes to meet theirs, you will appear submissive, shy or lacking confidence.

Good posture doesn't stop at the waistline. It also includes your lower body. Many people frequently stand with their weight resting almost entirely on one leg. This shifts their hips rearward over the leg upon which their weight is rested. This rearward shift creates an impression of withdrawal, disinterest or casual aloofness.

You will avoid this rearward shift if you rest your weight evenly on both feet and keep your feet directly under your shoulders. Also, when you keep your weight on the balls of your feet, rather than on your heels, you create a slight forward lean. The forward lean conveys the message that you are confident, alert, attentive and energetic.

Each of the techniques to improve your posture in a standing position applies with equal force when you sit. Sit upright, with your back straight, your shoulders back, and your head up. Don't sink into the chair, lean rearward or slouch forward in the vulture pose. Place your weight evenly across your buttocks. Don't favor one side or the other.

The way you walk also sends messages. We've all known people with that assertive, forceful walk that exudes confidence and capability, and others who seem as timid as a child in a Halloween spook house. Some people walk so slowly that they appear apathetic; others so quickly that they appear nervous.

The walking style that makes the best impression is neither too fast nor too slow, too bouncy nor too smooth. The barnyard strut doesn't show confidence, it shows cockiness. The schoolyard shuffle doesn't impress most adults as cool and in control, but as lackadaisical or bored.

Notice those whose walk strikes you as confident, professional and relaxed, and duplicate it. If you tend to walk slowly, pick up the pace a bit.

If you tend to walk fast, slow down. As you do, avoid unnecessary motions. Let your arms hang naturally and comfortably to your side. Don't hold them in front of you as if they were shields to guard against those you might encounter; and don't hold your hands behind your back as if you're a general in a battle briefing.

Most important: practice. If you really want to improve your posture and the impression you make on others, get out that video recorder and use it—the more the better. Remember, you have decades of bad habits to overcome. Accept that good posture may feel uncomfortable at first, but don't give up. Visualize how great you will look the next time you walk into a party or a sales meeting with perfect posture—and you will.

ENTHUSIASM

Think back to the bosses, politicians, teachers or coaches who most inspired you. They will all have one thing in common: enthusiasm. It is that singular quality that elevated John Madden, a portly, not very good-looking ex-football coach, to his immense popularity as a sports commentator and made a short, squeaky-voiced exercise phenomenon of Richard Simmons. It is also enthusiasm that makes Sam the number one salesman in the company; and Missy the one who always seems to motivate the members of the Women's League to invest their time and energy in its latest fundraiser.

Studies show that those who show enthusiasm are better liked, trusted more, are thought to be more capable and more effectively capture the attention of their audiences. Those who hold their emotional cards too close to their vests are seen as less honest, friendly and capable. Enthusiasm is particularly important when you deliver a content-laden message. Facts, figures and analysis presented in a monotone by an expressionless speaker won't be heard by an audience whose eyes have glazed over, ears have closed and minds have wandered.

Retention, not just attention, is improved dramatically as your enthusiasm increases. A teacher, coach, salesman, lawyer or CEO who stands behind the podium and reads a speech will not make contact with his audience. If he steps out from behind the podium, moves around the room, gestures and shows emotion, he will.

One of the greatest benefits of enthusiasm is that it is highly contagious. Your enthusiasm generates positive feelings of hopefulness, happiness and self-esteem in others. As Henry Wadsworth Longfellow noted, "Enthusiasm begets enthusiasm." In one study that demonstrates this process, passive, expressionless individuals were paired with more expressive animated people. Both members of each pair filled out a form to assess his or her mood at the inception of the experiment. The researcher then left each pair alone together for two minutes. When he returned, he asked each participant to again fill out a form to evaluate his or her mood. In just *two* minutes, the more passive tended to adopt the mood of the more expressive. When your enthusiasm rubs off on others, it makes them feel good, which makes you look good.

Our research demonstrates that effective enthusiasm requires:

- Physical, visual and aural stimulation;
- Focus; and
- Positive emotion.

PHYSICAL, VISUAL AND AURAL STIMULATION

Six-month-old babies intuitively know how to convey enthusiasm better than all of the world's greatest communications experts combined. They smile, wiggle, shake their arms, gurgle and squeal to communicate their enthusiasm. They leave no doubt about what excites and pleases them. This type of enthusiasm is not learned—it's natural. Open communication of their feelings through their voice and body motions touches and moves us, and draws us to them. It produces physical, visual and aural stimuli that are received and processed by our emotional brains.

You can imagine how much less attention a baby would receive if he sat stoically and showed no emotion. Yet that is precisely what we tend to do as we mature. Our research leaves no doubt: To convey and evoke enthusiasm, you must stimulate others' senses with broad strokes of as many of the Seven Colors as possible.

FOCUS

It's not a great idea for you to blow bubbles, coo and wiggle uncontrollably to show your enthusiastic support for your boss's marketing proposal at your next regional sales meeting; or for you to initiate the "wave" around the conference table to show your excitement. You must always balance the positive and negative aspects of each trait as you manage impressions. As important as enthusiasm is, enthusiasm without focus, purpose and appropriate restraint appears shallow, insincere, fanatical or immature. "Enthusiasm is of the greatest value, so long as we are not carried away by it," Goethe aptly noted.

Your enthusiasm may first touch others' emotional brains, but it has to make sense to their rational brains, too. We all have certain expectations of the reasonable range of enthusiasm in different circumstances. If the computer guru in the office pitches a proposal that the office should change its word-processing software, we don't expect his presentation to build to a passionate crescendo as if he were a football coach giving a last-minute pep talk to his team before they take the field for the national championship game. Yet if someone wins a ten-million-dollar lottery there is almost no level of enthusiasm that would exceed our expectations. But what would we think of a woman who has the same reaction upon winning the ten-dollar office football pool?

People aren't stupid. If your level of enthusiasm exceeds their expectations, they will find it immature, irrational or phony. If they conclude that you are immature, irrational and phony, they will find you neither trustworthy nor inspirational.

POSITIVE EMOTION

Enthusiasm comes from the enjoyment of what you do; and enjoyment of what you do comes from enthusiasm. When your enthusiasm is an expression of positive emotions, you create a whirl of excitement around you that invigorates and excites others. When your energy is directed toward negative thought and action, you create a whirlpool that pulls others down and is transformed from a Magic Pill to a poisonous toxin.

Hitler was enthusiastic. So is the rabble-rouser at work, or the vicious gossip. Those whose enthusiasm is negative may find allies among the bitter and disgruntled, but most of us fear and shun them. Their enthusiasm sometimes pulls others into the whirlpool they create; but their sway is usually short-lived, since most people find little long-term satisfaction or happiness in negative beliefs, feelings or actions.

Those whose enthusiasm sustains friendships, motivates employees and inspires confidence are always positive. They encourage us. They are like the calm breeze that cradles a kite and carries it aloft, not the tempest that wrenches it skyward and batters it until it disassembles in the fury. As we describe the various ways you can generate enthusiasm, bear in mind that the enthusiasm we encourage is not loud, dominant, controlling, repressive, negative or hateful. It is positive, uplifting, animated, attentive, engaging, encouraging and fun.

WRITE YOUR PRESCRIPTION

Now that you've finished this chapter, put it to use. Find an index card or scrap of paper and jot down the five Magic Pills.

- Eye contact
- Smiling
- Handshake and greeting
- Posture
- Enthusiasm

Tape it to a mirror where you'll see it every morning. Promise yourself that every day you will take each of these Magic Pills and you will display them to everyone you meet. Make this promise to yourself, day in and day out, until each of these characteristics becomes a habit. As you do, you will experience a healthy transformation in the impression you make on others and in your own life.

CHAPTER 6

Toxic Traits

Don was the hardest-working associate in his law firm. An Olympic-caliber athlete and graduate of one of the top law schools in the country, he was brilliant, hard charging and showed an unparalleled zeal for his clients' causes. He also had a quick wit and self-effacing manner, a ready smile and a warm "hello" for every occasion. He was thought by most to be the perfect associate, and a shoo-in to make partner.

The firm's employees were shocked when the partnership announced the list of associates who were invited to become partners. Don's name was not on it.

It seemed that two years earlier Don made a passing comment in jest to one of the partners' girlfriends at a firm party. He did not intend to offend her, and did not even know he had. But she commented to her boyfriend, who was an influential partner who had never worked directly with Don, that Don made a rude remark to her.

Two years later, her boyfriend still had the impression of Don that had been formed that evening. From one passing remark, this partner had judged Don and was able to influence enough other partners to block Don's admission to the partnership.

People tend to dwell on the negative. One harsh remark will be remembered long after ten compliments are forgotten. One selfish action will obliterate the goodwill accumulated through years of selflessness. One vulgar comment will taint the image of the most gracious host. It need not be something shocking. Even seemingly insignificant transgressions, as Don discovered, may supersede monumental good deeds.

Some characteristics carry such overwhelming negative associations that they overshadow everything else. There is no upside if you display them, only a downside. And there is only one way to manage the impression they make on others—just don't do it.

What follows are a number of behaviors that should be avoided like the plague. We call them "toxic traits" because they seldom, if ever, have any redeeming value, yet they consistently cause serious, often irreparable, damage to your impression. They fall into five categories:

- Offensive physical acts
- Unappealing word usage
- Insensitive communication
- Aggressive behavior
- Pettiness

There may be times when you think these behaviors are funny or witty, or you believe that they are justified in the heat of the moment. Yet even if others perceive them in that same light at some level, they will be seen in a negative light at other, more emotionally influential levels.

Early in relationships it is extremely unlikely that you will exhibit any of the traits that we discuss in this chapter. You don't swear, belch, tell off-color jokes, fly off the handle, or go out unbathed or in tattered clothes. You know that's no way to make a good impression. Unfortunately, as you become more comfortable in relationships, good manners slide.

Maybe you believe that once people have come to know you they will accept your less attractive behaviors, or at least take them in stride. In reality, it is not a function of acceptance; at best, it's a matter of tolerance. When you maintain good manners and avoid inappropriate behavior, you never weaken a relationship. So why not maintain these behaviors? You develop a limited amount of goodwill in every relationship. There always will be occasions when you will need to rely upon it to smooth over rough moments. Don't trade on it unnecessarily.

OFFENSIVE PHYSICAL ACTS

There are certain physical characteristics that no one views favorably. Bad hygiene, an outward display of tasteless behavior and excessive drinking are the three physical traits that we have found are at the top of most people's lists.

BAD HYGIENE

Several years ago Jo-Ellan worked with an attorney who dressed exquisitely. His hair was styled, fingernails manicured, and shoes always meticulously shined. But the first time he bent over to whisper something to her in court she nearly gagged. His breath was absolutely disgusting. The judge did not allow gum or mints in the courtroom, or Jo-Ellan would have offered them to him in the hope that he would get the message.

It is difficult to believe that his persistent bad breath had not been brought to his attention previously. The same is true of those with notice-able body odor, dandruff or other signs of bad hygiene. Apparently this man, like so many others, had either chosen to ignore the friendly (or not so friendly) hints by others, or discounted how important good hygiene is to Impression Management.

In our survey of 135 men and women who were asked to identify what characteristics led them to form negative impressions, bad hygiene came in second, behind only an uncaring attitude. The irony is that good hygiene is one of the easiest traits to address. Almost everyone can bathe regularly, wash her clothes, shampoo with a dandruff deterrent, comb her hair, wash her face, brush her teeth or put deodorizing powder in her shoes.

It makes no difference where you work or what you do, where you live, how much money you make, your race or gender—good hygiene never hurts. It may not be noticed when practiced. But when it's not, you will trigger a stereotypical chain reaction that will contaminate all of the qualities on which you're judged.

Tasteless Behavior

The first time Mark saw Derek scratch himself, he did a double take. Derek stood in the conference room in Mark's office in front of a large easel on which Derek wrote the key points he wanted to make at trial. Suddenly, he grimaced perceptibly, bent slightly at the knees and reached down with his left hand to—well, Mark wasn't sure exactly what he was doing. He suspected Derek was either scratching his crotch, or trying to reposition his jockey shorts. Mark was afraid to look closely enough to tell which. He wanted to make a good impression himself, and staring at his client's crotch wasn't part of his Impression Management Plan.

Mark's first thought was entirely professional—"That's an interesting behavior under these circumstances. I wonder if it's a nervous tic?" His next reaction was purely personal—"How gross."

As it turned out, this was something Derek resorted to regularly. Mark couldn't tell if it was a nervous habit, if it was prompted by some chronic skin condition, or resulted from poorly fitting underwear. Mark chose not to raise the issue and embarrass Derek.

As Derek took the witness stand to testify a few days later, Mark regret-ted his decision. Mark had this horrible image that Derek would step down from the stand to write on the easel to highlight his testimony for the jury. He could just see it: as Derek turned to face the jury he would execute a perfect plié as he reached down to give his crotch a firm tug. Fortunately, he did fine, and gave new meaning to a phrase lawyers have used for years: "He made it through his testimony without so much as a scratch."

We all have rashes, pimples, scabs and sores that we scratch, rub and pick, along with our noses, ears, teeth and just about every other part of our anatomy. We trim our fingernails and scrape an infinite variety of discolored residue from beneath them. We chew, bleed, spit, belch and pass gas.

If you find simply reading about these bodily functions gross and unnerving, that's the point. They are. Just imagine how others feel when they actually have to hear, see or smell your bodily processes up close and personal. If it has to do with your body's function, keep it to yourself. Some things just weren't meant to be shared.

Displays of any of these behaviors tend to be seen as low class, rude and insensitive, and indicate bad judgment. Since people generally associate truthfulness with dignity and class, these behaviors also tend to diminish others' impressions of your truthfulness. They adversely affect your impression in the caring and humility categories, as well. And, of course, rudeness, poor taste and bad judgment are antithetical to intelligence, competence and professionalism.

EXCESSIVE DRINKING

Marilyn was an attractive single mother who began her career as a stockbroker after her children were all in school. Between her responsibilities at home and at the office, she seldom had a chance to go out socially and relax. At office functions she made up for lost time. She drank heavily and was loud and flirtatious. At first, others just joked about her behavior. In time, the jokes became serious reflections on her judgment. Even though her behavior at the office never warranted any concern, her bosses found it difficult to distinguish between characteristics shown in one environment—social—and those revealed in another—professional. Her career suffered.

Many of us have looked for inspiration, courage, charm, wit or a good time at the bottom of a glass. We're often convinced we've found it—at least temporarily. Those around us, sober or not, don't always share our charitable view.

We don't advocate a return to prohibition, or advise that you become a teetotaler if you want to make a good impression. Moderate consumption of alcohol by adults meets with our societal expectations, and triggers no particular stereotypical reaction for most people. But you should avoid anything that might raise concerns that you have a drinking problem, since that will raise concerns about all four Compass Qualities.

Those who are thought to have a drinking problem are considered less trustworthy, not only because we associate drunkenness with dishonesty, but also because most of us have found those who drink excessively are less reliable. We also question the capability of those who drink to excess because we are all aware of the impact alcohol has on someone's ability to think clearly and act appropriately.

Where, when and what you drink may be as influential to impression formation as how much you drink. A generation ago, it was not as unusual to find businessmen drinking alcohol at lunch. Today, however, even one martini at lunch is unusual. As a result, most people don't expect anyone other than heavy drinkers to drink alcohol at lunch. A drink at lunch is much more likely to trigger associations with excessive drinking than consumption of the same quantity and type of liquor in the evening. Likewise, drinking hard liquor (particularly by a woman) more frequently leads to assumptions that someone is a heavy drinker.

UNAPPEALING WORD USAGE

Most words or patterns of words can evoke a broad range of reactions, depending upon the circumstances. Profanity and bad grammar, however, rarely trigger anything but negative stereotypes.

PROFANITY

Sixty years ago America gasped when Rhett Butler told Scarlett O'Hara at the end of *Gone With the Wind,* "Frankly, my dear, I don't give a damn." Profanity on the silver screen was unthinkable. Today, unless we limit our viewing to Walt Disney cartoons and the Nickelodeon channel, we are exposed to a level of profanity that our parents would have found unacceptable.

With frequent use of profanity has come an assumption in many circles that using foul language doesn't speak that poorly about a person anymore. There is a distinction, however, between our expectations of the way things *are* and the way they *should be.* The use of profanity in both business and casual settings does not raise eyebrows the way it once did.

But the perception that profanity no longer carries any particular social stigma because it is so commonplace is wrong.

Research has consistently demonstrated that the use of profanity detracts from each of the Compass Qualities. One study that sought to determine the effect of religious, excretory and sexual profanity on the listeners' attitude regarding a speaker's credibility found that profanity has a negative effect on the perceived truthfulness of the speaker, whether a man or woman. The attitude change was particularly pronounced if the speaker was female. This gender distinction was reinforced in another study that found that males were not only more likely to use profanity than females, but also more likely to consider it socially acceptable, particularly as a way to achieve dominance. Other studies show that most people find profanity offensive and that those who use profanity, in either professional or social settings, are considered less socially adept, less friendly, less intelligent, less competent and even less physically attractive.

BAD GRAMMAR

Sigismund, the leader of the Holy Roman Empire at the beginning of the fifteenth century, once responded to a bishop who criticized his grammar, "I am the Roman king, and am above grammar." He had a point. But for those of us who don't reign over half the civilized world, bad grammar is without virtue.

Surveys have found that those who do not use good grammar are considered less credible, confident and intelligent, obtain lower-paying positions and receive fewer promotions. We all know individuals who use poor grammar yet who do not fit these stereotypes. But we would rate those individuals even higher if their grammar conformed to our expectations of how intelligent, competent and trustworthy people speak. Good grammar is particularly important during the initial impression formation phase of your relationships when you don't have the luxury of time and experience from which others can overcome initial negative stereotypical impressions.

INSENSITIVE COMMUNICATION

Humans are the most emotionally frail of all of God's creatures. We are hurt, offended, slighted, disgusted, appalled, embarrassed, insulted or provoked at the drop of a hat. Sometimes those who seem most secure have the largest emotional Achilles' heel, and the thinnest skin. Insensitive remarks are like a scalpel wielded by a drunken surgeon. With almost imperceptible ease and swiftness they can make deep and enduring impressions.

The following behaviors each hold the potential to inflict irreparable damage to any relationship. They are toxins for which there is often no antidote.

GOSSIP

Man's deep-seated abhorrence of this poisonous trait is reflected by its almost universal condemnation in religious scripture, as represented by comments such as "Whether it be friend or foe, talk not of other men's lives," in the Bible, and "Neither let the one of you speak ill of another in his absence" in the Koran.

Others'"catty" sides make it easy for you to find a willing audience for your gossip; but it won't keep others from judging you harshly when you do. Most of us have common sense enough not to disclose much about ourselves to a gossip. We know she'll talk about us enough once we're out of earshot, without our providing her with the ammunition she needs. The reason for our personal discretion arises from our recognition of the most important of all Compass Qualities—trustworthiness. We simply don't trust gossips, since at some level we assume that if they speak poorly of others, they speak poorly of us as well. We don't expect loyalty toward us from one who displays disloyalty toward others. Without trust and loyalty it is impossible to forge lasting friendships or business relationships.

Gossip also triggers the stereotypical reaction that someone who talks about others is cruel and uncaring. He may smile, laugh and invite conversation. But we question his motives. Is he really interested, or is he just trying to gather yet another juicy tidbit?

As the old saying goes, "If you can't say anything nice about someone, don't say anything at all."

SARCASM

As George walks into work he's met by his coworker Phil, who says, "Did you get dressed in the dark this morning?" (Translation: Your outfit is mismatched.)

Ralph, recently divorced, joins a conversation in the lunchroom about what makes for a good relationship. Connie can't resist saying, "You're the expert." (Translation: What does somebody who failed miserably at his own marriage know about good relationships?)

Some of the most quick-witted people are also among the most sarcastic. It's as if they can't pass up an opportunity to display their sharp mind with a sharp tongue. They may or may not be vicious, but their sarcasm stings just the same.

It's little wonder that you will not be considered friendly, warm or compassionate if you rely upon sarcasm as a means of communication. To the contrary, you will be thought harsh, angry, hostile, bitter, jealous, frustrated and dissatisfied with life.

Sarcasm also often lessens others' impression of your intelligence, confidence, competence, professionalism and leadership. Secure, confident, straightforward individuals don't attack from the flanks. Yet sarcasm is typically used as a way to communicate indirectly a strongly felt opinion, belief or emotion. Indirect communication always adversely affects the speaker's trustworthiness. You do not want someone to think about you, "I wish when she has something to say, she'd just come out and say it." Yet once the pain from a sarcastic barb has subsided, that is often the reaction.

There are many ways to demonstrate wit, to communicate criticism, or to make a joke, without resorting to sarcasm. If you want to be seen as trustworthy, caring, humble and capable, keep your sarcastic remarks to yourself. Follow Thomas Carlyle's admonition: "Sarcasm I now see to be, in general, the language of the devil; for which reason I have long since as good as renounced it."

BITING OR OFF-COLOR HUMOR

Humor is a verbal Dr. Jekyll and Mr. Hyde. It can be biting, sarcastic, a powerful tool of aggression used to hurt and humiliate, a means to create distance and a reflection of cynicism. That's its dark side. But it can also bring people closer, diffuse awkward moments, help us relax and make us laugh—a wonder drug that requires no prescription.

Humor at someone else's expense never shines brightly on your image. Someone may laugh when he is made the brunt of your joke, but inside he's almost certainly wincing. He stumbles as he gets into the elevator. "Have a nice trip?" you joke. He spills a drop of soup on his tie. "I'll see if I can flag down the waiter and get you a bib," you chuckle. He takes it in stride. He may even think it's funny on some level. Yet on a much more emotional level, it hurts to be ridiculed, even "good-naturedly."

Don't feel you're safe to make jokes about individuals or groups who aren't represented in the conversation. Off-color or critical remarks often create poor impressions. Biting, cruel humor won't endear you to many, and it always presents a risk of unanticipated fallout. Just as your Impression Management Plan should include good-natured, positive humor, it should eliminate all potentially hurtful humor.

PUBLIC EMBARRASSMENT

Janice excused herself quietly from the table to use the restroom. The rest of our group hardly noticed as we continued to talk and nibble hors d'oeuvres on the outdoor patio of the restaurant. A few minutes later Janice returned with at least three feet of toilet paper trailing from the back of her skirt like the train of a wedding gown. As she approached, Jim glanced up. He broke into a broad grin as he announced in a voice loud enough that he was certain to be heard by everyone, "I think you've grown a tail." Janice glanced over her shoulder. We could hear an audible gasp, followed by a quiet, "Oh God!"

Embarrassment hurts. It makes us feel stupid and ashamed. Long after the event, it and the person who caused it are remembered.

If you want to make a favorable impression on others, you must meet their needs; and their number-one need is to feel important. When people feel important, they physically and emotionally stand tall, chest out, shoulders back, head up so the world can see them in all their glory. When you embarrass someone, you make her want to crawl into a hole and disappear. It's hard to conceive of anything further removed from a sense of importance.

There are times when it is necessary to correct someone's grammar, pronunciation, or misuse of a word. If your employees or children use words in ways that will adversely affect the impression they make on others, you have an incentive, and often even a responsibility, to help them improve their impression by correcting them tactfully. But you almost never need to do so in public if your action will result in embarrassment. When you are in conversation with someone whom you have no reason to correct, why feel compelled to correct him at all if he misspeaks? Why not just let it pass? To the extent it makes you seem smarter to point out his error, it will make him feel dumber. From an Impression Management perspective, that's not a good tradeoff.

Criticism, too, is a reality of life. Sometimes you need to be critical as a friend, lover, employee, coworker or parent. But how often does that criticism need to be expressed in public? The worst kind of embarrassment can't exist in private. It needs witnesses. Your private criticism of another may create a degree of embarrassment, since after all, at least you are there; but there is seldom any need to play to a larger audience. Follow Roman philosopher Publilius Syrus's advice: "Speak well of your friend in public, admonish in secret."

TABOO TOPICS AND TOUCHY SUBJECTS

When you make others feel uncomfortable, they don't like it. It may be that you disclose something personal about yourself that leaves them feeling, "That's more than I needed to know." Or perhaps, your curiosity or bad judgment gets the best of you; and you probe into areas that most people hold sacred, or at least private. In either case, the other person questions your judgment and social aptitude. She may think you're insensitive, pushy, vulgar or foolish.

In an intimate personal relationship almost anything goes; but even then, certain topics are generally unwelcome, unless absolutely necessary. In professional or more casual personal relationships many topics seldom are appropriate. There are no absolute rules, since the nature of your relationships varies from person to person; and each individual's sensitivities to touchy topics are different.

The best rule of thumb is to avoid taboo topics and tread lightly around touchy subjects unless you're *very* sure that the other person will be comfortable talking to you, or listening to you talk, about them. Until you're familiar enough with the person to make that assessment, the safest course is to follow his lead.

Taboo Topics

Just as no one wants to witness your body at work, they also don't want to hear about it. Nor do they want to share their physical intimacies with you. Discussions about menstrual cycles, hemorrhoids, diarrhea, constipation, sexual function, gas, rashes, pimples, "woman problems," prostate and phlegm are not the stuff of which great impressions are made. Save it for your doctor, or if necessary your spouse.

Other topics you should avoid in most situations include: how much money someone makes; how much something costs; a person's (particularly a woman's) age; physical conditions, surgeries and the like; someone's sex life, or whether they have a good or bad marriage. Many people will feel perfectly comfortable talking about some of these topics. Many others won't. Until you know someone quite well, you won't know which topics are fair game and which are off-limits. If someone feels comfortable with a particular topic, odds are before long she'll raise it. This will give you the green light to talk about it yourself. Until then, be discreet.

Touchy Subjects

There are many subjects that are not inappropriate topics of discussion, but are laced with the potential to trigger negative impressions. These are subjects about which people tend to be most passionate—topics like religion, politics and abortion.

Because these are topics about which many people care deeply, they are also common topics of conversation. Not only can't they be avoided, they shouldn't be avoided or you're likely to be perceived as either not forthcoming, disinterested, not very bright or boring. The problem doesn't arise because you discuss these topics of conversation. It surfaces when you express your opinions too adamantly, or show intolerance of others' opinions if they differ from yours.

As fervently as you may feel about highly charged topics, the person to whom you express your opinions may feel just as strongly to the contrary. It's natural to be threatened and challenged by conflicting beliefs and to interpret them as personal criticism. When you express a strong opinion contrary to another's view on an issue of great importance to her, her emotional brain will respond negatively, even if her rational brain might say, "Everyone has a right to his or her own opinion." If you express intolerance of the other person's contrary views, the conflict escalates.

We don't suggest that you can never express your opinions or differ with the opinions of others without making a bad impression. If expressed politely, thoughtfully and tolerantly, an articulate discussion of your views on important matters will favorably influence the impression you make. But remember, Impression Management requires that you maximize others' impressions of your positive qualities without introducing negative impressions. Extreme views, fervently expressed, always present the risk of extreme reactions.

AGGRESSIVE BEHAVIOR

There's a bit of the beast in all of us—that raw instinct to fight to defend our turf and to achieve dominance. We wondered if other creatures harbor resentment and anger when they have been beaten into submission or vanquished from the herd by its more aggressive and powerful members. We know that that reaction is remarkably predictable among members of the human species.

Our surveys and countless juror interviews confirm that aggressive behavior, while sometimes associated with confidence, gives rise to predominantly negative impressions of truthfulness, caring, humility and capability. People like to be led, not pushed. An aggressive, in-your-face, dominant approach is seen as an effort to achieve with force what cannot be achieved with reasoned, honest and caring behavior.

When you interrupt, talk over someone, shout them down, invade their personal space or show dominance with other body language, voice or action, you produce far more negative impressions than positive. Research shows that men are expected to be more aggressive than women, and that the overall negative impression aggressive behavior creates is therefore more pronounced when aggressive characteristics are displayed by women. But it's just a matter of degree. Both genders score poorly on all points of the Compass if they're overly aggressive.

Behavior that is perceived as aggressive does not necessarily have to be loud and forceful. Any conduct that seeks to establish intellectual or physical dominance causes negative reactions. Assertion of intellectual superiority through a know-it-all attitude, harsh criticism and anger or confrontation are among the most common behaviors that are associated with aggression.

THE KNOW-IT-ALL

According to legend, a student of Socrates once visited an oracle. When asked, "Why are you here?" the student responded, "I'm in search of the greatest teacher in all the world." The oracle replied, "Socrates is the greatest teacher." "But," the student questioned, "Socrates has said, 'One thing only I know, and that is that I know nothing.'" "That is why he is the greatest teacher," the oracle responded.

Like many myths repeated over the millennia, the oracle's message carries more symbolic than literal meaning. Obviously, someone who truly knows nothing, who has no opinions and can contribute little, will not be highly regarded. On the other hand, as Voltaire said, "He who thinks himself wise, O heavens! is a great fool."

When we encounter a know-it-all, he in essence says to us, "I am smarter, better informed *and more important* than you." He knows a better Italian restaurant than the one you've recommended, has seen a funnier movie, has an uncompromising memory of not only every event in his own life, but in yours and in the history of the world. Frequently, he is quick to give you unsolicited advice about how you should raise your children, where you should work, whom you should date or marry, what you should order off the menu, where you should vacation and what you should do when you get there. It's as if you were a small child who desperately needs his benevolent guidance in all things.

We all value intelligence, knowledge and experience in our friends and coworkers. But we resent the implication that we are somehow deficient in any of those respects. A balance must be achieved that the most respected people find naturally. It is a balance that you can obtain in every aspect of your life if you follow a few simple guidelines.

First, learn to distinguish between fact and opinion. In one respect, someone's opinion is always right. Opinions express how someone feels or believes. If I say, "I think *Gone With the Wind* is the greatest movie of all time," I'm absolutely right—that's what I think. You can have a different opinion, and express it as, "I like *The Godfather* better." That's okay. Yet if you say, "You're wrong; *The Godfather* is better," you have suggested that your belief is more *factually* valid then mine. When you express your opinion as a fact, you invalidate me. Learn to accept and view others' opinions and your own not as facts but as feelings.

Second, don't profess to be an expert on every topic. Most of us welcome the thoughts of those who have special knowledge, experience or expertise on a given subject. You probably have unique knowledge, experience and expertise on a number of topics that your friends and coworkers recognize. You may be a sports nut, follow politics closely or have a passion for wine. When you talk about sports, politics or wine, you will be given deference and respect. But anyone who professes to be an expert on everything loses credibility on all things.

The third guideline to keep in mind is to remember that it's not what you say but how you say it that often impacts the impression you make. People do not respond the same to those who reason with them and those who lecture to them. The distinction is often a function of different body language and semantics. If you invade someone's personal space, engage in intense eye contact, raise your voice, speak stridently and use words like "should," "must," "best," "worst" and the like, you communicate aggressively. On the other hand, if you show more relaxed body language, smile, engage in soft eye contact, use a more passive voice and words or phrases like "might," "consider," "can," "we" and "our," you can deliver the same message without appearing to force your views on others.

When you give others advice, keep this distinction in mind. It's one thing to offer suggestions or ideas for someone's consideration, and quite another to tell her how she *should* think, dress, sound or act. One effective technique to make it clear that you respect others' views is to ask for permission to give advice. "Can I offer a suggestion?" "If you have a minute, maybe I can help. I have a couple of thoughts on the matter." Statements such as these give the listener the opportunity to welcome your suggestions, rather than have you foist them upon her.

HARSH CRITICISM

"If you and I want to stir up a resentment tomorrow that may rankle across the decades and endure until death, just let us indulge in a little stinging criticism—no matter how certain we are that it is justified," Dale Carnegie wrote in *How to Win Friends and Influence People*. He was absolutely right. No one likes harsh criticism. At best, we tolerate it. But unfortunately, criticism is a fact of life. Sometimes it's absolutely necessary, sometimes justified but discretionary, and sometimes purely gratuitous. Sometimes you can achieve the desired objective without criticism. Sometimes there's no effective way to sugarcoat it; you just have to be critical.

Even so, if an employee dresses inappropriately at work, there are different ways to communicate that you would like her to change. The first would be to say critically, "Your dress is inappropriate and unprofessional. Change it." The second would be to counsel, "I've given some thought to how we might improve our image in the eyes of our customers. I think we should all increase our effort to dress more formally, and to make sure that our clothing is always clean and pressed." Most employees will get the message and won't need to be personally attacked.

If the employee doesn't get the message, and continues to wear dirty, crumpled and inappropriate clothes, there will come a time when more direct criticism is necessary. Even then, it doesn't have to be delivered in an overly harsh or personal attack. Compare "Your clothing is too casual, and sometimes not as clean and neat as I would like in order to project the most professional image possible of our company" with "You have to clean up your act: you look like you sleep in your clothes." In the first instance, the criticism is depersonalized to the extent possible. It is directed toward *the clothing*. In the second example, the criticism is very personal. It attacks the individual.

Honesty doesn't mean brutality. Whatever strides you may make in the candor category will be offset by losses in others' opinions of your kindness and tact. Criticism that has no productive purpose and is therefore unnecessary and gratuitous will not enhance anyone's impression of you. On those occasions when criticism serves a legitimate purpose, there are ways to blunt the blow. Your criticism will always be more effective if you are understanding, positive, gentle and show that you can take as well as give criticism.

Be Understanding

Criticism should have a purpose. The purpose should be to alter another's behavior positively. Some things people can change; some they can't. When you identify what someone is able to change, you can gently prod her toward transformation. When you determine that some characteristic cannot be changed, don't create expectations that the other person can't meet, which will leave both you and him frustrated and resentful.

At some point, you need to stop trying to force a square peg into a round hole. On the other hand, if the person is incapable of change, you won't overcome his limitations by beating on him. On the other, if he's capable of change but refuses to take action or responsibility, he will consider your continued nagging insensitive, unfounded and unfair. Either way, he will have a poor impression of you.

Reciprocal tolerance is perhaps the most valuable by-product of tempering your criticism with understanding. Most people believe one good turn deserves another and embrace the opposing concept, "An eye for an eye, and a tooth for a tooth." When your criticism of others reflects no understanding of the reasons for their perceived inadequacies, they are unlikely to treat you any more charitably when the roles are reversed. But when you are understanding, especially when harsh criticism is warranted, you accumulate a reservoir of goodwill that will temper their judgment of you.

Keep Your Criticism Positive

Psycholinguistic researchers have found that a person will understand a positive statement in approximately two-thirds the time it takes to understand a negative one. Even if your only objective in life is to motivate others to do what you want them to do, constructive criticism will carry you much further than a negative attack.

As former Speaker of the House Sam Rayburn once said, "A jackass can kick a barn down, but it takes a carpenter to build one." Successful individuals are carpenters who build barns, not jackasses who kick them down. Every criticism can be expressed in either positive or negative terms: If someone has done something half right and half wrong, emphasize how great the end product would be if he consistently employed the techniques that worked well. If someone's clothing is attractive and classy, but her makeup looks like it was applied at Le Salon de Barnum & Bailey, compliment her on the tastefulness of her attire; and if you have a legitimate need to change her appearance, suggest that she would look even better if she conformed her makeup to her clothing style. Offer solutions, not just criticism; and give others the chance to take the hint. If they don't, you can always ratchet the criticism up a notch or two until they do.

Be Gentle

Criticism need not be harsh, and is seldom as effective when it is. Abrasive, insensitive or abrupt criticism is more likely to be perceived as unfair, unkind, egotistical and incorrect, than kind, reassured counsel. As a result, it is also more likely to be ignored.

Some people are more thick-skinned and open to criticism than others. They need not be criticized with the same degree of finesse. But when you address sensitive topics, or sensitive people, don't believe for a moment that blunt criticism will be appreciated, respected or admired, even if someone assures you that it will. At least start gently. Depersonalize your criticism, as we explained earlier. Choose your words carefully. Let others know your criticism is motivated by a desire to help them succeed. Show them you care.

Learn to Take Criticism

Learn to take criticism graciously. There is nothing more frustrating than to sit down with someone in the hope of effecting change, only to be met by interruptions, inattention or defensiveness. Whether you like it or not, if you're being criticized, someone apparently believes you need to change. It may be your boss, your friend or your spouse. If your response is a steadfast unwillingness to recognize his need, he will naturally assume that no real change will be forthcoming. To the contrary, if you accept criticism, or at least carefully listen to what might motivate what you believe to be unwarranted criticism, you show that you are anxious to please and improve.

ANGER

When psychologists prepare their short lists of basic human emotions, anger always makes the cut. Anger, as your most aggressive emotion, triggers a response by those against whom it is directed that is unparalleled by any other emotion.

If you demonstrate that you are able to communicate your frustrations, disappointments, animosity or indignation calmly and rationally, you will be considered more trustworthy, caring, humble and capable. When you are quick to express anger, you detract from each of these qualities, since people perceive anger, particularly at unwarranted levels or inappropriate times, as a loss of rational control. Without rational control, your objectivity, believability and trustworthiness will be placed in doubt, and you will be considered less reliable and competent.

Expressions of anger, particularly by men, often are viewed as an effort to intimidate, dominate or control. This gives their anger some rational purpose, but it is a decidedly negative focus. Because women who express anger openly or frequently fall outside our normal expectations, the negative response to their outbursts is even greater than the reaction to men's anger.

Anger may intimidate others into submitting to your will in the short run, but will leave a lasting scar on your victim, and a poor impression of you by him and any witnesses to your attack. Anger also has a unique way of begetting anger. Voices escalate, gestures become more pronounced, and strong words are exchanged until a relationship is destroyed. Anger is never defused by anger; nor does either participant in a confrontation find the other's behavior acceptable simply because it mirrors his own. Others will respond positively to you when you defuse angry confrontations, and poorly when you escalate them. Of the peacemaker we think, "He handled that well." Have you ever thought the same of someone who allowed herself to be drawn into an angry exchange?

In our research we came across an interesting study that demonstrate that your attack on another will enhance his image, while diminishing yours. Individuals were asked to watch someone give a speech during a debate. When the speaker's opponent shook his head, grimaced, rolled his eyes, mouthed disagreement or showed other signs of disapproval, the speaker was thought to be more credible and likable than when his opponent did not. Though the experiment involved behaviors that would more appropriately be characterized as disagreement than anger, we're certain that if the opponent's behavior had escalated to more obvious signs of anger, the speaker's ratings would have increased even further at the opponent's expense. When faced with disagreement, and particularly angry disagreement, keep this study in mind. It may be difficult to control your emotional response, but if your objective is to come out on top, maintain your composure.

Some techniques to avoid potentially angry confrontations and maximize your impressions of trustworthiness, caring, humility and capability are:

- *Maintain your composure.* Tell yourself that nothing positive comes from anger.
- *Don't be offended by disagreement.* As Mark Twain said, "It were not best that we should all think alike; it is difference of opinion that makes horse-races."
- *Look for common ground.* In almost every confrontation, there can be some agreement. When you establish even a tiny foothold of common ground, you help defuse emotions. Agree not to agree on everything, and search for some partial solution that will lessen the emotions of the moment.
- *Listen carefully.* Your attention shows your opponent that you respect his opinion, though you may disagree with it. Vest him with that feeling of importance and you will lessen his resolve to conquer you.
- *Admit when you're wrong.* Nothing defuses anger more quickly than a heartfelt, "I'm sorry, I was wrong."
- *Don't be defensive.* Keep an open mind. It will allow you to understand the other person's perspective better and respond in more productive ways. Look for compromise.
- *When all else fails, retreat.* As Abraham Lincoln once said, "Better give your path to a dog than be bitten by him in contesting for the right. Even killing the dog won't cure the bite." Or as grandpa used to say, "Never wrestle with a pig. You'll just get muddy, and he'll enjoy it."

Sometimes, as we watch people maneuver for position in relationships at home or in the workplace, we are reminded of Civil War battles like Gettysburg, in which thousands of soldiers dutifully formed lines and advanced on enemy entrenchments with a remarkable show of courage, loyalty and patriotism. At the end of the day, thousands of soldiers from both camps lay dead, and many thousands more injured and maimed. At most, one small hill on one desolate battlefield either was defended or fell under the human onslaught. No one could tell the victor from the carnage. But somewhere, in dimly lit battlefield tents, one general counted himself the conqueror and the other the vanquished.

This is called a "pyrrhic victory," after Pyrrhus, the king of Epirus, who said solemnly after his bloody victory over the Romans at Asculum in 280 B.C., "Another such victory over the Romans, and we are undone." Yet most of us are all too willing to suffer pyrrhic victories—battles won at the price of others' respect, admiration and affection for us, and ours for them.

Don't shout others down, beat them into submission or intimidate them into surrender. None of these techniques will create an image worth maintaining. They are not the tools of a leader, the solutions of the wise or the habits of the friendly or humble. Learn to accept disagreement and to resolve it in a positive fashion.

PETTINESS

The witness was an actor who had just concluded an acrimonious divorce from his wife, a successful Hollywood movie producer. Along with the marriage, the wife had terminated her ex-husband's contracts to star in two of her upcoming movies. He sued.

During trial, her lawyer, a lanky, balding man with a wry sense of humor and quick wit, began questioning the actor about the conversation in which she told him his services were no longer welcomed in bed, or on the set. After a few minutes, the lawyer asked, "Did she explain why she didn't want anything more to do with you?"

"She just said that's the way it was going to be," the actor responded sarcastically. "She thinks she's so high and mighty with her big house and fancy parties that she doesn't owe any of us mortals an explanation about anything. She's such a princess!"

"Oh," the lawyer said thoughtfully, as he turned from the witness and took a step back toward counsel table. Then, with an exaggerated wrinkle of his brow and a quizzical look on his face, he turned back and asked, "Do you take every opportunity you have to say something bad about your ex-wife?"

"No," the actor said indignantly as he straightened in the witness chair.

"Oh," the lawyer said in that same almost whimsical tone, as he once again turned toward the podium. He again stopped and pivoted toward the actor. He looked puzzled as he mused out loud, "Are you saying you pass up an opportunity to say something bad about her every once in a while?"

No one in the room, except of course the actor, could suppress his or her laughter. In that brief exchange the witness had done more damage to his impression of trustworthiness, caring, humility and capability than in the remaining two hours of cross-examination. He had shown himself to be envious, jealous and resentful.

Pettiness can be displayed in many ways: jealousy, envy, resentment of others' successes, celebration in others' losses or failures, gloating over your own victories—and even overly competitive behavior. However clothed, pettiness gives rise to very predictable stereotypical reactions.

Pettiness creates two somewhat distinct impressions. First and most obvious is: If you resent others' successes, celebrate in others' failures or gloat about your own accomplishments, you will lead others to conclude that you are neither caring nor humble. You will seem so full of yourself that there is no room for charitable thought of anyone else.

Second, and somewhat more subtle, is the connection between pettiness and insecurity. Our first thought of someone who is petty may be, "What a jerk"; but followed closely on its heels is often, "Boy, is he insecure." If you appear insecure, you won't project capability. Others wonder, "If he's really intelligent, competent, confident and professional, why does he resent others' successes, or gloat so blatantly about his own?"

Trustworthiness also is placed in doubt by petty behavior. Would you trust a petty coworker to stand up for you, to give you credit when credit is due or to speak well of you? Would you welcome a personal relationship with such a man or woman?

Petty behaviors strike to the very heart of others' feelings of importance, and your ability to meet their needs. In times of personal success or failure, remember:

- *Celebrate others' successes.* Send them congratulatory notes. Stop by and pat them on the back. Tell them you're happy for them, and *be* happy for them. Send a memo around the office to make sure everyone knows of their accomplishments. Throw a party. Take them out for a celebratory dinner.
- *Accept your own accomplishments graciously.* Don't gloat or grab all of the glory. Give credit for your accomplishments to others when due. Thank those who have helped you achieve your objectives.
- *Compete for the sport, not the conquest.* No matter how much you despise losing, think not of your opponent's success as your loss, but as her victory, and celebrate it with her.

CHAPTER 7

Physical Appearance

"God, he'll be here in less than two hours," Marcia whispered. "I just have to look perfect." A shower and shampoo began the ritual. Marcia then carefully rolled and pinned each curler in place. She applied her makeup like a portrait artist for another half an hour before she began the quest through her closet for just the right dress. Marcia pulled out one after another and held it up to her neck. "I look like an old lady," she muttered; "too business"; "ummm, sexy, but sleazy." Finally she announced, "Perfect!"

The ritual was repeated with her underwear, purse, shoes and jewelry. After fifteen more minutes of combing, brushing and primping, her preparation was complete, just as the doorbell rang.

Even though Marcia spent almost two hours and more thought than she had devoted to any task at work in weeks to assure she made "just the right impression," she didn't give a moment of thought to what she would say, how she would say it, or what she planned to do once her beau arrived. Her focus was on one thing. What do you think she noticed first about her date? You guessed it—his appearance.

The first thing people usually notice about you and what they examine in the greatest detail is how you look. The more care and attention they give to their own appearance, the more likely they are to judge you by yours. This, coupled with the lasting quality of a first impression, should make your appearance more than a casual concern if you want to make a great impression, particularly on someone who is appearance conscious.

THE IMPACT OF PHYSICAL ATTRACTIVENESS

Attractive men and women are thought to be more honest, intelligent, competent, friendly and professional than less attractive men and women—even though less attractive people are generally perceived to be harder working and more reliable. Others also tend to defer to attractive people more readily and respect their authority. Research demonstrates that attractive people of both sexes are hired more quickly, promoted more often and earn more money than less attractive people with similar qualifications. One survey conducted by America's foremost expert on the effect of dress and appearance in business settings, John Molloy, author of *Dress for Success* and a half-dozen information-packed sequels, found that attractive women were 20 percent more likely to be hired by another woman, and 300 percent more likely to be hired by a man. Other studies show the wide-sweeping effect of appearance in every arena:

- Both men and women, but particularly men, believe interactions with attractive individuals are more pleasant;
- Those who are more attractive are thought to have better developed social skills, whether or not they really do;
- Attractive people are considered more extroverted, warm and agreeable;
- Attractive children who display the same discipline problems as unattractive ones are nonetheless considered less naughty; and
- Attractive criminal defendants receive significantly lower sentences when convicted of most crimes than less attractive defendants.

On the flip side:

- While those who are only moderately overweight suffer from no significant negative stereotypes, anyone who is obese (often defined as more than 20 percent overweight) is judged less intelligent, industrious, detail-oriented, competent, self-confident and socially adept.
- Those with obvious blemishes (prominent moles, acne, scars) fall victim to essentially the same stereotypes as overweight individuals.
- Women who don't wear makeup, both men and women with unattractive hairstyles/haircuts and those with crooked or discolored teeth or other unattractive features also are judged more harshly in each of these categories.

As strong as these biases are, most people don't even recognize that they hold them, as shown in a study of the voting patterns of the Canadian electorate. The researchers found that the better-looking candidates received an average of 250 percent more votes than the less attractive candidates, yet 73 percent of those who cast their votes in the elections adamantly denied that appearance played any role. This same pattern has been seen in other research in which interviewers who clearly favored better-looking applicants were equally insistent that appearance was irrelevant to their hiring decisions.

Physical attractiveness is definitely an asset. Yet we don't recommend that you use it as the foundation of your Impression Management Plan even if you are among the blessed. If others believe that you trade on your good looks rather than good character, your otherwise favorable impression will fade quickly. We have seen many lawyers and witnesses who have become accustomed to deference because of their good looks fail miserably before a jury that detects either that they rely on their appearance to manipulate others, or that they expect to be held to a different standard than the rest of us because they have been graced with beauty. The same is true in all environments.

While good looks are advantageous, beauty—particularly striking good looks when openly flaunted—often spawns negative associations. Very beautiful women are not taken as seriously and are not thought to be as professional or intelligent as their less gorgeous counterparts. The same bias exists, but to a lesser extent, toward particularly good-looking men.

Another frequent bias harbored against attractive individuals is that they are self-centered and arrogant. Most of us have noticed some correlation between physical attractiveness and arrogance. It's natural for us to then engage in what psychologists call "heuristic thinking," or what we call "shortcut thinking." Rather than evaluate each person separately to see if our preconceptions are justified, we simply incorporate our biases into our first impression of any beautiful person we meet. Once we have stereotyped a particularly attractive individual as arrogant and self-centered, a secondary association that he or she is also less caring often follows.

Frequently, extremely attractive people don't know how to look, speak and act to best manage their impression on others. They assume that because they are attractive they will make an excellent impression, even if they don't display the four Compass Qualities. Just the opposite is true. The very beautiful must often display trustworthiness, caring, humility and capability even more than the rest of us to be thought of as favorably, and the slightest attempt to trade on their appearance can subject them to criticism and doubt.

HOW TO ENHANCE YOUR PHYSICAL APPEARANCE

Matthew Arnold wrote: "Character is capable of being taught, learnt, and assimilated; beauty hardly." We disagree strongly.

Before you say, "There's nothing I can do to be more attractive," take a hard look in the mirror and ask if that is really so. Can you "do something" about your hair? Are exercise and a better diet really out of the question? How much thought do you give to how the clothes you wear affect your overall physical impression? It's not a matter of *if* you can become more physically attractive, it's a question of whether you want to be more attractive. There is always room for improvement if you try.

There also are many ways you will be perceived as more physically attractive that do not require any changes to your face, body or even wardrobe. Research has proven that your physical attractiveness is influenced significantly by many factors that don't show up in a photograph—factors like voice, competence, intelligence, success and dignity and grace. Many other behaviors, like smiling, friendliness and good posture, are not within the unique province of beauty queens and leading men; yet they also significantly enhance others' perception of your attractiveness.

In one of our surveys, we asked both men and women what trait most contributed to their first impression that someone was "sexy." Physical attractiveness was the most common response, but it accounted for only 37.2 percent of the answers. How someone dressed and their body language tied for second at 13.8 percent. Their smile, eye contact and personality qualities such as confidence, intelligence, compassion and charisma were also mentioned frequently. Almost two-thirds of the respondents identified traits that had little, if anything, to do with inate physical beauty. Among those traits are:

- Clothing
- Weight and physical condition
- Posture and other body language
- Smiling, eye contact and other facial expressions
- Hygiene
- Voice
- Intelligence
- Dignity and grace
- Environment

Each of these traits can be enhanced with Impression Management. And, unlike the impression of attractiveness created by physical beauty alone, these traits when well managed not only will make you appear more physically attractive, they will have a positive effect on others' assessment of each of the Compass Qualities.

SEXINESS

If Freud is to be believed, sex is our most powerful motivator. Our conscious or unconscious awareness of its potency is a natural invitation to use it to our advantage in both social and business settings. Women, more than men, have been socialized to believe that they can, and should, capitalize on their sexual allure in interpersonal relationships. Many women, on at least some level, rely on that technique.

But be forewarned. When you sexualize your appearance, you will attract some people, but not without a price. Substantial research has explored the effects of sexual dress and behavior on others' perceptions of qualities such as trustworthiness, competence, intelligence and professionalism. The overwhelming conclusion of this research, which is consistent with our own experience from interviewing jurors about their attitudes toward witnesses and attorneys who sexualize their appearance, is that those who use sexual appeal to draw others' attention to them are thought to be less trustworthy, caring, humble and capable.

One survey of 137 women revealed that approximately one-third were "openly hostile" toward other women who wore sexy and revealing clothing. In another study, the majority of men, and an even greater number of women, thought women who dressed "sexy" were ineffective businesspeople, and manipulative. Another study in which women wore conservative gray or blue suits, but with miniskirts, surprisingly found that most women judges found their attire appropriate; but 90 percent of the men surveyed said that a woman dressed in a short skirt would make them feel uncomfortable, and that they would not take her to an important meeting dressed that way.

Sexual attire and behavior have the same negative effects in both professional and blue-collar jobs. In social settings, where sexual suggestiveness is more expected, it does not produce adverse responses of the same magnitude; but to a lesser degree the same attitudes exist.

On those occasions when you want to make a favorable impression at every level, there are certain guidelines that you should follow to desexualize your appearance.

- Your makeup should not be too dramatic. It should bring out your natural beauty, and look as if you're wearing no makeup at all. Eye shadow should be flesh toned, not colored. Eyeliner should be minimal. Studies indicate that women make a better general impression when they wear lipstick. Wear lighter and softer colors during the day and for business functions. Darker shades are more acceptable at night, or on social occasions.
- Like lipstick, women's nail polish should be clear or a relatively conservative color.
- Long, flowing hair is also considered sexual when worn by a woman.

Studies have shown that shoulder-length, simple styles of hair for women, and shorter conservative cuts for men, better enhance overall perception.

- Tight and revealing clothing should be avoided. Tight sweaters or shirts, form-fitting pants, short skirts for women and tank tops for men are obvious signatures of someone who is sexualizing his or her appearance.
- Women typically should not wear high heels other than on social occasions when they are accepted as normal style. Otherwise, they will sexualize their appearance.

BEYOND BEAUTY

No one "look" is right for every person, or every occasion. Each "look" evokes many stereotypical associations which, if neglected or managed poorly, may lead others to unwarranted conclusions. The impression you make through your appearance involves constant trade-offs. One style or color will make you appear more professional, but less friendly; another more authoritative, but less humble; and another more expressive, but less reliable. The look that best serves your objectives will depend upon many factors. With the knowledge of how your appearance influences others' impressions of you, you can find the balance that creates just the right impression for each occasion.

CONFORMING TO EXPECTATIONS

Mark had known Bob for almost ten years when Bob's transformation occurred. Bob had always fit the mold of a big-firm litigator. After receiving a law degree from a top law school, he joined the most prestigious and conservative law firm in town, where almost all of his clients were Fortune 500 companies. For almost twenty years his uniform was blue and gray conservative suits, white shirts, simple patterned ties and lace-up black oxford shoes. Athletic and tan, with a short conservative hairstyle, Bob fit in perfectly with the firm and its clientele.

As Bob's kids left home and his marriage disintegrated, he faced midlife in search of a new identity. What he settled on left him almost unrecognizable. His hair crept down well below his collar; he hung up the classically tailored business look in favor of double-breasted suits that were then at the cutting edge of style for business attire; he added colors and patterns to his suits, shirts and ties, which, though tastefully coordinated, gave a noticeable flair to his outfits; woven leather, tasseled Italian loafers took the place of his classic oxfords; and, topping it all off, he began wearing a small diamond stud earring.

Bob believed he had paid his dues. He had proven to his firm, and to his clients, that he was a superb lawyer: bright, aggressive, creative and hard-working. For his first forty-five years he played life by other people's rules; and now it was time to express himself—to literally let his hair down. To some degree, Bob was right that those who knew him for years probably would not draw the same conclusions from his new persona as would strangers who met him for the first time. On the other hand, those who witnessed his transformation would have questions strangers never would—questions like: "Is he still committed to the practice of law and his clients?" "Have his priorities changed?"

New acquaintances who had no history with Bob would have nothing else on which to base their opinion apart from how he looked when they first met. What they would see was a forty-five-year-old man, dressed at the height of fashion, with long hair and an earring. The overall style of Bob's appearance would not conform to his clients' expectations. As a result, the typical Fortune 500 client would tend to form certain conclusions and impressions about Bob that he never intended or anticipated.

We use the word "expectations" frequently because the concept often holds the key to how you will be perceived. Bob's appearance at a board meeting with a Fortune 500 client, dressed in a shimmery double-breasted suit, bright-patterned shirt and tie, Italian loafers, long hair and an earring would deviate from the board members' expectations. They would expect a lawyer with well-trimmed hair, free of jewelry apart from a watch and at most wedding ring, who wore much more conservative attire—because that's the way they and their other lawyers look. On the other hand, if Bob were an executive at a Hollywood studio or a salesman in a trendy clothing store, his appearance might actually meet others' expectations.

There's nothing inherently wrong with being individualistic, creative or expressive; but few people hold nonconformity, even if it reflects creativity and expressiveness, in high esteem if it detracts from the four points of the Compass. And that conflict can be expected when your appearance deviates from others' expectations. Many people think that they'll get ahead if they break from the pack. This is seldom true. We are not unlike the other members of the animal kingdom whose suspicions are immediately drawn to anything unusual or unexpected in our environment.

The Impact of Style

Style is almost undefinable, and includes many distinct components. However, we have found that three aspects of style are most influential to impression formation: trendy or classic, casual or formal and cultivated styles.

Trendy or Classic

Studies show that high fashion and cutting-edge trendiness often raise questions about your trustworthiness, caring, humility and capability. Such styles tend to set you apart and, ostensibly, above your peers. People don't trust those who seem dramatically different from them.

People who dress either more or less stylishly than their coworkers tend not to get along as well in the workplace as those who do. They are not seen as team players, and are often thought to be egotistical or antiauthority. Extremely fashionable clothes when out of place in an environment also project an image of shallowness. People assume that those who spend a substantial amount of time, money and energy reading fashion magazines or shopping at the trendiest stores to put together just the right outfit reflect their true priorities—style over substance. This can affect others' assessment of your intelligence, competence and professionalism.

As always, there are exceptions to the rule. First, what is "trendy" varies from job to job. Your job may call for creativity. If that's the case, trendiness *is* conforming and expected. This is true in any avocation or environment in which creativity and artistic bent are valued, such as the theater, advertising and the arts. But those of us who work in other professions are expected to conform to normal custom.

One of the rare occasions when it can be beneficial to dress above your peers is if you aspire to rise to a higher level within your company where people typically dress differently. For example, studies show that middle managers who hope for a promotion to the executive ranks have greater success if they mirror the styles worn by those in the positions they covet. We are drawn to, and more comfortable with, those who reflect our own characteristics. Many American executives are relatively fashion conscious. They may think someone who dresses classically and conservatively lacks creativity, imagination and self-confidence. Subordinates who share their fashion flair are more readily given a key to the executive washroom. This is more true of women who assess the fashion flair of their female subordinates than it is of men who evaluate the garb of either their female or male subordinates.

This concept doesn't apply just to professions whose members wear suits to work every day. Last year Jo-Ellan watched as a large construction crew gutted and rebuilt the interior of the office suite across the hall in the building where she works. A dozen or more different workers regularly came and went. The foreman always wore a well-pressed collared work shirt that was carefully tucked into his jeans. Most of the other workers typically wore T-shirts that were often dirty or stained. Occasionally they wore the company-issued collared work shirt, but when they did, it was frequently dirty and often looked sloppy. One worker was an exception. He was always dressed like the foreman.

Jo-Ellan had no idea whether this worker was in fact harder working, better at his trade or more reliable. Whether he was or wasn't, his personal appearance made him appear in a better light than his coworkers. If he'd shown up to work in slacks and a dress shirt, he also would have distinguished himself, but not in a positive way. Jo-Ellan would have assumed that he didn't roll up his sleeves and work as hard as the others, and that he was more concerned with appearance than getting the job done.

Whether a teacher, gardener, retail clerk, banker, lawyer, secretary or accountant, there are a few general principles of style that will serve you well.

- Don't try to set yourself apart from the pack by excessive trendiness.
- Dress as stylishly as the top 70 to 90 percent of your coworkers.
- If the position to which you aspire requires different dress than the job you currently hold, show the decision makers that you have "all the right stuff." Dress as they do, but recognize that this may alienate your coworkers. To manage their possible resentment, show them that you are a team player in every way possible.

Casual or Formal

Twelve strangers come together in a jury with a single purpose: to decide the fate of those who appear before them. They spend days, weeks or sometimes even months chatting in the hallways, gathering in groups for lunch, talking about their children, their jobs, their hobbies, their lives. When the day finally arrives for them to enter the jury room and deliberate, their first task is to choose one from among them who will lead them in their deliberations. He or she must be likable, fair-minded, socially adept, able to build consensus and intelligent. In other words, they select someone who embodies the qualities all of us hope to project.

We always try to predict who will be selected foreperson. Will it be the college professor, who probably will be assumed to be the most intelligent? Or the woman whose smile and friendly "good morning" distinguishes her as the most friendly and outgoing? Or the man who, as senior manager at the power company, is the most accustomed to taking charge and directing others? To the extent that there is any single predictive characteristic, it is that the foreperson is almost always among the more formally dressed of the jurors.

Our courtroom observations and post-trial interviews with jurors conform to the studies that have been performed outside of the courtroom. Those who dress more formally generally are considered more honest, confident, intelligent, respectful and competent. They are thought to be leaders and more professional.

More formal dress speaks of authority and leadership. And others listen. The influence of formal attire is illustrated by a study in which a man jay-walked across a crowded downtown street dressed in either an expensive business suit or a work shirt and pants. The researchers found that three and a half times more bystanders took the man's lead and followed him across the street against the red light when he wore the expensive suit as opposed to the work shirt and pants.

Before you run out and buy a tuxedo or formal gown to wear to work tomorrow, you should be aware of the flip side. Those who dress more formally than would be expected on a particular occasion are considered less friendly, approachable, likable and humble.

The institution of "casual day" in many workplaces has complicated Impression Management for both men and women. It has raised the question for both employers and employees: "What is appropriate wear for casual day?" Over the past five years we have spoken with many employers about their experience with casual day. The most significant concern that has been voiced is that employees don't understand that "casual" does not mean "sloppy." There is a difference between "personal casual," and "business casual."

When in doubt about appropriate dress for casual day, err on the more formal side. Don't take casual day as a license to ignore your appearance. Once a casual day "climate" has been well established in your office from which you can gauge appropriate dress, choose among your options bearing in mind that how you appear on casual day is at least as important as the rest of the week.

To optimize the impression you make on others, the watchwords are "appropriateness for the occasion." Both underdressing and overdressing affect the impression you make in different ways. Whether in a professional or casual setting, the best rule of thumb is to dress as formally as the top 70 to 90 percent of those in the environment. If in doubt about appropriate dress, ask. No one will think less of you for it, and it's definitely better than showing up dressed differently from anyone else.

Cultivated Styles

For most of us, our "image" is the natural by-product of the family in which we were raised, our cultural heritage, our regional origins, and other life experiences. Others cultivate an image or style intentionally. No particular style has a monopoly on positive or negative qualities, and none is free of them. Every cultivated style carries with it a number of stereotypes, as borne out not only through our interviews, but also by the way those who project various images are portrayed in the media.

- *The sophisticate:* She tries to set herself apart and above the rest of us. She has an air of intelligence, but is seen as snooty and arrogant. As a result, she's thought to be less trustworthy, caring and humble.
- *The cowboy:* He's down-to-earth and friendly, but not very intelligent. He scores well in the trustworthiness, caring and humility categories, but slips when it comes to capability.
- *The GQ Man:* He's egotistical, shallow and self-centered. He may or may not be capable. But we doubt that he cares about anyone but himself; and who can trust someone like that?
- *Mr. and Mrs. Hollywood:* They're just so cool, "with it" and trendy that they can't possibly value trustworthiness, caring, humility or capability.
- *The punker/grunge monger:* He wants nothing to do with civilized society, and has no place in it. He follows his own rules, not ours. If we turn our backs on him, he'll probably rob us blind, or worse. He almost certainly has never worked an honest day in his life.
- *The jock:* He's strong, confident and powerful, but he couldn't have been graced with both brawn and brains. Why do you think people are surprised when they hear about a professional football player who was a Rhodes scholar?
- *The ethnic poster child:* She shows her ethnic background in every way possible. She's nonconformist, antiestablishment and angry. She obviously has her own agenda. We don't trust her, and we're sure she could care less about us.
- *Daddy Warbucks:* Rich, yes, but what did he have to do to get there? Now that he's arrived, he's full of himself.

We don't defend these or any other stereotypes, but we can assure you that we have seen many witnesses testify who had cultivated these images. And when we interview the jurors afterward we always get a healthy smattering of these stereotypical reactions. As a society, we have tended in recent years toward greater acceptance of ethnic, cultural and social diversity. In many areas, we have actively promoted it. Still, any style that varies significantly from the social mainstream tends to stoke up old biases.

HAIRSTYLE

Your hairstyle is often the first feature of your physical appearance others notice, particularly if it is unusual. After years of reading people based upon all of their features, including their hairstyle, we have found that hairstyle in isolation can often lead to invalid assumptions about someone's personality, particularly a woman who may perm her hair one month, dye it the next and cut it short the month after that. Her fundamental character doesn't change as she experiments with different looks, but those who encounter her on any given day will tend to make fairly predictable associations between her hairstyle and her character. Because of those strong associations, your hairstyle should be an important component of your Impression Management Plan.

In this section we discuss hair length, style and color, which are the three key components to the impression your hair makes on others. We also discuss the impact that facial and body hair have on the impression made by both men and women. As you review our conclusions, you may find that the stereotypical associations we attribute to particular aspects of your hairstyle aren't a fair characterization of your personality. We understand that. But whether or not they are accurate, these stereotypical associations are fairly universal.

HAIR LENGTH

Long hair on a man carries associations of independence, irresponsibility, loose morals and a host of other negative impressions. If you wear your hair long, expect that many people will assume you are less trustworthy and less capable. If long hair is a common style among your professional or social peers, it may be seen simply as part of your "uniform," and will not be given as much weight. For example, a man who works in the fashion or entertainment industries, or even a man who works in the construction trades where many of his conservative coworkers sport long hair, will be viewed by his peers without any negativism. Those outside his peer group won't be so charitable.

On the other extreme, research has demonstrated that people judge bald men not only to be older than their chronological age, but also to be less intelligent than men with a full head of hair. Any attempt to counter balding with dramatic comb-overs or toupees accentuates the negative reaction. The man's judgment, common sense and realistic self-assessment are then doubted. There was a time when a man who shaved his head would have been thought to be radical and nonconformist, just like the long-haired hippie of the sixties. In the post–Michael Jordan era, a balding man who shaves his head is more frequently seen to have adopted a socially acceptable hairstyle. A man who shaves his head and also dresses the part of a "skinhead," however, will be assumed to follow an ultra-radical right-wing ideology. That image carries with it extremely pejorative associations for most of us.

If you are a man and keep your hair closely cropped, but not shaved, you may be thought to have a military or law enforcement background, especially if you have other traits that support this image. The look carries with it certain associations. Men from a military or law enforcement background are viewed as trustworthy and capable, but less emotional, outgoing and friendly. If you prefer to keep your hair short because it looks neat, clean and is convenient, or if you wear your hair in the same kind of buzz-cut to which you became accustomed after years of military service, you may not want to change anything, but keep these stereotypes in mind, and compensate for them. Accentuate other traits that display caring and intelligence.

Long hair on a woman has always been associated with femininity, sexuality, youth, vibrancy and health. This image is accentuated if a woman's hair is styled in a way that makes it even more noticeable—curled, permed, wavy, woven or teased.

On a younger woman, longer hair does little to affect others' impressions of her, apart from her sexuality. However, as women age we *expect* that their hairstyles will change as well. Consequently, when we see an older woman with long hair, our antennae quiver. Something doesn't fit. Is she insecure? Doesn't she accept her age gracefully? Does she keep her hair long in the hope that it makes the rest of us think she is younger than she really is? Doesn't she realize her hairstyle is too "young" for a woman her age?

Because long hair on an older woman doesn't meet our expectations, older women who wear their hair long are judged as less competent, sophisticated and socially adept. If you are an older woman and prefer to keep your hair long, and want to avoid these harsh and often unfair judgments, wear it in a bun or similar style, particularly in any professional setting.

Studies have shown that women, particularly older women, are perceived as more credible, friendly and competent when they wear their hair shoulder length or shorter, and in relatively simple styles and cuts. Particularly short, chic, styled hair can look very professional, and scores well in the capability category as well, although it appears more harsh and unfriendly.

Short hair that is not styled is often seen as a sign that a woman is not feminine, and may be a lesbian. Bear in mind that in a recent *National Law Journal* survey, more than three times as many people acknowledged that they would find it difficult to be fair to gays and lesbians when compared to any other minority group, including African Americans, Hispanics and Asians. Whenever someone harbors a strong bias or prejudice toward a particular group, he or she will tend to rate those who fall within that group poorly with regard to each Compass Quality. Whether the assumption is made that a woman with a butch haircut is a lesbian or particularly masculine, a very short, nonstyled haircut on a woman is typically taken as a reflection that she is less friendly and less approachable.

DRAMATICALLY STYLED HAIR

Women in our culture are expected to style their hair. Those who don't are more likely to draw attention to themselves than those who do. Very trendy or dramatic hairstyles affect others' impressions much the same as do trendy and particularly expressive clothes. Women's hairstyles that are less dramatic generally make the best impression.

Men, on the other hand, generally don't style their hair. They get haircuts. They wash their hair, comb it and that's it. Men who pay unusual attention to their hair, like those who receive manicures or pedicures, are generally seen in a negative light by those who don't. They're thought to be cultivating the power image that shows others how successful, wealthy and important they are. They are seen as untrustworthy, uncaring, egotistical and shallow. Those men we have seen appear before juries with the coifed look always prompt a barrage of negative remarks in our post-trial interviews.

HAIR COLOR

Men seldom color their hair for any reason other than to cover their gray. Women color their hair for many reasons, but like men, the object is typically to rid themselves of gray. That's a good idea. Gray hair makes both men and women look older. For men, this is a mixed blessing. On the positive side gray-haired men are seen as more mature, wise, experienced, distinguished and often even more attractive. On the negative side, they are thought to be less energetic, active, creative and spontaneous. Since it's a bit of a mixed bag for men, graying hair generally doesn't significantly affect others' overall impression of them.

If a man chooses to color his hair, it should be colored professionally and he should avoid the jet-black, shoe polish look. Since we accept men with gray hair readily, those who obviously dye their hair are considered vain. If an older man appears to be trying to recapture his youth with artificially dark hair, others not only will perceive him as vain, but also will question his judgment and self-awareness.

Women, however, don't fare so well when they turn gray. Studies show that they are considered older, tired, less creative and less capable. Unlike men, there are no corresponding positive associations when women's hair turns gray. Women with striking white or silver hair in short, chic hairstyles avoid the negative associations that generally apply to women who have grayed. But for those whose hair has turned gray or salt and pepper, hair coloring will significantly improve their image, particularly in the professional arena.

Anyone who colors his or her hair should be careful not to allow the roots to show, or the negative associations made with poor grooming will tend to attach. Women also should carefully consider the color they dye their hair. The bleached-blond look, particularly if it results in damaged and frizzy hair, like artificially appearing red hair, generally is perceived as unprofessional, lower class or attempting to look sexy.

BODY AND FACIAL HAIR

One of the most common questions men with facial hair ask us is how beards and mustaches impress others. As "people readers," we have found that the presence or absence of common variations of facial hair usually says little about a man. In our experience, it normally reflects a personal cosmetic choice. The man simply thinks he looks better with a beard or mustache.

However, if someone has a particularly long or unkempt beard or mustache, it suggests either radical leanings or a lack of attention to personal grooming. Since people are suspicious of anything different, a long, unkempt beard, a large mustache or a goatee will tend to adversely affect others' assessment of a man's truthfulness and capability. On the other hand, a conservative, close-cropped mustache or beard shows that a man tends to detail, is concerned with his personal hygiene and may in fact be quite conservative.

That's our analysis as people readers. As image managers, however, we caution that for many there is still a stereotype that men who sport facial hair are trying to hide behind it, and are therefore less honest, forthcoming, friendly and open. This book is about perception, and that is how many people will perceive you if you choose to wear a beard, and to a lesser extent a mustache. If that is still your cosmetic choice, manage the potential negative impression by accentuating open and friendly body language, communication style and actions.

Other facial hair on a man, and any significant facial hair on a woman, usually affects others' impressions poorly. Bushy, unkempt eyebrows on either a man or a woman, excessive nose or ear hair (typically only a problem for men) and facial hair on a woman fall beyond our normal expectations. We therefore tend to wonder why someone hasn't done something about it. Don't they realize how noticeable it is? Do they care so little about their appearance that they can't be bothered to trim or remove unattractive facial hair? Don't they care what others think? If you happen to be someone who has a problem (which you may not see as a problem at all) with what most people would characterize as unusual or unwanted facial hair, don't think for a moment that people don't ask these questions about you.

Those of us in the United States notice women with unshaved underarms and legs immediately. American women who do not shave their underarms and legs are seen as nonconformists. They may be viewed as feminists, liberal naturalists or simply people who don't care about their appearance. As with anyone who deviates from societal norms, this will raise questions about their character. The feminist may be perceived as harsh, the naturalist as caring but not very capable and the person who doesn't care about her appearance as socially inept, less intelligent and generally less capable. These are admittedly harsh and oftentimes unwarranted characterizations. But they exist. Unless the statement you choose to make by not shaving is particularly important, this is one concession to American social custom that we strongly recommend.

BODIFICATIONS

Twenty years ago men in the military, bikers and biker chicks represented the segments of society with whom we associated tattoos. As recently as ten years ago, a single earring in the lobes of a woman's ears was the extent of mainstream body piercing. Today, a young college student, a bank teller or the girl who baby-sits your children might be among those who adorn their bodies with tattoos and multiple body piercings.

American society has just begun to accept that this practice is no longer reserved for the rebellious and nonconformists among us. While the bias against them is softening, tattoos and body piercings continue to trigger strong negative stereotypes.

The negative stereotypes associated with tattoos apply more to women, since tattoos have traditionally been worn only by American men. For the same reason, body piercing, including ear piercing, is more accepted for women than men. For both men and women, any Impression Management Plan that includes visible tattoos or multiple body piercings will be hampered from the start.

CLOTHING AND ACCESSORIES

Your clothing and accessories have a tremendous impact on how you are judged by others. The importance of dress as an element of your Impression Management Plan is demonstrated clearly in the research. For example: studies have found that most hiring decisions are made based upon the job applicant's appearance; entry-level salaries of those who make a better physical appearance are higher; and those who dress best at work are more likely to be promoted. Notwithstanding the clear evidence to the contrary, most interviewers and managers deny that someone's physical appearance is particularly important to them, which demonstrates that many of the messages conveyed by different styles, fits, colors and fabrics are not conscious.

Our comments about what is or is not the most effective dress in various circumstances are not gospel, but they are based on the results of hundreds of studies, surveys and interviews and will provide you with a good foundation from which to build your Impression Management Plan. As you review the impact various aspects of your attire will have on your image, assume that you can start fresh with an empty closet and an open mind. As you replace your wardrobe, incorporate flexibility to create different but consistently great impressions for different occasions.

SUITS, PANTS AND DRESSES

As a high school teacher since she graduated from college twenty years ago, Mary had never given much thought to the clothes she wore to work. Everything from jeans to dresses was within the range of acceptable attire for teachers at her school. When she decided to apply for a job at the school district's administrative office, she recognized that if she were to make the transition from the classroom to the district office, she had to rethink her wardrobe.

We told Mary that if she were to invest in just one outfit, it should be a conservative but feminine blue suit, and off-white silk blouse. She should wear flesh-tone nylons and black closed-toed pumps with one and one-half-inch heels, and a simple necklace with either gold stud earrings or gold earrings that hang no more than one-half inch below her earlobe and should carry a medium-sized black purse. This is a classic professional look, and one that is perfectly suited for a middle management position. Women who wear ladylike (as opposed to girlish) feminine-cut suits, or skirts and matching jackets with simple white, off-white or pale-colored blouses are not only seen as strong and confident, but also as trustworthy, likable and humble—the best of all worlds.

This isn't ideal for all positions, however. In more high-fashion professions, the suit should be more stylish, with more expressive accessories such as a tasteful gold brooch, a scarf or a slightly more dramatic necklace. When a woman reaches for the glass ceiling, the look should change. The goal is a "ladylike" professional look: Suits should be soft and feminine and strike a balance between understated and conservative, feminine and fashionable. Colors can range from navy, gray and blue to butternut and mahogany. Jewelry should be expensive, simple, appropriate and elegant. The look should be rich but businesslike.

The male equivalent of Mary's new outfit is a navy blue or medium-gray wool or wool blend suit, a white stiff-collared dress shirt, and a simple patterned or striped tie. Black lace-up oxford shoes and a three-quarter-inch black leather belt with a small gold buckle completes the look. If a man needs to own no more than one dress outfit, this would be it. It would serve him well at a wedding, funeral, job interview or formal holiday office dinner party.

To snaz this outfit up, the man could add a blue shirt, a brighter, more distinctive tie or matching pocket square, French cuffs and tasseled loafers. Presto, the conservative business suit has become the foundation for an expressive, creative and imaginative outfit that looks less "professional," but is certainly more high-styled.

When a man wants to project a greater sense of approachability than what is conveyed by a formal business suit, a blue blazer and either gray, camel or tan slacks is a good alternative. It is less formal, and less professional than the blue or gray suit, but scores nearly as high in the credibility department as a classic "sincere blue" suit. On balance, it's an excellent choice when professionalism and approachability are both essential, such as in sales positions that bring you in contact with those who don't wear conservative suits themselves. There is no "right" choice between a suit and a sports coat and slacks. Choose one or the other depending on those qualities that are most important for you to convey in a particular situation.

Generally speaking, both men and women should interview dressed in clothing slightly more dressy than what they would customarily wear to work. If they overdress they may raise questions about whether they will fit in at the position. For example, if Mary had interviewed for a clerical position at the district office, instead of an entry-level management position, we would have recommended that she replace the suit with a skirt and complementing jacket, which would appear professional, but less formal. Otherwise, the ensemble would remain the same.

For men who wish to dress formally, the choices are fairly simple: either a suit or a sports coat and slacks. Women, however, can choose from a much more extensive menu. The style of women's suits varies dramatically. Women also have the option to wear a skirt and jacket, a pantsuit or a dress. Each projects a different image.

The unisex look has become popular as women have entered male-dominated work environments in greater numbers over the past three decades. Many women's suits have the look of their male counterparts. Women who dress in masculine-cut suits, particularly in black, dark blue, or gray, are seen as stronger and more professional, but also as more severe and less friendly. In professions like law, accounting and banking, this look is anticipated as part of "the uniform," and therefore does not result in negative stereotyping to the same degree as it does in less formal or less male-dominated occupations.

The harshness of a dark masculine-cut suit can be softened, while still preserving its professional appearance, if a woman wears a feminine, light-colored blouse, rather than more masculine colors like white or gray, or wears a brightly colored scarf and feminine brooch. Frilly blouses, puffy sleeves and feminine trim like lace and felt, however, detract from a professional image and are advisable only on social occasions.

Traditional male styles such as bow ties, straight ties, dark pinstripes, long straight lines, and pants may have the opposite effect intended by most women who favor them. Many women think that this is the female equivalent of the "power look," since it borrows heavily from masculine styles. Studies indicate, however, that women who dress too masculinely are thought to be less creative and to have less self-esteem and confidence than those who wear more traditionally feminine, but professional, styles.

Over the past ten to fifteen years women have begun wearing pantsuits, or slacks, a blouse and jacket more frequently in professional settings. In the *New Woman's Dress for Success Book,* Molloy cites several studies that should give you pause before you dress in pants for your next important business meeting. In one of the studies, for example, 53 percent of the men polled had a negative reaction to a businesswoman dressed in pants.

At the other end of the spectrum are women who wear dresses, rather than either suits, pantsuits, or skirts and a jacket. Particularly imposing, assertive or aggressive women may benefit if they wear dresses when they want to emphasize their caring nature, since dresses tend to soften the go-getter image of more aggressive career women. But if you prefer dresses, at least add a jacket for the work setting.

Women should bear in mind that the impression they make will be influenced by their choice from among the many options that are available to them.

- A masculine-cut suit reflects more power and authority, but will be interpreted as more aggressive and domineering and less creative.
- A feminine-cut suit will show more expressiveness, and a heightened level of approachability, yet maintain a high degree of formality, professionalism and confidence.
- Either slacks and a jacket, or a dress and a jacket is even more approachable, but less professional.
- A pantsuit is less professional still, and generally will not enhance your image of approachability or friendliness.
- Finally, a dress without a jacket is the least professional alternative, and will not enhance others' impressions of your professionalism, competence or confidence. As the most feminine of the alternatives, however, it will most strongly evoke a sense of honesty, caring and humility.

SHIRTS AND BLOUSES

Few generalities can be made about shirts for men to wear to work when they don't have to wear a jacket and tie, and even less about appropriate shirts to wear in casual occasions. It's best simply to keep in mind the general observations we made earlier. Avoid trendiness unless creativity and individuality are more valued by your peer group than other qualities, and adhere to the general rule that you should dress as formally or trendily as 70 to 90 percent of your peers. Other factors such as fit, color and fabric, which are discussed later, also should be considered.

While there are no hard and fast rules that apply in other situations, substantial research provides excellent guidelines for those men who wear a shirt, tie and jacket to work.

- A man's dress shirt should be cotton, or a cotton blend. Cotton or cotton blends look more professional than silk or synthetic fabrics, and they absorb odor better. Cotton blends tend to show less creasing.
- Collars should be plain, and either button-down, or thick and stiff. Collar length has varied from time to time, but the most professional look consistently has been a mid-length pointed collar.
- A man's shirt should not be shiny or patterned, particularly if the fabric is thin. An undershirt should be worn to ensure that it is not see-through and to help obscure perspiration.
- Men's dress shirts should be long-sleeved. Short-sleeved dress shirts are considered less professional. The other extreme, French cuffs, are trendy. If you choose to wear them, wear them with simple gold, silver or stone cufflinks.
- Monograms are another flair that can be added to shirts, but with the same effect as French cuffs. If you prefer monograms, they should be subtle, placed on the sleeve, not the breast pocket, and the same color as the shirt.
- For a traditional conservative look, a man's shirt should be lighter than his jacket. White, off-white and pale blue are the most professional and conservative colors. Darker colors, patterns and stripes are more casual and trendy.

There also are no hard and fast rules for appropriate blouses for women to wear on casual occasions. Once again, be guided by the general principles discussed elsewhere. But for professional occasions keep these rules in mind, all of which are supported by the research.

- Silk blouses in white, off-white, light blue, beige, champagne, peach, pink or other pale colors are judged more professional.
- Women's blouses with lapels tend to project more authority and competence. Blouses without lapels, or collarless blouses, are more feminine, and project a friendlier image.
- Women's blouses should not be sleeveless if intended as part of a professional package.

- A slip or camisole should be worn if a woman's bra or bra straps would otherwise show; and for professional occasions the neckline should never be low enough to be the slightest bit revealing.

ACCESSORIES

As any good salesperson will stress, accessories can make the outfit. Both men and women, but especially women, can impact their overall image with a variety of accessories—belts, ties, scarves, handkerchiefs or pocket squares, socks, purses, attachés, suspenders and even eyeglasses.

The most notable accessory for a man is a tie, if he wears one. The same suit or sports coat can be made elegant and classic with a conservative solid, patterned or striped tie, or can be given a noticeable flair with bright-patterned or geometric designs, or transformed completely by the Mickey Mouse tie his son gave him for Christmas. Which you select should depend on the image you want to project.

- In a professional setting, silk ties are preferable. They should be neither too wide nor too narrow, or they can make even the most conservative outfit look trendy. They should accent but not repeat the pattern or color of your suit.
- As a symbol of authority, the "power tie" is typically fairly bright and bold. Yellows and reds are the most common colors associated with this image. However, if they are too bright and bold, they detract from a professional appearance.
- Ties should be tightly knotted and extend just below the belt buckle. If you don't know how to tie a good knot, ask someone to teach you. Sloppy, loose or uneven knots will detract from your image.

Pocket scarves can add flair to even the most conservative suit. A classic blue wool suit with a bright pocket scarf will leave much the same impression as a more trendy suit. If your goal is to hit a conservative professional note, at most incorporate a plain white or dark solid-color pocket scarf that either accents or matches the colors and patterns in your tie.

For most occasions, men's belts should be black or brown leather, and free from any adornment. Woven fabric belts, however, are appropriate with more casual outfits. The width of buckles should correspond closely to the width of the belt, and should be plain metallic colors, such as brass, gold or silver. The width of casual belts is generally between three-quarters of an inch and an inch. Belts worn with slacks and suits should be at least one-half-inch, and no more than one-inch wide. Belts that are either too thin or too wide keep your outfit from looking "well put together," unless they fit an overall "look," such as a wide leather-tooled cowboy belt with an over-sized silver buckle when worn with western wear.

Men often give very little thought to their socks, but they are an important part of the total ensemble. For casual wear, or at work when a suit and tie is not required, plain cotton socks that match the color of your shoes or pants are appropriate. With a suit, or slacks and a sports coat, bulky cotton socks are too casual, and will detract from the professional look. Instead, choose a thin dress sock with either a very subtle pattern, or a plain color that matches your shoes or pants. Socks should always extend far enough up your calf to assure that no skin shows when you sit down or cross your legs.

Women's belts come in a wider variety of colors, shapes and styles than men's. Some outfits include a belt that may be either the same color as the outfit, or an accenting color. Women's belts may be fabric, leather or metallic. Regardless of the style, they should not be gaudy, and should not dangle or make noise. When worn with dress slacks, women's belts, like men's, should be simple, thin and incorporate unobtrusive buckles. Generally, for professional attire, women's belts should match or accent their shoes.

Attachés, like belts and shoes, should be plain, no-frill leather for the most conservative look. Black, brown or cordovan are perceived as most professional. Large boxy briefcases look less professional. Women should favor a thinner attaché, which should not be carried with a purse. Choose one or the other.

A woman's purse should also be selected with care. Leather purses are consistently judged as more professional than fabric or synthetic purses. Black or brown leather is not only more versatile, but also the most professional. Many women favor purses that match the color of their outfit—red with their red blazer or green with their favorite green dress. Colorful purses are stylish, but are more appropriate for casual occasions.

Women should wear pantyhose with a dress or suit, and pantyhose or knee-high stockings with slacks. Flesh tones are preferable, though navy and black, if they accent the outfit, are appropriate. White and other colors detract from a professional image.

How you express yourself by your choice of eyewear also cannot help but be noticed. You may be tempted to choose an expressive or particularly trendy fashion, but we don't recommend it. Both men and women who wear eyeglasses are considered more professional and intelligent than those who don't—unless the eyeglasses are gaudy, trendy or outlandish. Don't lose the single benefit that results from your need to wear glasses unless an image of expressiveness is more important than an image of intelligence and professionalism.

JEWELRY

When men wear more than a wedding band, school ring or wristwatch, their jewelry is usually noted, and seldom in a positive light. Gold bracelets, necklaces, earrings and even particularly showy watches or rings consistently prompt negative associations. People tend to think that men who wear excessive jewelry are "slick," which adversely affects their trustworthiness. They also react to men's jewelry much as they do to coifed hair and manicured nails, thinking that they reflect egocentrism and shallowness.

The response to women's jewelry is more complex. We are accustomed to women who wear bracelets, necklaces, pins, earrings and an assortment of hair ornaments, as long as they are not particularly massive or gaudy. Studies show, however, that women are rated more professional when they wear less jewelry. A simple, high-quality necklace or bracelet, a tasteful watch and earrings that do not dangle far below the earlobe are considered more professional than more expressive and noticeable jewelry. The higher up the corporate ladder a woman climbs, or wants to climb, the more tasteful and expensive her jewelry should be.

Each piece of your jewelry should complement the others. A woman should wear all gold, or all silver, but not mix the two unless one or more of the pieces is two toned. Simple but elegant jewelry, such as pearls, should not be combined with more gaudy jewelry, such as sequined brooches. Decide on a look that you want with a particular outfit on a given occasion, and use jewelry to compliment that look.

Accessories are an excellent way to accentuate or minimize traits as part of your Impression Management Plan. For example: a strikingly beautiful woman who may be considered arrogant and shallow should wear more understated jewelry to minimize that impression; a smaller woman who may tend to go unnoticed can benefit from more dramatic jewelry; and a wealthy man who is concerned that he may be perceived as arrogant or untrustworthy can appear more trustworthy and friendly if he wears a less-expensive watch for occasions when there is no legitimate reason for him to emphasize his financial status.

SHOES

There are too many different jobs and types of footwear to begin to catalogue all those that might be appropriate or inappropriate in various professional or social settings. There are, however, a few general rules that apply on all occasions, and several more specific guidelines that should be followed in professional or social settings where dress shoes are required. First, some general observations:

- Trendy shoe styles give rise to the same associations and stereotypes as any other trendy part of your wardrobe. Balance your desire to appear fashionable, exciting, fun-loving and creative against the need to be seen as professional, reliable and humble.
- More functional shoes will tend to enhance your image with regard to all four Compass Qualities, as long as they are not dowdy or out of style. Less functional but more stylish shoes send a message that you are more concerned with appearance than performance.
- Women's shoes with more than a two-inch heel lengthen and accentuate a woman's legs, which contributes to an overall "sexy" image. If the heels are spiked, this image is enhanced even more.

When dress shoes are required, for either professional or formal social occasions, studies show that you should keep the following in mind:

- Don't wear boots with dress attire unless they are *very* frequently worn by others in your professional environment. For example, men in Dallas frequently wear dress cowboy boots as part of their professional wardrobes.
- For men, lace-up wingtips or oxfords in brown, black or cordovan make the most conservative appearance.
- Men's slip-ons can be quite conservative, but as tassels and patterned leather are added, they become more trendy and less professional.
- Women's shoes that are simple and elegant perform best in tests designed to gauge professional image. Closed-toed pumps with one and one-half-inch heels in conservative colors and styles top the list. Shorter women can wear two-inch heels to be more noticeable, but the heels should not be spiked. Taller women may prefer one-inch heels to minimize their dominating presence, particularly if they have otherwise powerful traits.
- Don't try to match your shoes with brighter-color clothing. Stay with basic colors.
- Avoid anything that is particularly fancy, frilly or busy, as people tend to take those dressed in such styles less seriously.
- Always keep your shoes clean and polished. If the soles or heels are worn, repair or discard them.

COLORS

Always consider the colors you wear. The studies that demonstrate the associations people make between particular colors and those who wear them are too persuasive to ignore. Many of these associations are reflected in common phrases like the following: *red* hot; calm as the deep *blue* sea; peaceful as a *green* meadow; innocent as the driven *white* snow; *black*-hearted; and sunny *yellow* disposition.

Research into the psychological effect of color has resulted in many changes in the world around us, from the color of fire engines and hospital wards to the suits candidates wear at televised presidential debates. Strong correlations have been found between different colors and how they affect our impression of such traits as status, effectiveness, attitude, loyalty, honesty, credibility, friendliness and intelligence. Most colors can be grouped into one of six general categories, each of which conveys a distinct set of messages. It may be helpful to envision these colors on a spectrum with jet-black and dark gray on the far left, and pastels on the far right. Between the two extremes, moving from left to right are navy blue and light gray, bright colors, light colors and earth tones.

Power and	◀ Black –	Navy –	Bright –	Light –	Earth –	Pastels ▶	Friendliness and
Authority	Dark	Blue	Colors	Colors	Tones		Approachability
	Gray	Light					
		Gray					

- Black and dark charcoal gray are strong authoritarian colors. Those in positions of leadership or authority will project an image of no-nonsense confidence, strength and power if they wear black or dark charcoal gray. Studies even show teachers control their classrooms better when they wear dark colors.
- Black is also seen as serious, secretive, mysterious and depressing. For that reason those who dress in black are not rated as warm and friendly. In our seminars, the most frequent comment we hear about the impressions colors make is that black is stylish and sophisticated and makes you look thinner. That's true, but its popularity doesn't overcome the stereotypes and emotional responses it evokes.
- Lighter shades of gray and navy blue are also associated with power, authority and leadership. Unlike dark gray and black, however, studies show that they are warmer and more approachable. This is why the "sincere blue suit" is generally thought to be the single most versatile

professional garment. It strikes a balance between power, authority, competence and leadership on the one hand, and sincerity, warmth and friendliness on the other. For men, navy blue is definitely preferred; but for women, a medium shade of blue is ideal.

- Bright colors like red, turquoise, purple, bright blues and greens and fuchsia are sexy, energetic, hard-charging and aggressive. They generally are not considered as professional as darker colors, or lighter shades of colors.

- Lighter shades of blue, green and yellow, as well as tan and beige, convey a sense of warmth, friendliness, approachability and trustworthiness. They do not communicate the same sense of authority, power or leadership that dark blues or grays project. Subtle tones, however, can be very effective to combine friendliness and professionalism.

- Autumn colors—like rust, brown, gold, muted shades of yellow, olive and burgundy—are perceived as trustworthy, caring and humble. Autumn colors don't pack much of a punch, and generally test poorly in the strength, competency and leadership categories. These colors, however, are a good choice for caring professionals such as psychologists or counselors, or anyone whose first priority is to be approachable.

- Pastels are the most feminine of all colors. Not surprisingly, stereotypical feminine traits are associated with them, such as caring and nurturing on the positive side, and weakness and immaturity on the negative. They are also viewed as lively and fun-loving. Pastels are effective if you want to show your fun-loving, vivacious, youthful side, but they're a poor choice if your primary objective is to be viewed as serious, intelligent, competent and professional.

You may have noticed that the colors of expensive clothing tend to be richer, deeper and more vibrant than the colors of less expensive clothes. The difference results not only from the use of higher quality dye, but also because more expensive fabrics tend to take the dye better. If you compare the jet blacks, royal blues and bright reds of inexpensive and expensive garments, you'll see that the difference is obvious.

Studies show that the variations between different shades and qualities of the same color have a significant impact on the impressions they trigger. Rich, deep colors project an image of class, quality, competence, success and professionalism. The less vibrant, almost faded look or the brash, gaudy appearance of inexpensive clothing is perceived as lower class, less competent and less professional.

In one study, two women each interviewed with twenty-five recruiters. They both wore black skirts, white blouses and red jackets, though one jacket was purchased at an upscale Fifth Avenue store in Manhattan, and the other was purchased at a discount house. The jackets looked almost identical, but the color of one was deeper and richer. Each of the women interviewed with twelve recruiters before they switched jackets and interviewed with the thirteen remaining recruiters to assure that their personal appearance and mannerisms did not influence the recruiters' responses. When the women wore the more expensive jacket, they received two job offers and seven call-backs from the twenty-five interviews. When they wore the inexpensive jacket, they received one call-back and no job offers. They also were treated with less respect by the receptionists and interviewers when they wore the less expensive jacket.

There are many ways that colors can be used as an integral part of your Impression Management Plan. If you have a number of traits that can be interpreted as overpowering or threatening, such as large size, powerful voice or assertive mannerisms, lighter colors will soften your impression; but won't cause you to lose your image of confidence and control because your other traits will continue to send that message. On the other hand, if your traits suggest a lack of confidence, control, authority or capability, you should wear darker colors to create a stronger authoritarian image, or brighter colors to show more energy and enthusiasm. A dark suit with a more colorful tie or scarf can combine both elements.

The impact of different colors was demonstrated a number of years ago when the New York City Police Department changed the color of its officers' uniforms from dark blue to light blue in an attempt to reduce the number of assaults on police officers. The theory was that dark blue was an intimidating color that tended to promote hostile reactions by those who felt threatened by the police. The theory proved true. With the change from dark blue to light blue, the number of assaults on police officers dropped. Unfortunately, police officers complained that the respect they were shown by the public also declined, since the light blue uniforms were less authoritarian.

Don't minimize the contribution of color to your overall image. The findings of the New York City Police Department can be applied to almost any situation, whether professional or casual. Take advantage of the opportunity to use different colors on different occasions to emphasize different qualities. As you prepare both your general Impression Management Plan and individual Impression Management Plans to apply in specific circumstances bear in mind:

- Wear dark colors if you want to command authority or stress intelligence and leadership in situations in which friendliness and approachability are secondary.

- If you want others to relax, feel comfortable and think of you as likable and humble, wear lighter colors or autumn hues.
- If you want to create excitement, enthusiasm and call attention to yourself, wear bright colors, but with the recognition that you will seem less professional and less humble.
- Wear rich, dark colors. You're better off owning fewer pieces of high-quality clothing. Once you've learned to tell the difference between high-quality colors and low-quality colors, you will be able to find garments with high-quality colors in many discount outlets at affordable prices.
- Evaluate whether your image will be enhanced or diminished when you wear darker or lighter colors. Unless your traits collectively are quite overpowering, in professional environments you will almost always be well advised to wear darker colors.
- Always bear in mind that different circumstances will call for different emphasis. You may want to command authority and respect with a no-nonsense dark suit one day, and favor a softer color on those days when you want to be approachable.

FABRICS

Many people view synthetic fabrics, and those who wear them, in a negative light. Natural fabrics like wool, cotton, silk and linen convey a more honest, warm and professional image. Choose from among the wide assortment of natural fibers depending upon what is most appropriate for a particular occasion, keeping these guidelines in mind:

- Silk with a bright sheen tends to look slick, and detracts from all the Compass Qualities.
- Less shiny silk material lends itself well for casual occasions, but should be avoided for dress shirts, suits or jackets.
- Silk blouses, ties, scarves and pocket squares are definitely preferred, and they don't have to cost a king's ransom. Beautiful and classic scarves and ties can be found at reasonable prices.
- With the exception of men's cotton dress shirts, cotton and linen tend to be too casual for formal business occasions. They also wrinkle easily, which makes them difficult to keep pressed and looking sharp. But they are warm and approachable for casual occasions.
- Tightly woven wool and wool blends stay relatively wrinkle-free, absorb odors well, as do all natural fibers, and have that classic look that helps build credibility.

- Any fabric that tends to be smooth and shiny will seem less warm and approachable. Thicker, bulkier and softer weaves reflect friendliness and caring.
- Any dramatic or loud pattern in a fabric not only raises questions about your taste, but also your trustworthiness, caring, humility and capability.

FIT

In our interviews with jurors after trials, we have found that they frequently comment about lawyers' and witnesses' clothing. Fit is among the most common observations because it makes a strong impression, and gives rise to certain associations on a fairly consistent basis. Poorly fitting clothing detracts from the impression you make, notwithstanding how appropriate your clothing is otherwise.

Men's clothing that is too short in the sleeve, leg, jacket or tie makes a particularly poor impression. Your ties should come down just below your belt buckle, and no further. Jacket sleeves should be approximately four to four and one-half inches above your extended thumb when your arms are at your side. Your shirt sleeve should extend slightly below the jacket sleeve. Your shirt should be long enough that at least one, and preferably two buttons fall below the belt line. This will keep the shirt from coming untucked.

The front of a man's slacks should always touch the top of his shoes when he stands. Some men prefer more of a "break" in the fabric of the pants above their shoes than others. Some prefer a more straight-leg look. Either is acceptable, though more break, up to a point, gives a more casual look. Too much break looks sloppy. In either case, the pant leg should extend over the back of the shoe to within one-half to one inch from the ground. Whether your pant legs are cuffed is also a matter of personal preference, though cuffs are more classic and conservative, and cuffless hems in trousers are more sporty.

While the length of women's pants varies dramatically depending upon the style, women's dress slacks should cover their ankle entirely, and for the most professional and conservative look should touch the top of their shoes. Unlike men's slacks, women's dress slacks should have little or no "break," and the hem should be horizontal to the floor.

Skirt length is always an issue for women. Unlike men's fashions, women's fashions, and particularly skirt length, change every few years. For a professional look, stay mainstream. Today, for example, the Ally McBeal miniskirt is occasionally sported even by women in professional settings, but it sexualizes a woman's appearance and detracts from her competence and professionalism. At the other extreme, skirts that extend to the ankle are seen as dowdy and unprofessional unless worn by an older woman or as part of a casual look. Whether you wear your dress skirts a few inches above or a few inches below your knee is largely a matter of personal preference, and a decision that should be based on what looks best on you, and with what you feel most comfortable.

One of the most common fashion faux pas is to wear clothing that is too tight. This is seen as either an effort to be sexy or a sign that the person doesn't know better or can't afford to buy properly fitted clothes.

Collars should be loose enough to stick two fingers comfortably between the collar and your neck, but not so loose that they show any significant space between the collar and your neck when you stand. Shirts and jackets should not strain against the buttons and there should be no gaps or puckering between the buttons as you move naturally. Pants should be tight enough so that you don't feel compelled to hike them up from time to time, but not so tight that the pockets spread or creases appear on the sides or across the back. Your underwear or pantylines should never show. But pants that are too baggy, like any other clothing that is too loose, tend to give the impression that you are sloppy.

Unfortunately, you can't always rely on the salespeople at the clothing store to assure that you leave with perfectly fitting clothes. Sometimes they are afraid they will lose a sale if they tell you that the clothes you have selected don't fit well. Don't rely exclusively on a salesperson. Shop with a knowledgeable friend, or compare how your clothing fits you with the fit of the clothes worn by the salesperson who probably knows how clothes should fit, and with the fit of the clothing worn by your friends and colleagues who appear to be most clothes conscious.

WRITINGS, LOGOS AND PICTURES

One quick way to project an image is to emblaze it on your clothing. Any graphics or embroidery on your clothing suggests not just your interests, but your personality. Before you slip on that silk-screened T-shirt, consider what others will assume that it says about you. Here are a few examples.

- *Designer Labels:* A giant "Gucci" may be seen as an attempt to establish status.
- *A Butterfly:* An archetypical image of honesty, caring and humility, it also suggest the wearer is passive or frail.

- *Sexual Motifs:* They are seen by most as crude and in poor taste. You may find sexually suggestive sayings or prints funny, but many others won't.
- $E = MC^2$: The latest addition to the logo realm, egghead T-shirts, say that the wearer is intelligent and intellectual. But there is also the assumption among many that eggheads aren't socially adept.
- *New York Yankees:* A jock. Strong, aggressive and confident, but probably not that smart.

MAINTENANCE

We recently noticed an ad for Sears HomeCentral in *Time* magazine that illustrates the prevalence of the stereotypical associations we make with how well someone maintains his or her clothing. The ad depicted a smiling repairman standing at the front door wearing a crisply pressed uniform shirt emblazoned with the Sears HomeCentral logo. Across the middle of the ad were the words: "If the starched uniform doesn't impress you, the ironclad guaranty will." The research that no doubt led to that advertising slogan reflects the impression that well-maintained clothing generates. A starched uniform is compared to an ironclad guaranty. Both instill trust and confidence.

Even costly, tasteful and perfectly fitting clothing won't overcome a negative impression if they are not properly maintained. A man who wears a custom-tailored suit that bears the wrinkles of months of wear without dry cleaning, or a woman whose designer purse looks as if it was substituted for the ball at her son's soccer games all last season won't make a good impression.

Wash and press your clothes regularly. If they are frayed or worn, throw them out. If you travel frequently, purchase clothes that don't hold wrinkles, like high-fiber-content wools and knits, or make arrangements at your hotel either to send them out to be pressed, or have an iron and ironing board delivered to your room and do it yourself. If this isn't an option, carry a travel steam iron. Make sure you use a brush to remove lint and pet hair. Carry one in your car, or keep it at your office if you share your car with a pet. Shine your shoes regularly. If they have worn heels or soles repair or replace them. Remember, there are a lot of people out there who have shoe fetishes.

PUTTING IT ALL TOGETHER

Deep in discussion with his friend Joel about this chapter, Mark tagged along with him while he had his hair cut at the salon across from where they had just finished lunch. Joel's stylist, Toni, is a tall, attractive woman with a thick black mane that cascades just below her shoulders. Joel told Mark that Toni was rather "outgoing," and he didn't exaggerate. From the moment they walked in she laughed and joked about their conversation about the importance of personal appearance. Their exchange drew Silvia, the stylist in the next booth, into the conversation as well.

As Toni finished sweeping beneath the barber's chair she turned to Mark and asked, "Okay, what do you think about the way I look?" Toni's question brought Silvia to a halt mid-snip as she turned to hear Mark's response.

"Well, you're wearing black, which is normally not a very friendly color. It can be intimidating and a bit authoritarian, especially for a woman who is physically imposing. But you're such a friendly, outgoing person that I don't think you have to worry about people thinking you're the dragon lady."

"How about me," Silvia asked, as she fingered the lapel of her red blazer.

"Red is a sexy, vibrant, active color," Mark answered. "But it's not as professional as some others. You are a petite woman, and sometimes bright colors like red are necessary for small women to get noticed. Besides, you're a hairstylist, not an investment banker. It's more important that people see your lively creative side than for you to appear professional, but stodgy. You can let your professionalism come across where it matters most, in your tasteful hairstyle."

Many generalities can be made about how style, color, fit, cost and the other characteristics we have described in this chapter can affect your image. They are just that—generalities that are not applicable to every person or every occasion. The exchange with Toni and Silvia is a good example of the various factors that must be taken into consideration as you evaluate how to make the best possible impression from your appearance.

To make the best impression, candidly view your entire bundle of traits. How you incorporate your appearance into your Impression Management Plan will depend on all of those traits in combination. Some features that might detract from another person's image might complement yours and vice versa. For example, small women can wear black or red with less concern about appearing overly aggressive or domineering. A more imposing woman, who should shy away from black or red on most occasions, can wear lighter colors and still be taken seriously. A friendly, outgoing man can wear dark colors and still be approachable; whereas a sterner man would be wise to favor lighter colors that make him appear less severe. A good-looking, but not stunningly beautiful woman, can enhance her overall image with flattering clothing and jewelry. The shockingly beautiful woman who does, however, may be seen as shallow and arrogant.

If you start with a fundamental understanding of how your appearance makes favorable and unfavorable impressions, you can manage your traits to make the desired impression. As you do, keep these basic concepts in mind:

- Be as physically attractive as you can be, unless you are already gorgeous, in which case be careful not to flaunt it.
- Don't set yourself apart, and especially above, your peers.
- Always dress appropriately for the occasion.
- Opt for traditional styles, fabrics and colors unless creative flair is clearly essential.
- Buy the most expensive clothes you can afford, even if that means less variety.
- Don't emphasize sex appeal.
- Give as much thought and attention to your casual wear as you do to your professional wear.
- Don't try to be a trendsetter.
- Always be clean and neat.
- Dress as formally and trendily as the top 70 to 90 percent of those in your environment.

CHAPTER 8

Body Language

Your body has hundreds of moving parts that are set in motion at times by your rational brain, and at other times by your emotional brain. The choice to enter a room, shake hands or give someone a hug is a product of rational thought. Yet you blush, your pupils dilate and you sweat based on emotional reactions. Other actions, such as when you turn toward or away from someone who speaks to you, lean forward or backward, smile, avoid eye contact or shake your head, can be triggered either unconsciously or consciously.

Just as you may display body language either consciously or unconsciously, others may attribute meaning to it either consciously or unconsciously. They may consciously think that you don't maintain eye contact because you are nervous or lying, for example. They also may believe, without thinking about it whatsoever, that you are nervous or lying only because their emotional brain has noticed your lack of eye contact. Research demonstrates that often your body language will be interpreted by others entirely on this noncognitive level. Since their emotional brains tend to assume, "what you see is what you get," your ability to control your body language will help you convey the impression you hope to make on others at both a conscious and subconscious level.

If you don't intervene to control the messages sent by your body language, your psychological makeup is programmed to express many of your emotions and personality traits through preset physical reactions, much as your home printer is set to display a particular font, print size and margin unless it is overridden. If you ignore the printer, it will print in a very predictable fashion. You can choose to override your printer's default instructions, and, within the printer's limitations, dictate the style, color and format of the end product. Similarly, with conscious attention and effort, you can control most of the messages your body language sends to others.

Most body language can have several different meanings. The true meaning of body language, therefore, is seldom derived from isolated motions, but from a pattern of body motions and facial expressions that in concert project particular qualities. In this chapter we have identified seven pairings of opposite traits that significantly affect how people perceive the Compass Qualities. Although we've expressed each category in a range from one extreme to the other, few of us fall at one end or the other of the range within any category, but rather somewhere in the middle. How you display these traits in combination will have a remarkable effect on others' impressions of you.

The seven different categories are:

- Physically aloof or physically familiar
- Closed or open
- Nervous or relaxed
- Disinterested or attentive
- Controlled or expressive
- Shy or outgoing
- Submissive or dominating

PHYSICALLY ALOOF OR PHYSICALLY FAMILIAR

Stand in the corner at any event where men and women mingle and watch the crowd. You will identify those who are physically aloof. They never initiate contact and avoid it whenever possible. Those who are physically familiar welcome and pursue physical contact. They shake hands, touch others on the arm, back or shoulders, hug and kiss. The extent to which someone welcomes physical contact can also be seen by where he positions himself within the room. How far away from others does he stand when he is in a group? How close does he stand when he talks to someone one-on-one? Does he join in groups where he is surrounded by others, or does he seek isolation?

Physical contact at appropriate levels (which we'll discuss shortly) enhances all the Compass Qualities. Trustworthiness is established by the physical bond and the measure of intimacy touching creates. Caring is promoted by appropriate and welcomed physical contact that satisfies the fundamental need to feel important. Humility is enhanced by interaction, since aloofness is equated with egotism. Even capability is promoted by physical contact and proximity that reflects security and self-confidence, and also allows you to communicate more effectively on both emotional and rational levels.

But it's not all good news. Before you hug and kiss everyone in sight, be aware that too much physical contact can have catastrophic consequences. Studies have consistently shown that those who are too physically aggressive, overly sexual, don't respect others' "personal space" or act artificially familiar create bad impressions. They're considered phony and untrustworthy, insensitive, uncompassionate and tasteless. They're even thought to be less intelligent and competent. Physical intimacy is a privilege, not a right. Those who ignore that principle are thought to be socially inept and egotistical.

If you demonstrate an appropriate amount of physical contact, others' perception of you will be enhanced. If you show too little physical contact, or too much, your image will suffer. It's as simple as that. But that's the easy part. The challenge is to strike the appropriate balance.

As we discuss the elements and impact of touching and personal space in the sections that follow, we will repeatedly caution you to pay particular attention to the circumstances under which physical contact takes place. What may be perfectly appropriate, and even expected, in one situation may be shocking and inappropriate in another. How much physical contact is enough, too much, or too little depends most predictably on three factors:

- Are you in contact with a new acquaintance or an intimate friend or lover?
- Are you or they male or female?
- Are you at a social, casual but professional, or formal professional event?

TOUCHING

Studies conducted by Richard Hesslon identified five different types of touching: (1) functional; (2) professional/social; (3) polite/friendship; (4) warmth/love; and (5) intimacy/sexual arousal.

- *Functional touching* describes what is needed to do a specific task, such as when a doctor examines a patient, or a railroad employee assists an elderly woman up the steps into the railcar.
- *Professional/social touching* is most commonly evidenced by a handshake, and reflects the degree of physical contact that is expected between new or casual acquaintances under normal social or professional circumstances.
- *Polite/friendly touching* is similar to professional/social touching, but is

more personalized, such as a gentle pat on the back or a playful tap on the arm. In general, professional/social or polite/friendly touching is appropriate for casual acquaintances. Which of the two is more appropriate will depend upon the nature of the relationship, the genders involved and the setting.

- *Warm/loving touching* reveals personal affection, but in a nonsexual way. It is the type of touching common between siblings, parents and children and close friends. Firm embraces, particularly those that last more than a few seconds, and pecks on the cheek generally fall in this category if not accompanied by any more intimate touching.
- *Intimate/sexual touching* is reserved for spouses or lovers. Kisses on the lips and prolonged or firm hugs, especially when coupled with rubs on the back or shoulders, buttocks or waist, are intimate and sexual in nature.

In normal social situations most of us have clear expectations about which of these five types of touching is appropriate for us to initiate or for others to direct toward us, depending on the nature of our relationship, the genders of the people involved and the setting. If we think of the five degrees of touching as a continuum, with the first purely functional, and the last entirely sexual, most of us wonder whenever anyone slips very far up or down the continuum. Because appropriate touching enhances trustworthiness, caring, humility and capability, you want to assure that you don't fall short of others' expectations. But since overly familiar touching can be very offensive, you should be even more careful not to slide too far up the scale.

There is a significant difference between the expected and appropriate level of touching between male/male, female/female, and male/female. A man usually will welcome more intimate touching from a woman than from a man, and as a woman will tend to accept more intimate contact from another woman than from a casual male acquaintance. If you're a woman, when you greet another woman or a man, you can slide up the scale of intimacy somewhat with relative safety. If you're a man, until your relationship is clearly defined, you should err on the conservative side.

Similarly, in purely social environments more intimate touching generally is welcomed. In professional settings that same level of touching generally would be inappropriate. The recipient might feel it puts her in a less professional light. If you make her feel awkward, you will appear insensitive and unprofessional.

There are exceptions to every rule, including the appropriate level of touching. For example, a hug, or even a touch on the waist, generally will be considered inappropriate and unprofessional if initiated by a male boss or coworker toward a female subordinate or coworker. But that isn't always the case. If a visibly upset female employee came into her male boss's office and asked for time off to tend to an ill or injured child, it might be appropriate for her male boss to give her a comforting hug, in a very nonsexual way. In fact, if he didn't, he might seem uncompassionate, particularly if she initiated the hug and he withdrew from it.

As you evaluate the ideal degree of touching in different circumstances, these rules are reliable.

- For a new acquaintance, avoid more than minimal touching. The more familiar the relationship, the more physical you can be without risk.
- Male-to-female, or male-to-male contact should be kept on the low end of the scale, while female to female, or female to male touching can be slightly higher on the scale than normal; though anyone who makes inappropriate physical advances will jeopardize his or her impression.
- Touching in professional settings should be lower on the scale than touching in purely social environments.

PHYSICAL DISTANCE

Dr. Edwin Hall identified four separate "zones" where we can approach others in different circumstances without making them uncomfortable. The first, and most intimate, zone is within eighteen inches from their bodies. Unwelcomed invasion within the "intimate zone" causes nervousness, fear, discomfort and a host of other negative reactions.

The second zone, called the "personal zone," extends from one and a half feet to four feet from our bodies. Dr. Hall divided this zone into two subzones. The first subzone ranges from one and a half to two and a half feet, and may be invaded by close friends or during social gatherings without causing defensive reactions. The second subzone within the "personal zone" lies from two and a half to four feet, and is the area in which most of us feel comfortable in casual settings where proximity is required to hear and be heard. If you approach someone closer than is required you may trigger defensiveness or anxiety.

The third zone, which Dr. Hall calls the "social zone," ranges from four to twelve feet. This is the area in which most of us feel comfortable with relative strangers. For example, unless required by physical constraints, if you stand closer than four feet from others upon entering an elevator, you will probably make them uncomfortable.

The last zone is the "public zone." This zone begins at twelve feet, and extends to the point where communication is no longer effective. This is the distance from which people typically address a group of strangers.

These zones serve as excellent starting points, but they are only general rules. Once again, the nature of the relationship, the genders involved and the social or professional context must all be considered. Gauge the distance to which you approach someone, not only based upon whether the contact is "intimate," "personal," "social" or "public," but also in light of the specific nature of your relationship, the genders involved and the circumstances under which the encounter takes place. As with touching, you can slide further into someone's inner zones if you have a long-standing relationship, or if you are a woman and if the contact takes place in a social environment. But if you are in contact with casual acquaintances, or strangers, if you are a man or if the encounter takes place in a purely professional setting, keep a comfortable distance. Under these circumstances, if you move slightly farther away than normal out of an abundance of caution, you will not appear unfriendly, unapproachable, distant or shy.

CLOSED OR OPEN

Body language can be used to maintain both physical and psychological separation. We display closed body language when we feel threatened, challenged or defensive. We close our body to others like an armadillo who rolls into a ball to shield itself. Like little children playing hide and seek, we prefer to peek out from behind our protective walls only when we feel safe. When we withdraw, we appear less honest, friendly and capable. To the contrary, when we show that we are eager to make contact and willing to let down our guard, we enhance virtually every positive quality and (unless our actions are obviously excessive) diminish none.

As with every trait, there can be too much of a good thing. Yet after two decades of talking to jurors about their reactions to those who have appeared before them, we rarely have heard anyone comment negatively about open nonverbal behavior. People will feel uncomfortable if you share too much of yourself too quickly. But openness doesn't require that you wear your heart on your sleeve, and it isn't needy, aggressive, overpowering or pushy. When you open your body physically, you should *let* others see your emotions, but you shouldn't *force* your emotions on them.

When you find yourself engaged in closed nonverbal behavior, stop, take notice and step out from behind the wall. Until people see you in the open, they won't see you in the best light.

To use body language effectively to communicate openness you must assert conscious control over each of the many separate body movements within your arsenal. We have divided your body motions into four general categories:

- Movement within your environment and among others;
- Torso movements;
- Head and limb movements; and
- Facial expressions.

As you develop more open nonverbal behavior, keep these four categories in mind, as it will make it easier for you to identify when you slip back into your armadillo mode.

MOVEMENT WITHIN YOUR ENVIRONMENT
AND AMONG OTHERS

To show you are "open" you should welcome and initiate contact. Don't stand in the corner of the room. If you're approached, maintain contact. Don't just participate to the extent minimal social protocol requires, and then move on. Seek out others, both individually and in groups.

When you approach others, face them directly. Square your body to theirs, chest to chest, eye to eye. Studies have shown that considerably less communication takes place between people who face in the same direction shoulder to shoulder than occurs between those who face one another. Open people seem to know this instinctively. If it's not an automatic behavior for you, make it a conscious one.

When in groups, face toward the center, where you can see and speak directly to everyone in the group, and everyone in the group can in turn see and speak to you. Don't whisper or huddle in small groups. Don't turn sideways—the effect will be to point your shoulder to the center of the group and your face away from it—or continuously glance around the room as if you are uncomfortable in your surroundings. Welcome new members to the group. Turn to face them as they approach, and gesture them to join you.

You should always avoid invading others' personal space; but you will appear more open if you come near to the edge of the applicable comfort zone. When you speak with a close friend, eighteen inches to twenty-four inches is appropriate. If you talk to someone you've just met for the first time, don't stand farther away than four feet, or you will seem to withdraw.

The essence of openness is to allow people to make contact with you and you them. Particularly rapid movements within your environment will prevent this. If you walk quickly through a crowded room you send the message that you don't want to stop, don't want to talk and don't want to be open. Walk slowly with your arms comfortably at your side. Keep your eyes open for those who might try to signal you to stop and chat. Be accessible.

TORSO MOVEMENTS

To convey openness, keep your shoulders back, chest out, back straight and head up. A slight forward lean will enhance the appearance of openness as well. Show the world that you have nothing to hide, and that you welcome contact, conversation and friendship.

HEAD AND LIMB MOVEMENTS

When people do something embarrassing or foolish, they'll frequently bring their hands over their eyes or other portions of their face as if they don't want you to see them, or they you, in their moment of shame. When people are angry, defensive, frightened or nervous, they tend to cross their arms, legs and ankles, once again as a way to shield themselves from unwanted emotional contact. When they are ashamed, lie or become submissive, they lower their heads and draw their limbs inward, circling their head and limbs like emotional wagons drawn into a protective formation. When challenged or defensive, they may either pull their limbs and head inward like a turtle into its shell for protection, or thrust out their arms, point or engage in other pushing or repelling motions to maintain physical and psychological distance.

You must avoid all of these gestures if you want to project an impression of openness. Your arms should be kept at your side. If your legs are crossed, they should not be turned to the side, which conveys avoidance or withdrawal. Your head should be kept up, and your body squared to others. Objects like purses, books or notepads should not be held in front of you like shields, but at your side, in your lap or on the table in front of you. Hand gestures and arm gestures should be open with palms up. Your hands should not be in your pockets, which suggests discomfort, nor should they rest on your hips, which can be seen as defiance; nor should you hold them behind your back, which generally is viewed as a sign of dominance or control.

A lot to remember? Not really. Just remember, if you want to appear open, you should not have anything—your arms, hands, legs, purse or objects like flowers, glasses or centerpieces—between you and others.

FACIAL EXPRESSIONS

The most "open" form of eye contact is soft but sustained. Intense eye contact appears dominant and intimidating, and will impede open communication. Evasive eye contact will be viewed as an attempt to avoid interaction.

Smiles should be natural and relaxed. Forced smiles don't look open, and if displayed along with other comparable body language, can look phony or uncomfortable. Yet an expressionless face that shows no pleasure, confusion, interest or other emotion at appropriate times, sends a message that the person behind the face is not open to the communication. A deadpan expression is a closed expression. Keep your face turned to the others, and let them share in your emotions, and allow yourself to share in theirs.

NERVOUS OR RELAXED

Nervousness, whether caused by dishonesty, embarrassment, fear, stress or any number of other emotions, is revealed by a common cluster of traits. Discomfort leaks out from our bodies like water from a cracked vessel. For some, it pours forth in a torrent. For others it's only subtle seepage. But it's there.

Many of those characteristics that signal nervousness parallel those that are revealed by the "closed" person. However, you can show signs of closure when you are not nervous: you may be bored, indifferent, unfriendly or reserved. When you are nervous, however, you typically will display your anxiety through many traits in addition to those adopted by the closed person.

There are scores of traits that in combination will place you either on the nervous side of the spectrum or on the relaxed side. As with the open or closed grouping of traits, they generally fall in four categories: how you move within your environment and among others, your torso movements, your head and limb movements and your facial expressions.

MOVEMENT WITHIN YOUR ENVIRONMENT
AND AMONG OTHERS

In most respects, someone who is nervous will move within her environment, and among those who share it, much as a person who is closed moves. She will tend to avoid people, since interaction increases her anxiety. She won't join in groups, or make any effort to welcome others into her conversations. She will frequently distance herself at the far end of the "zone" of personal contact. When approached by others, her conversations will be brief. She will often turn her body away from others as they talk to decrease the intensity of the physical contact.

Those who are nervous frequently pace. Some walk quickly as if anxious to escape or avoid contact. Others will tend to walk slowly and tentatively. People who are nervous often hold their arms rigidly at their sides, or hold their hands or arms together in front of their bodies as they walk.

To convey a sense of relaxation, avoid these behaviors. Everyone who engages in them is not nervous, but if you engage in these behaviors, most people will conclude that you are.

There are many ways you can convey relaxation and confidence, as can be illustrated by something as simple as how you enter a room full of people gathered for a business meeting. When you enter the room, stand tall and erect, shoulders back and arms comfortably at your side. Linger for a moment as you enter, and take advantage of the opportunity for everyone in the room to notice you. If you stand in the room while others are seated you will draw attention to yourself. This will create the appearance of confidence and control, but will also project egotism if the position is sustained for no apparent reason. You don't want to sacrifice your humility; so maintain this position for only a moment.

After you enter the room and before you seat yourself, greet those in the room with a smile and a handshake. Don't sit down until you've completed the circle. You may be tempted to seat yourself and then simply wave across the table, but you will have lost the opportunity to reveal your comfort by the personal contact shared with a handshake and a one-on-one exchange.

Where you sit after you enter the room can also influence others' perception of you. Don't sit in a low or deeply padded chair or sofa, which will cause you to sink down and disappear both visually and psychologically, and will make your body appear to roll into a protective ball. This will make you appear tentative, nervous and not in control. When you sit upright, but relaxed, in a stiff-backed chair you will appear more confident.

When you sit at a table with a number of people, consider where to sit.

The head of the table is recognized as the position of greatest power and authority. The person who sits next to the head of the table is often perceived as the least dominant and authoritarian. If you want others to know you are comfortable, relaxed, and in control, assume a position of authority and sit at the head of the table.

Walk at a moderate pace, and let your hands move freely at your side. Don't swagger or strut. Approach others. Don't wait to be approached. Take the opportunity to include new participants in your conversation. This reflects that you're at ease not only with yourself, but with them; and will further the primary objective of making them feel important.

TORSO MOVEMENTS

Your body should be neither too rigid nor slouched to convey relaxation. Rigidity shows nervousness. The complete absence of muscular control may be considered an indication that you are completely comfortable and at ease; but it also can be seen as a sign of withdrawal. In all but the most casual circumstances it frequently is seen as a sign of disinterest—disinterest, which is associated with arrogance, not confidence. Don't lean too far backward or too far forward. Strike a comfortable balance. If you lean too far forward you may appear overeager. If you lean too far backward you will seem to withdraw.

Your breathing should be slow and rhythmic. Rapid or shallow breathing is a clear sign of severe nervousness. Tension in your chest makes it difficult for you to take deep sustaining breaths. To counter this, force yourself to exhale completely and slowly take a full breath. Until the pressure subsides, try not to talk. For most people, it will take only a few breaths before the tension eases.

HEAD AND LIMB MOVEMENTS

Here's where nervousness most frequently leaks out. There are a number of common symptoms that most people will notice either consciously or subconsciously. The first is any type of fidgeting, including crossing and uncrossing arms, legs or ankles; finger or toe tapping; touching, rubbing or scratching your nose, ears, mouth, face, chin, or the back of your hand, head or neck; twirling your hair; straightening or pulling on your collar, tie or sleeves; picking at lint, clothing or cuticles; or rubbing your hair, eyes or forehead. Nervousness also will be perceived if you swallow frequently, stretch, or hold objects, such as a purse, between you and others. Rapid nods or shakes of your head are another common sign of nervousness, especially if it rises to a level that you nod "yes" and say "no," or vice versa.

People tend to watch others' hands as they speak. As a consequence, what you do with your hands will affect others' impression of whether you're nervous or relaxed. Rubbing or wringing your hands, rapid or exaggerated hand motions and putting your hands in your pockets are among the more common characteristics associated with nervousness. Clasping and unclasping your hands will also reveal nervousness, though when you hold them together in what is called the "steepling" position, with your fingers intertwined and index fingers extended, most people will see it as a sign of concentration, not nervousness.

To show relaxation through your limb and head movements, avoid any rapid, excessive or exaggerated fidgeting, gestures and other body movements. On the other hand, a number of studies have demonstrated that when people attempt to obscure lies or other causes of nervousness they consciously decrease subtle body movements. Many people notice this consciously. Many more make this association at an unconscious level. As a consequence, others will be suspicious if your body movements appear unnaturally controlled or suppressed. They expect that you will be somewhat expressive if you truly are relaxed, confident and honest. Avoid both rigidity and excessive movement, both of which are viewed with suspicion.

FACIAL EXPRESSIONS

It's difficult for people who are nervous to sustain eye contact. They always seem to look around, up, down or sideways, like a caged cat. A comfortable gaze is essential to convey relaxation. But your eyes can reveal nervousness in other ways beside eye contact.

Rapid eye movement, even if accompanied by frequent eye contact, is a classic sign of nervousness that most people recognize. Blinking is another frequent expression of nervousness. Louise Woodward was a young English nanny tried and convicted in 1997 for the death of a young child in her care. As we watched her deny at trial that she ever dropped, shook or hit the baby, we noticed that she blinked and held her eyes closed for much longer than normal before each answer. The rest of her body language was very controlled, in fact unusually so. This rigidity made her look nervous, but it was her slow blinks through which her nervousness leaked out most obviously.

When you are nervous, you may try to force a smile in order to alleviate the pressure. When you do, out comes a crooked, awkward and nervous mouth-only smile. Such a smile is better than none at all for the overall impression you make. But it diminishes your appearance of relaxed confidence. If you have not mastered the full-faced smile, don't try to force a smile if confidence is more important in a particular exchange than friendliness.

DISINTERESTED OR ATTENTIVE

Boredom is the most common cause of the classic nonverbal signs of disinterest. But disinterest can also arise from preoccupation, or even arrogance. Signs of boredom or disinterest are particularly toxic because it is a short mental leap to interpret them as signs of arrogance, disdain or contempt. Nothing is so flattering as rapt attention; and few things make us feel less important than disinterest in us or what we have to say. Any display of disinterest must be avoided scrupulously in favor of the many ways you can show others their importance by your attention.

MOVEMENT WITHIN YOUR ENVIRONMENT AND AMONG OTHERS

Most of the nonverbal behaviors that display openness also convey attention. It is particularly important that you stay as close as possible to someone when you speak (without invading his personal space), listen intently as he talks and keep your body square to his. It's also important to avoid too much movement. When someone is attentive he tends to keep his entire body relatively still, not just his head, limbs and face. If you shift your weight back and forth from one foot to the other, or move away from someone as he talks, you will broadcast, "I'm tired of this, can I leave yet?"

The nonverbal behavior that diminishes the appearance of attentiveness most strongly, yet one that is surprisingly common, is the failure to show undivided attention. "Focus," is the watchword to convey attention. Don't read your mail, straighten your desk, watch TV, make phone calls or be distracted as people walk by. We know it's tempting to do more than one thing at once. But the odds are if you try, you won't do anything well; and you certainly won't convey interest.

TORSO MOVEMENTS

To convey interest and attention, keep your torso still. A slight forward lean is most commonly perceived as a sign of attention, though a slight rearward lean that is not accompanied by other signs of inattention will not be interpreted as disinterest. An excessive rearward lean, however, normally will.

HEAD AND LIMB MOVEMENTS

When you fidget, doodle, rub or scratch, you reveal inattention. These are nonverbal behaviors that are perceived at an emotional, if not rational, level as a lack of focus and therefore a clear sign of inattention. Likewise, when you fold or unfold your arms, legs or ankles, turn your head to look around the room or otherwise engage in unnecessary body motions, you send the message that you are not engrossed in what another has to say. Even something as subtle as pointing your legs away from another signals a "disconnect," which can be interpreted as inattention.

A common gesture that can be interpreted as either a sign of attention or inattention is placing your hands behind the back of your head when you are seated. If you place both hands behind the back of your head and lean backward without eye contact, your mind will appear to be elsewhere. However, if you maintain good eye contact in the process, most people will perceive your actions as a sign of concentration or contemplation, and a positive indication of attention.

An appropriate level of touching also lets the other person know that you are paying attention to him or her. In some situations, you can touch someone on the arm or hand during a conversation to make a connection. In more formal situations, or where touching may seem sexual, the benefit of such contact is usually not worth the price.

Because what you do with your hands while someone speaks to you is usually noticed, it warrants particular consideration. Perhaps one of the most common signs of inattention is "twiddling" your thumbs. Everyone is familiar with the image of someone who sits with his or hands clasped and rotates one thumb around the other. We all know not to do that if we want to appear attentive. Yet essentially the same impression is made if your hands are "busy" doing anything else while someone speaks, such as, picking at your nails or rubbing your fingers or the back of your hand.

Perhaps the best way to display attention is to show an immediate and appropriate emotional response to what someone has said. When you nod your head, lean forward or gesture with your hands in response to what someone says, you give her instant confirmation that you are listening.

FACIAL EXPRESSIONS

When someone speaks to you, particularly from close range, she can see the slightest hint of inattention. The most obvious is loss of eye contact. Even with good eye contact, if your facial expressions don't reflect that you have heard and understood what the person has said, she will doubt your attentiveness. The two best ways to show others that you are paying attention are eye contact and letting her clearly see an emotional reaction to what she has said reflected in your face.

CONTROLLED OR EXPRESSIVE

Apathy is rooted in the Greek word "pathos," meaning emotion, and is defined as a lack of feeling or emotion, interest or concern. Many people who are very controlled in fact feel very deeply, but for a host of reasons either choose consciously, or are directed unconsciously, to keep those feeling to themselves. When they hide their emotions, they appear apathetic even if they are not.

Just as you can appear apathetic without being apathetic, you can be very high energy, yet not particularly expressive, as was the case with Alice, a young attorney who worked with Jo-Ellan on a case almost ten years ago.

Alice was fresh out of law school and eager to please. She was a tiny woman with short cropped dark hair, a whisker-thin mouth, and small dark eyes that constantly darted around the room. She reminded Jo-Ellan of a small mouse. Like a mouse, Alice's high energy was so consistent that it was impossible to determine whether she felt joy or sadness, doubt or confidence, attraction or disdain. She wasn't controlled, but she also wasn't expressive, except for her nervous energy.

To impress others with your positive qualities, you have to allow them to "read" you. If you control the outward expression of your emotions too much, you deny others that critical glimpse of you, and their reaction to you will be much the same as it is to "closed" people. Even worse, if your lack of expressiveness is interpreted as apathy, you may be subject to the even harsher judgment reserved for those who are disinterested or inattentive.

But don't go overboard in an attempt to express energy and emotion. If you are overly expressive, you may be thought to be less socially adept, less sincere and less professional. If your emotional energy is focused too intently on someone, you can also appear pushy and overpowering.

We have asked many people who showed very controlled nonverbal behavior why they adopted that approach. Some have explained that they feel more comfortable and in control if they don't let others know how they feel. Their attitude seems to be that life is a game of cards, and a poker face gives them the advantage. Others have told us that they believe controlling their emotions conveys confidence, intelligence and competence.

It's true that when you suppress any outward display of emotion, others will not be able to trade on your emotions to your disadvantage. The problem is that they may not care to have a relationship with you in the first place. Almost everyone we have surveyed has said that someone who keeps his cards too close to his chest is unfriendly, self-absorbed and less trustworthy.

Those of you who fall into the category that believes an image of confidence, intelligence and competence is promoted by stoicism should also think again. In fact, a much more common reaction is that a person who does not express his or her feelings *lacks* confidence, intelligence and competence, as well as truthfulness. Expressiveness, on the other hand, enhances all of those qualities. But it does even more. It makes you a more effective communicator.

Numerous studies have examined how others' retention and comprehension of what you say is affected by the emotional content of your delivery. The consistent finding is that if you speak to others about something that is of great interest to them, or about values they hold dear, they will understand and retain what you say whether or not you accompany your words with expressive nonverbal behavior. You don't need to generate emotional interest in such topics through your nonverbal presentation because your audience is already emotionally invested. But if your message is not something that already intrigues your audience, your ability to communicate your ideas is dramatically diminished if you don't generate emotional contact through expressive nonverbal behaviors.

As with other characteristics, expressiveness is shown in the manner in which you move within your environment and among others, your torso movements, head and limb movements and facial expressions. Those traits typical of an open, relaxed and attentive person all require expressive nonverbal behavior; but then, so do many of those traits typical of a closed, nervous or disinterested person. While expressiveness is essential to the creation of an excellent impression, bear in mind that the objective is to express the positive traits that reveal openness, relaxation and attention, and not their opposites.

SHY OR OUTGOING

Of the various traits that we discuss in this chapter, shyness is perhaps the most difficult to overcome. But unless you do, you will create a barrier to personal and professional success.

In the abstract, you would think most people would find it difficult to distinguish between shyness and other characteristics like disinterest and apathy, which involve emotional and physical disengagement. You would even think that people would confuse the type of nervousness shown by an intensely shy person in most environments with the kind of nervousness shown by someone who is normally at ease but finds herself in a particularly intimidating environment. However, most people easily distinguish between someone who is just shy, and someone who is closed, controlled, apathetic or temporarily nervous.

Unlike nervousness, the nonverbal behaviors shown by someone who is shy are typically not random or repetitive. There isn't a lot of tapping, rubbing and scratching. The signs of shyness are more similar to those displayed by someone who is closed and pulls himself inward, like a spider exposed to a flame. The signs are also different from those revealed by someone who is disinterested. While eye contact may be minimal due to the discomfort that curses a shy person, her eyes typically will not wander, but rather will settle on one or two points that provide the distraction that she desperately needs. Nor are the signs of shyness similar to those demonstrated by the controlled or apathetic person. Emotion is written all over the shy person's face, and spoken by every part of her body. She's uncomfortable; and it's clear.

The most significant difference between shyness and closed behavior, nervousness, disinterest, a lack of expressiveness, and apathy, is the way people will perceive you if you are shy, relative to how you will be viewed if you convey those other characteristics. Shy people aren't thought to be dishonest, arrogant, bored or uncaring. But they are often thought to be less intelligent, competent or professional than those who are more outgoing. If you're shy, the reality is that you will be tarred by those stereotypical associations, whether or not they are justified, unless you learn to display more outgoing characteristics. This doesn't mean you need to adopt a gregarious persona. For most shy people, that's impossible.

There are many ways shy people can manage the impressions they make. Shy people adopt characteristics that help them avoid uncomfortable contact. They also adopt many characteristics that don't really avoid contact. For example, a shy person may develop poor posture as a form of *emotional* withdrawal. To some extent it may convey unapproachability, which keeps people at a distance. But a shy person's poor posture makes a poor impression without normally protecting him from the contact he resists. Likewise, shy people often place their hands over their mouth, chin, cheeks or other portions of their face as a way of creating psychological distance. In fact, movement of their hands to their face actually draws attention to them. The same is true when they cross their legs or arms.

If your shyness concerns you, begin to manage the impression your shyness makes by reviewing the list of traits that show physical aloofness, a closed nature, nervousness and disinterest. Note any that you display frequently. Begin to manage your impression by creating two lists. First list the traits that truly help you avoid uncomfortable contact, such as standing at the outskirts at a gathering. Second, list those traits that, if eliminated, would not really expose you to any greater contact with others, such as posture and movement of your hands to your face. Begin to manage your impression by eliminating those traits that are no more than ineffectual psychological crutches, and don't really protect you from unwelcomed contact with others.

Then review the traits that reveal physical familiarity, openness, relaxation and attention. Once again, you will identify a number of traits that will help eliminate your appearance of shyness, without actually exposing you to a greater degree of contact with others. Continue your metamorphosis by adopting those traits. For example, you can keep your body square to others as you speak to them, and gesture more freely. Slowly add traits that are characteristic of a more open, relaxed and attentive person until you work your way up to traits, like strong eye contact and a broad smile, with which you are currently uncomfortable.

You don't need to move from a dead stop to full throttle instantaneously. If you currently avoid eye contact, start by engaging in eye contact for a few seconds at a time, and don't try to focus on the other person's pupils. Instead, begin your quest for excellent eye contact by looking at the eyelids, corner of the eyes or bridge of the nose. Likewise, you won't magically transform yourself overnight into someone who feels completely comfortable smiling. Begin with a very faint smile. If you try to force a broader smile, it will appear strained. A faint smile will appear more natural, even if it isn't.

SUBMISSIVE OR DOMINATING

Martin is one of the best trial lawyers in the country. He attributes his success in equal parts to his meticulous preparation and his authoritarian demeanor. He shared with Jo-Ellan that his philosophy was to control the courtroom from the moment he entered it until the moment he left. He believed that jurors would be drawn to, and ultimately vote with, whoever became the most dominant, powerful force in the trial. His nonverbal behavior, though polite, was far from warm. It varied remarkably little, whether he spoke to the jury, opposing counsel, witnesses or even the judge. A former military officer, he carried himself with the bearing of a base commander addressing the troops—dignified, powerful and completely in control.

Over the years we've seen many men, and progressively more women, assume a similar approach, with varying degrees of success. From our interviews about typical responses to this type of demeanor we can draw some reliable conclusions about when, how and why dominant nonverbal communication is perceived in either a positive or negative light.

The key lies in how the behavior melds with other characteristics that impart trustworthiness, caring, humility and capability. What makes Martin's dominant approach effective is that while he controls the environment around him, he treats everyone within it politely and with dignity. Those who seek to dominate an environment by overpowering or controlling people, rather than letting them choose to be controlled, fail. Those who are rude, push, shove, cut in front of people, show disinterest, display boredom or interrupt may get their way in the short run, but they earn no one's respect. There is a clear distinction between control through the power of your presence, and domination by intimidation or force.

Those who encourage others to yield to them by their confident and dignified manner are believable and reliable. They're the ones who are asked to chair committees, lead PTA fund-raising efforts, and attract mates who want to partner with someone who will carry his or her share of the load in the relationship. They're seen as honest, competent and reliable. That is why Martin has found that jurors more frequently vote his way. They believe not only that what Martin says is true, but also that whatever he says is reliable, since a man with his confident bearing presumably doesn't make even honest mistakes.

It can be difficult to adopt a powerful bearing without appearing uncaring and egotistical. But it's not impossible. It depends upon whether you treat others with respect. Power, confidence and leadership are enviable qualities. We're attracted to those who possess them. And we want people who possess those qualities to like us and consider us important. If they show us respect, they say, "I owe you proper treatment, because I am no better than you." That's a distinctly positive message when it comes from someone we admire. Someone we respect is able to make us feel much better about ourselves, and hence make a better impression on us, than someone we don't respect.

Just as dominant traits carry with them certain risks, submissive characteristics can adversely affect your impression on others. Submissiveness is not the same as shyness, apathy or disinterest, though there are many nonverbal behaviors common to each. Submissiveness is defined as "yielding to governance or authority." Its Latin root *submmissio* means *a lowering,* and that is what frequently happens to the esteem in which you are held by others when you are too submissive and nonassertive.

The most severe handicap overly submissive individuals face in their quest to project all four Compass Qualities is submissiveness's effect on the perception of capability. Their reluctance to express their views freely, or their tendency to adopt whatever opinions, desires or decisions are made by those who are more assertive, leads to questions about their intelligence, competence and reliability. The same phenomenon occurs in a business meeting or neighborhood gathering. When you sit quietly in the corner, watch but never contribute, agree with one opinion, then the next and seldom proffer any ideas, you will not appear intelligent, competent and professional, even if you are.

Where the balance lies between overbearing and submissive behavior depends upon the circumstances.

- If you are in a position of authority, you will be allowed more control over the space in your environment without resentment. Others will tend to expand your personal space and allow you within theirs.
- Men, who are expected to be more dominating, are usually afforded greater latitude than women, both in their control of physical space and other nonverbal behaviors. More dominant behavior, therefore, won't result in the same negative reactions toward men as toward women. On the other hand, submissiveness or a lack of assertiveness will do more damage to a man's image than a woman's.
- In social environments, deference to others will typically be viewed as a matter of common courtesy and not submissiveness. Likewise, dominance over others in social situations will be less well tolerated, whether by a man or woman.
- Many nonverbal traits reflect dominance or friendliness depending entirely upon the circumstances. Protracted and intense eye contact and intrusion into the personal space of another, for example, will be viewed as dominant behavior in a business negotiation, and intimate in an exchange between close friends.
- In those situations where another engages in dominant behavior toward you, studies show that your reaction will tend to define your relationship. If you yield to another's domination, you will send the

message that you are prepared to assume a subordinate role in the relationship. If you adopt the same dominant behaviors, you will assert your status as an equal.

Domination and submissiveness are shown by many of the same traits we have highlighted in earlier sections of this chapter. Domination results from extremes of physically familiar and open behavior, and submissiveness from extremes of the opposing traits. But domination has an aggressive edge not required of open or confident behavior. And submissiveness is not always shown through the withdrawal typical of aloof, closed and disinterested behavior. Many submissive people are very eager to please, and search out opportunities for contact. But when they make contact, they assume a subordinate position. As we highlight the traits that reflect domination or submissiveness, watch for these distinctions.

MOVEMENT WITHIN YOUR ENVIRONMENT
AND AMONG OTHERS

You will appear dominating if you invade others' comfort zones by standing or sitting too close. Similarly, any unwelcomed physical contact, such as touching, pushing, bumping or shoving reflects not only physical domination, but also psychological domination. Any behavior that tends to put you in a position of control also projects domination, as when you sit at the end of the table, position yourself in a group to force the majority of others to face you, or stand when others sit. Extremely confident behavior, such as walking with a forceful pace or with your hands held behind your back will also create this impression.

If you incorporate any traits that reflect physically aloof, closed or inattentive behavior, people will assume that you are shy, lack confidence or are aloof. They will also make a secondary association from these traits that you are submissive. If you avoid contact, position yourself at the fringe of groups, walk tentatively, maintain a physical distance from others outside of the normal comfort zone, always yield to others when you pass through doorways or select a seat, take a position of less authority at a table, or favor cautious or halting body movements, you display a tendency to yield to others, which is at the core of submissiveness. There is no bright line between showing others deference and appearing passive and nonassertive. But the more of these characteristics you consistently display, the more likely you will be seen as submissive, not just polite.

Torso Movement

Exaggerated versions of any of the traits that reflect physical familiarity, openness and attention will carry you into the realm of the domineering. Exaggerated erect or upright posture, or a significant forward lean as you speak with someone, convey power and control. Torso movements such as turning your body at an angle when you speak with someone, slumping or slouching, leaning backward, as well as most of the other traits typical of physically aloof, closed or disinterested behavior will support the inference that you are submissive.

Head and Limb Movements

Many head and limb movements clearly convey domination. Others are likely to assume that you have a domineering personality if you tilt your head back as you speak with them, which forces you literally to "look down your nose" at them, place your hands on your hips or behind your back, make pushing gestures with your hands and arms, force their palms up or pull their hands toward you when you shake hands, point or make fists, gesture with your thumbs up when you speak or engage in any form of excessive touching.

Submissiveness is suggested if you have a weak handshake; tend to hold your hands, arms or other objects in front of your body; cover your face, mouth or eyes with your hands; clasp your hands in front of you; lower your head or turn it away; hold your hands in your pockets; gesture with your palms out or constantly nod in approval.

Facial Expressions

Intense or prolonged eye contact is the facial expression that research reveals is the trait most commonly associated with domination among humans, as well as most other beasts. Its effect is amplified if accompanied by a smug or ingratiating smile, a set or clenched jaw, a stern look or other dominating body movements.

Poor eye contact is also the first facial expression on the list of traits that are associated with submissiveness. A nervous smile, timid or anxious expression, and other submissive body movements will heighten this impression.

BODY LANGUAGE—THE MIRACLE CURE

You may have noticed that each of the Magic Pills we discussed in Chapter 5—eye contact, smiling, posture, the handshake and enthusiasm—are communicated by your body language. The message is clear: If you are to communicate each of the four Compass Qualities effectively, you must assume conscious control over the many ways your body communicates your emotions, character and values. Master these techniques and you will communicate the four Compass Qualities at the most primal level—the level at which the emotional brain functions.

CHAPTER 9

Voice

You worry about your hairstyle, shop for hours to buy the right clothing, try to anticipate the questions and answers you think might arise in an interview or a meeting, act in ways you believe will project a desirable image and clean up your house and car to make a good impression. Yet when was the last time you gave any thought to what you could do to better your voice—either to improve its positive characteristics or address its weaknesses? If you're like most of us, you can't remember. If that's the case, you haven't been putting your best foot forward.

We tune in or tune out voices based upon what emotional chords they hit. We are repelled by irritating, harsh, loud, quiet or boring voices, and are attracted to deeper, more resonant, energetic, clear and moderately paced speech. We do the same thing emotionally when someone speaks to us as we do consciously when we receive a radio signal on our car's radio. If it's irritating static-filled or unclear, we change the station. If the signal's crisp and clear, we listen.

Those with more favorable vocal qualities are consistently judged more physically attractive, honest, exciting, friendly, confident, intelligent, persuasive and successful. Even those blessed with tremendous talents in other respects achieve greater success when they incorporate positive vocal qualities.

Can you imagine a news anchor whose livelihood depends on his or her image of honesty, confidence and intelligence with a weak, high-pitched voice, or one who speaks too fast or too slow or mumbles? What would you think about him or her? Would he or she be as attractive, credible, interesting, engaging?

Examples of the powerful impact our voices make exist everywhere, but nowhere more publicly than in politics and on the silver screen. Many actors who recognize the importance of their vocal qualities have worked diligently and effectively to improve them. When former Mr. Universe Arnold Schwarzenegger began his acting career, his weak voice was inconsistent with his otherwise masculine image. Through vocal training he developed a much more powerful and distinctive voice, yet retained his vocal personality, including his Austrian accent. Actress Fran Drescher, best known for her starring role in *The Nanny,* had a distinctive nasal, high pitched, New York–accented voice that caused her to be typecast. Motivated to expand her opportunities to other roles, she consciously modified her voice to the one that she now has, a natural, soothing vocal quality, though she can revert to a nasal whine at will when required to play a part such as her role in *The Nanny.*

A number of the stars of the silent screen found out just how important voice is to overall image when they were unable to make the transition from silent movies to the "talkies." John Gilbert, who was one of America's hottest leading men when his audience relied solely on his appearance, disappeared into obscurity after his first talking movie revealed a weak, thin, high-pitched voice. Even his masculine good looks could not overcome the perception of weakness his audiences' emotional brains associated with his thin voice.

A weak or high-pitched voice will have greater impact on some individuals than on others, depending upon the image they want to convey. We have listened to many popular motivational speakers over the years, and have noticed that several ingredients are normally required for success in that arena. Among them is a strong and powerful speaking voice. Most motivational speakers teach people how to succeed in business, as well as in life; and their message is generally one of confidence, control and the power of positive thinking—a "can do" attitude, which they communicate not only with their body language and words, but with their voice.

Among the most popular speakers on the circuit today is one man who certainly has broken the mold. John Gray, author of the best-seller *Men Are from Mars, Women Are from Venus,* draws thousands to his weekend seminars designed to help them build healthy personal relationships. Gray's speaking voice is soft and high-pitched, not at all powerful or forceful, but because the image upon which he relies is one of compassion, caring and concern, his weak speaking voice actually contributes to the impression of a caring and nurturing nature in which his primary audience of women finds comfort and reassurance. If Gray promoted the power of positive thinking, or how to close a sale, his voice would present an insurmountable obstacle, just as the motivational speakers with high-octane voices could not effectively convey Gray's message.

The first step to a better voice, and your ability to use it as an effective tool to manage the impression you make on others, is to identify your vocal characteristics. To do that, you must listen to yourself. Anyone who has ever heard his or her recorded voice is aware that we don't sound the way we think we do. As we speak, our voice travels to the receptors in our brains not just through sound waves that are picked up in our ears and transferred to the brain through the normal auditory channels, but also by vibrations that pass through the structures in our face and jaw, which cause distortion.

So turn on a tape or video recorder, sit down with a friend, and chat for half an hour. At first you may be conscious of the recording device, but after a few minutes you will ignore it and your true voice will come through. Play the recording back and listen carefully.

Listen for each of the six separate characteristics of your voice.

- Vocal Emotion
- Volume
- Tone and Pitch
- Pace
- Other Vocal Qualities
- Accents

VOCAL EMOTION

The love of music is almost universal. It has strummed the emotional chords of mankind since the beginning of human history. The harps of the ancient Egyptians, flutes of the Inca's, horns of the Romans, harpsichords of seventeenth-century Europe, and electric guitars of the rock and roll era have moved us to dance, laugh, cry and dream. Can you imagine a world in which music was confined to a single octave, a repetitive pace, an unwavering volume and a consistent tone? The lyrics might vary from song to song, but the score would have almost no variety. It wouldn't be music. It wouldn't convey emotion.

Your voice has the same capacity to reach out and touch others' emotions with its variety and power as a musical instrument. It can generate excitement, contemplation, confidence, joy, apprehension and comfort—if you play it well.

Most people surveyed say they strongly dislike monotonous, boring voices. Monotonous voices don't simply annoy others, they trigger a broad spectrum of negative associations and stereotypes, all of which arise because monotonous voices show no emotion or enthusiasm. Those who speak in monotonous voices are thought to be slow, lazy, apathetic, bored and boring—and less sincere, friendly, intelligent and competent.

People not only trust and like those with more expressive voices, they also hear and retain more of what they say, particularly when complex ideas are communicated. Those with emotionally expressive voices are therefore more effective teachers, salespeople and managers. They also more effectively communicate their ideas and beliefs in social conversations.

An emotionally expressive voice offers a variety of range, volume, pace and tone. To be emotionally expressive, you need to break out of your vocal rut. Turn on that tape recorder, then pick up the morning newspaper and read it aloud in your normal voice. Now, read it again. This time, don't read it as if you were reading a textbook. Read it as if you were the anchor on the evening news. Sound authoritative, credible, definitive. Now, read it as you would read a children's story to your five-year-old. Show emotion, enthusiasm, emphasis.

When you play back the tape, hear how different each segment sounds. Listen to how emotion is communicated. If you're like most, in the first reading you'll sound like Sergeant Friday, communicating "just the facts." In the next, you'll hear greater confidence and control. In the last, there will be excitement and enthusiasm and a level of "entertainment value" not present in the first two.

In your everyday life a "just the facts" voice is seldom the best option. You wouldn't talk to your children or your best friend at lunch as if you were Dan Rather reporting on the latest NATO summit. Nor would you deliver a presentation to a new customer as if you were reading *Green Eggs and Ham* to your toddler. Each situation calls for different emphasis, depending upon the impression you want to make. Unless you're aware of the full range of options, and are able to use them all, you won't be able to "play" your voice effectively.

Now that we have said that, we caution you against vocal schizophrenia. Once again, the watchword is "expectations." No one expects you to change your vocal melody during the course of a conversation for no apparent reason. If you do, people may think you're emotionally expressive, but they will find it difficult to process and derive meaning from your emotional message.

There are times in the same conversation when you may want to slow the pace and lower the volume and tone of your voice to communicate sincerity or seriousness, and later, possibly even in the next sentence, become animated to show excitement and enthusiasm. But your variations can't be haphazard. They must make sense. They must be consistent with the ebb and flow of your overall message.

Vocal emotion requires energy, but not an unrelenting barrage of energy that will overwhelm your listeners and make it impossible for you to communicate subtle emotions. Give others an occasional break. A well-timed pause can add suspense, interest and a moment of reflection. It can emphasize a point, create suspense and pique the listener's interest in what you will say next. A two- or three-second pause may seem unnatural if you tend to speak quickly and rarely pause. Don't be concerned that you will lose the listener's attention or sound hesitant. You won't, particularly if you maintain good eye contact and open body language during the pause.

VOLUME

Studies have consistently confirmed that the optimal volume of speech is in the moderate range. For example, in one study, 148 adults were approached by three female graduate students at airports and train stations in Denver, New York City and Philadelphia. The three women said to each stranger, "Excuse me (slight pause), I'm running late. Would you please mail this for me?" as they handed him or her a postcard. The strangers more frequently took the card if the women used a moderate voice, rather than a voice that was either in a softer or louder range.

Strong volume reflects confidence and self-assurance, competence, commitment, assertiveness and leadership. However, if your voice is too loud, it can be intimidating and overwhelming, and convey aggressiveness, insensitivity and an effort to control or dominate. A loud voice also may be considered rude and unfriendly. A loud voice at inappropriate occasions, such as in public places or when you speak about private matters, also can cause embarrassment and is considered tacky and lower class. At a subconscious level, we make many of the same associations toward anyone who talks too loudly as we do toward a "loudmouth drunk."

At the other extreme, if you speak too softly you will irritate those who must strain to hear and understand what you say. Your soft voice also may be associated with a lack of self-confidence, shyness, lower competence and intelligence, a lack of assertiveness, boredom or disinterest, weakness, a lack of commitment to what you say, nervousness and even dishonesty.

Softer voices also trigger some positive associations. They are perceived as more friendly, approachable, humble and compassionate. In situations when a soft voice would be expected, as in a private conversation between friends at a restaurant, these negative associations will not arise, and a soft voice will have a distinct positive effect.

These general stereotypes are influenced significantly by the other traits you display as you speak. Aggressive body language, such as intense eye contact, invading personal space and a marked forward lean, will accentuate the negative associations made with a louder voice. More passive, less intimidating body language, like soft eye contact, a smile and slower or more open gestures, will temper the negative impact of a loud voice. Likewise, a soft voice accompanied by open, confident and expressive body language will tend to nullify the negative associations normally made from a soft voice, just as submissive or closed body language will accentuate them.

Use body language to manage your impression when circumstances call for a particularly loud or soft voice. If you're in a crowded room or speaking to a large group and must raise your voice to be heard by those who are farthest away, avoid the impression that you are overbearing by displaying calm, nonthreatening body language. If you must talk softly to keep strangers from overhearing a private conversation, show your emotion with more expressive body language and facial expressions.

Other vocal qualities, including tone and pace, can also have a significant impact on how a person with a loud or soft voice is perceived. A harsh, grating voice is much less attractive and inviting than a deep, resonant baritone at the same volume. Those with harsh voices will benefit from speaking softly. Those with soft voices can eliminate most of the negative stereotypes associated with poor volumn if they incorporate a clear, more rapid and confident tone.

The content of what you say will also affect the impression made by the volume of your voice, and vice versa. Aggressive, forceful, definitive, unwavering dialogue, coupled with a loud voice, will accentuate the impression of aggression, egotism and domination—while more conciliatory, thoughtful and friendly language, even spoken at a high volume, usually won't put people off. Raise or lower your volume to compensate for the aggressiveness or passivity of your messages, and choose your words to compensate for any extremes in the volume of your voice.

Even your appearance should be considered as you manage the impact the volume of your voice will have on others' impressions of you. A woman with a particularly soft voice, for example, will not be considered as authoritative, confident, competent, strong or forceful. If she tends to wear light colors or pastels, she will accentuate those negative impressions. However, if she wears darker or brighter colors, she will show more power and energy and help compensate for her weak voice. Someone with a particularly overpowering voice should not wear black in situations when friendliness and approachability is more important than confidence and control. In such situations, she might opt for lighter colors or autumn tones to help tone down the dominating image her voice projects.

TONE AND PITCH

Ronald Reagan has been called "the great communicator" because his relaxed, congenial and warm voice convinced us that everything was okay. He had it all under control. His voice was deep, full and rich. It was almost a perfect voice to communicate confidence, friendliness, likability, trustworthiness and control. Yet it wasn't at all overpowering.

Lower-pitched voices, for both men and women, consistently have been equated with those same positive qualities projected by President Reagan's voice. By their very nature, they are more pleasing to the ear and tend to minimize irritating nasal qualities that frequently accompany higher-pitched voices.

High-pitched voices trigger few positive associations. In some circumstances, they can show the bubbly enthusiasm and innocence of youth. But more frequently, high-pitched voices in women bring to mind stereotypes of the dumb blond bimbo or excited Valley girl. In men, they're associated with weakness.

High-pitched voices in both men and women also trigger stereotypical associations of lower intelligence, a lack of confidence, nervousness and agitation. Voices tend to increase in pitch when we feel strong emotions. As a result, we associate high-pitched voices with the same characteristics that frequently cause emotional stress—lying, anger, agitation and excitement. High-pitched voices, particularly the sing-songy variety, also are thought to reflect an effort by women to be coy or manipulative, which adversely affects their trustworthiness.

Before you resolve to duplicate James Earl Jones's deep bass voice, or the sultry breathlessness of Greta Garbo, a word of caution: A sustained attempt to speak in an artificial and unnatural low-pitched voice will place a tremendous amount of strain on your throat and vocal cords. Eventually hoarseness and even more serious problems can develop. But most people can safely lower the pitch of their voice if they learn proper techniques. Try a quick exercise and you'll see what we mean.

First, say "hello" in your normal voice several times without any effort to lower its pitch. Cup your throat in your hand as you do. You should feel only slight vibration and tension in your throat. Now, try to lower your voice without breathing more deeply than normal. In fact, to accentuate the effect, first exhale most of the air from your lungs and abdomen, and then say "hello" two or three times in the lowest pitch possible. You will feel a strong vibration in your throat like the vibration that occurs when you turn up the bass on your stereo. After a few "hellos," you will feel some fatigue in your throat.

Now, take a deep breath and fill both your chest and abdomen with air. As you exhale slowly, say "hello," lowering your voice, not by straining the muscles in your throat, but by exhaling more fully as you speak. If the exercise is done properly, you should be able to lower your pitch, without feeling any strain in your throat.

This is but one of many exercises voice specialists like Dr. Morton Cooper, Dr. Lillian Glass and Arthur Samuel Joseph have used to help actors, politicians, business notables, and hundreds of people just like you and us achieve a richer, fuller but still natural and safe vocal tone. If you don't have a deep, rich, full voice, consult one of their books, or find a voice coach in your area. We don't profess to be experts on "how to" develop better vocal tone without inflicting vocal damage, but from our experience and research, and that of countless others, we can assure you that when you incorporate positive tonal qualities into your voice, you will enhance the impression you make on others.

PACE

It's difficult for others to get a word in edgewise when you speak too fast. They may have a comment they would like to make, but there is never a pause long enough to interject their thoughts without interrupting you. Eventually, they just give up, and settle into what becomes your monologue, rather than a dialogue. Many times, they also become tense or agitated.

There are some positive elements to rapid speech. It reflects enthusiasm and commitment to what is said. Those who speak rapidly, up to a point, also are rated more intelligent if their rapid speech makes sense, since it takes a certain degree of mental horsepower to convert thought to words in rapid-fire order.

On the flip side are slow speakers, those who seem to take forever to finish a sentence. They don't necessarily pause frequently; they just talk as if their mind and tongue are on a leisurely stroll. Just as we often assume that fast talkers are more intelligent because they're able to fashion and communicate their ideas quickly, slow talkers are rated consistently less intelligent, less competent, and less confident. They also are thought to be more submissive, boring or tired.

There are a few whose appearance, demeanor, vocabulary and sophisticated thought process belie the impression of a lack of intelligence, even when they speak very slowly. Those individuals, however, sometimes fall victim to an entirely different stereotype. We don't question their intelligence. But they can seem preachy, self-absorbed and egotistical; as if they have the sense that whatever they have to say is so insightful that we should hang on every word. They seem to hold court as they grace us with a glimpse of their wisdom.

Apart from those slow talkers who impress others as arrogant and self-absorbed, slow talkers usually are perceived as more friendly and approachable. Slow speech also reflects calmness, and is usually easier to understand than rapid speech.

Halting, hesitant, stop/start speech raises a different cluster of stereotypical assumptions. As discussed earlier, the pause is a very effective tool to add emphasis and interest to a conversation or presentation. To be effective, however, the pause must be timed appropriately. A pause that is inserted mid-thought doesn't create the positive impression of additional emphasis, or an attempt to be precise and thoughtful. Instead, it suggests that you are unsure of yourself, nervous, confused, dishonest, unfocused or unable to maintain your train of thought.

The impression you make when you pause is influenced considerably by your body language. If your pause is coupled with nervous gestures, a loss of eye contact or facial expressions that are associated with doubt or confusion, the pause will be interpreted negatively. On the other hand, if you maintain eye contact, and your body remains relatively still, the listener will make the positive associations that a pause can produce.

If you find yourself in one of those awkward moments when you have lost your train of thought, or must pause to collect your ideas to be able to articulate them more clearly, don't panic. Make sure your eyes don't dart around the room as if the answer is written on the walls, and don't scratch your head or pick imaginary lint from your sleeve. Instead, remain focused on your listener and keep relatively still. Your listener will interpret this not as mental panic, but as focus and concentration, and will await the product of your efforts.

OTHER VOCAL QUALITIES

The other day we saw an advertisement on TV for the Men's Wearhouse, a national chain of men's clothing stores. The owner, Paul Zimmer, has acted as the company's spokesperson for years. We've always wondered why he turned to the camera at the end of his commercials and barked in a nasal tone, "I *guara*-n-tEE it." I'm sure his vocal quality and body language were intended as a confident assurance of satisfaction. But he came across like a hard-sell salesman.

In the last version, as the commercial ended, Mr. Zimmer was shown in profile sitting comfortably in a chair. He still closed the ad with the words "I guarantee it." But they were spoken slowly and calmly. It was as if he were reassuring his young son that he would be there to catch him if he fell from the jungle gym. What a difference!

Zimmer eliminated one of the vocal qualities to which particularly negative stereotypes attach—that grating, usually hard-sell, often cocky quality that seems to be a favorite among those selling knives at the county fair. But there are many other vocal qualities that also produce almost exclusively negative associations.

MUMBLING

Mumbling can be caused by poor enunciation, lowering your voice, covering your mouth with your hand as you speak, or looking away. When you mumble, you force your listeners to work hard to understand you, which irritates them. People associate mumbling with a lack of confidence, insecurity, self-consciousness, laziness, an inability to articulate thoughts, a lack of competence and dishonesty. Generally, mumblers' body language is equally passive, weak and unexpressive, which compounds the negative impression.

If people ask you to repeat yourself frequently, or if you determine that you're a mumbler when you candidly assess your speech pattern either with or without audio feedback, make a concerted effort to speak clearly and loudly, and to enunciate each word. In the privacy of your home, car or office, exaggerate your enunciation. If the problem persists, seek professional help. If you think your characteristic mumbling is "no big deal," simply ask yourself how many dynamic leaders or successful men and women you have known who mumbled.

ROUGH VOICES

Gravelly, rough, harsh voices are not well received. The Greek physician Galen once said, "The voice is the mirror of the soul," and at some level most of us believe he was right. People tend to think that if someone's voice is rough and harsh, it is because he or she is rough and harsh, as reflected in the raspy voice of the stereotypical life-hardened cocktail waitress seen on television and in the movies.

Harsh, raspy voices are often the result of physical maladies—allergies, bronchitis or years of smoking. Sometimes, however, your voice becomes hoarse and rough because you abuse it by not speaking properly. If you have a hoarse, rough voice, consult a physician or speech coach and see if it is possible to improve it. If that's not possible, incorporate other techniques to soften your image as part of your Impression Management Plan.

WHINING

Try as we might, we can't think of any redeeming quality associated with a whiny voice. We have come to the conclusion that God gave us the ability to whine for the same reason he gave infants an ear-piercing cry—to irritate others so we can have their way, if for no other reason than just to shut us up. Whining is interpreted as either an attempt to manipulate someone to do what you want or an effort to express your feelings and thoughts indirectly. In either case, when you whine you appear less trustworthy, caring, humble and capable. If you have something to say, say it. Don't whine it.

PRETENSION

Stereotypes are often reflected by how particular traits are portrayed in the media, and in particular by comedians. Fran Drescher's nasal New York City whine, the dumb blonde with a squeaky voice, the egotistical news anchor with an artificially deep voice, all play to our stereotypical associations.

The pretentious vocal quality of Mr. and Mrs. Howell on *Gilligan's Island* broadcasts arrogance as perhaps no other trait can. The blue blood, preppy quality of pretentious speech may suggest success, sophistication, intelligence, wealth and upper-class status, but we can assure you that it's not a good trade-off. Success, dignity and class are admirable qualities. A pretentious voice is no way to communicate them.

BREATHINESS

During normal speech your breath is not audible, either when you inhale or exhale. When it is, others will notice it. Most often, breathiness is due to exercise or illness. Extreme degrees of emotion, such as anger, excitement, nervousness, anxiety, frustration or disbelief also can result in breathiness. Some people also exhale audibly as a way to communicate disgust, disbelief or indifference. Finally, breathiness can be consciously adopted as an attempt to convey sexiness, such as when Marilyn Monroe sang "Happy Birthday" to John F. Kennedy. Apart from exercise-induced heavy breathing, each of these causes for breathiness carries negative connotations.

- *Illness:* Any physical condition that is severe enough to cause audible breathing will affect others' assessment of your physical well-being which can have a negative impact on their assessment of your capability. If you have a temporary medical condition that causes noticeable breathing, you should explain its origin to others if it is not obvious, rather than allow this concern to arise. If your condition is permanent, compensate by wearing more energetic colors, utilizing more expressive body language, vocal qualities and even words to show that you have the strength and energy to deliver whatever others may need from you.
- *Powerful emotion:* People naturally assume that if emotions have taken hold of you to the point that you breath heavily, your rational brain has lost its grip. If emotions take hold, take a moment and relax before you begin to speak. One technique we've used with lawyers who become nervous and breathe heavily is to suggest that they stop and engage in some distracting behavior for a few seconds until it passes. They can walk over to a table and pick up a file, glance through a stack of exhibits, or pour a glass of water. It doesn't matter what you do, as long as you do something until the wave of emotion subsides.
- *Purposeful exhaling:* Whether you use this technique to show disbelief, disgust or frustration, almost everyone will find it irritating, offensive and even demeaning.
- *Marilyn Monroe breathiness:* The breathiness of the movie sex goddesses of the forties, fifties and sixties is associated with sexiness, but at a very blatant and unsophisticated level. Most people find it more comical than seductive.

ASSORTED VOCAL NOISES

When you habitually smack your lips, whistle through your teeth when you exhale, click your tongue or make similar noises, you add nothing positive to the impression you make. Such vocal tics create much the same impression as facial tics. They are associated with nervousness and a lack of confidence and self-control.

If you have a vocal tic, stop every time you catch yourself and pause for a second. The pause won't be as distracting as the tic; and in fairly short order you will eliminate it. Your friends can also help. Ask them to mimic you each time you have a relapse. This will help you rid yourself of the problem even more quickly.

ACCENTS

America's diverse, multicultural and multilingual population is affected constantly by the stereotypical associations made regarding accents and regional dialects. The stereotypes associated with particular accents are usually offshoots of the stereotypes that are directed toward race and ethnicity, although other factors also influence the extent to which accents affect impression formation.

In a study conducted by Dr. Lillian Glass and published in her book *Talk to Win,* forty-one participants between the ages of twelve and seventy-two were asked if they liked each of thirty different accents "a lot," "a little," or "not at all." Dr. Glass's findings reflect that over a third of the accents listed were disliked by a majority of the respondents.

The accents that were favored were generally those incorporating sounds that are typical of English and other "romance languages." Those accents that were most disliked incorporate sounds that are not prevalent in English phonics, such as the comparatively choppy sound of Asian languages, throaty guttural sounds common to Middle Eastern languages, or the harsh sound of Germanic and Slavic languages.

This is not surprising if we consider that our emotional brains don't feel as comfortable when they process foreign data as they do when they receive familiar stimuli. Studies show that, with a few exceptions, the more different an accent sounds from our own, the more likely we are to equate it with lower socioeconomic class, less competence and lower intelligence. Not surprisingly, people with such accents on average receive lower pay and attain less success in the work environment. Those with non-standard accents often judge others with different nonstandard accents just as harshly as anyone else.

Those with accents that are the standard in the community, on the other hand, are perceived as more competent, confident, intelligent, friendly, ambitious and successful. They also are assumed to have a higher socioeconomic status, and what they say is thought to convey more substance. Studies also show that teachers with "standard" accents are better understood by their students, who remember what they say longer. They are also considered more dynamic.

Over the last twenty years we have seen countless witnesses and lawyers in court speak with every imaginable type of accent. Many of these individuals were rated very highly by juries on each of the Compass Qualities. Others fell victim to many negative stereotypes associated with nonconforming accents. After speaking with jurors about the bases for their conclusions, we have identified three elements that most frequently trigger negative accent-related stereotypes.

The first characteristic of a poorly received accent is that it is difficult to understand. Just as others will make a broad range of negative associations if you mumble, talk too fast or otherwise make them work too hard to understand what you say, so too, if your accent makes it difficult for others to understand you, they will become impatient, irritated and form derogatory associations with regard to your intelligence, capability, friendliness and competence. If you have a distinct accent that is still easy to understand, much less bias will arise.

The second factor that influences negative accent-related associations is directly tied to the ever-important concept of expectations. If we meet a person from a foreign country who has been in the United States for a relatively short period of time, and as a result struggles with the English language and speaks with a heavy and sometimes incomprehensible accent, we seldom judge the person harshly because of his accent. We expect someone who is learning a language to have difficulties. But when we encounter someone we know to have been in the United States for an extended period of time, or who has a job that requires him to communicate with others in English, we expect him to be able to communicate in English without his accent presenting a barrier. The typical reaction is to assume that if he has had a reason and opportunity to learn to speak without a heavy accent, but has not, it is either because he is not intelligent enough, industrious enough or friendly and thoughtful enough to have done so. These are strong negative associations, and perhaps even unfair, but they exist as a function of our expectations.

The final cause of negative associations with accents is that they accentuate whatever racial or ethnic biases and prejudices people otherwise harbor. Many people have significant racial and ethnic prejudice and bias, and tend to make strong stereotypical associations with any members of the groups who are the victims of those biases. We'll know that there are no longer such biases when at the end of a racial joke everyone looks puzzled and says, "I don't get it, what's the guy's race got to do with the joke anyway?" Until then, racial and ethnic biases will be a reality that can be addressed with Impression Management.

Our interviews with hundreds of individuals about witnesses with different racial and ethnic backgrounds have demonstrated that ethnic biases often are the product of associations made at an emotional level. Heavy accents accentuate this emotional brain response. When someone has no identifiable accent, her race or ethnicity is much less frequently even considered. Test our experience against your own.

Think of individuals you know who come from particular ethnic or racial backgrounds. Focus on one or two of them who have perfect English accents, whether they are Asian, Middle Eastern, African American or of some other race or nationality. If you're like most people, you seldom think about their background. Then consider a few individuals you know who have heavy accents, and you probably will find that you think much more frequently about their race or ethnicity. Those who have eliminated their accents have helped remove their race or ethnicity from others' minds, and with it the lingering biases others may harbor.

If you have an accent that is (1) so heavy that it's difficult to understand, (2) heavier than one would expect of someone who has had the opportunity and practical need to acquire a standard English accent, or (3) reflects a racial, ethnic, regional or other cultural background toward which strong stereotypes apply, your accent will affect the impression you make on many people.

We are not suggesting that people abandon their cultural heritage, or that a standard English accent is in any way superior to others. But we do want to impress upon those who have accents that a heavy accent will affect impression formation, particularly if the accent is associated with a racial or ethnic group toward which significant prejudice exists. If you eliminate your accent, you will decrease many of the negative stereotypes to which you are subjected. If you choose to retain your accent, you should recognize that your Impression Management Plan should incorporate traits to offset the negative stereotypes that your accent may trigger.

THE IDEAL VOICE

What is the ideal voice? We'll give you a hint: Walter Cronkite, Peter Jennings, Kathleen Sullivan, Harry Reasoner, Dan Rather, Katie Couric, Sam Donaldson and Jane Pauley.

The broadcast media have spent tens of millions of dollars searching for the perfect voice. They have found that the ideal voice must show emotion, be lower pitched, be moderately paced and have a standard English accent. It must be free of distracting qualities, clear and have moderate volume. This "ideal" voice consistently rates highest when tested by social scientists and has proven to be the most persuasive, credible and likable to the thousands of jurors we have interviewed.

Before you throw up your hands and say, "I will never sound like Walter Cronkite or Katie Couric," take heart. Each of the elements of the ideal voice is within your control. You can add emotion. You can turn up or turn down the volume, and increase or lower the pace of your voice at will. You even can change the tone, pitch and accent of your voice, though this will require more effort. At first, you may lapse into your habitual patterns; but with practice, you can and will change those patterns.

You may have spent twenty, thirty, forty or more years without a second thought as to how your voice projects your personality. But it's never too late to start. If you don't learn to paint a positive picture of yourself with your voice, you will be like Rembrandt removing the red paint from his palette before he sat down to his day's work.

CHAPTER 10

Communication Style

You control the ebb and flow of your conversations with your communication style—how well you listen, whether you talk (and for how long), whether you direct conversations or follow along passively, whether you volunteer, whether you are blunt or indirect. The importance of communication style is highlighted every time we hear a juror comment after a trial, "He seemed incapable of answering a question directly"; or "The way he rambled on, you could tell he was lying"; or "He was so defensive." Your body language, tone of voice, and the words you use all contribute to your overall impression, but your communication style is crucial to the mix.

Almost no one communicates the same way in all situations. You may communicate very differently at work than you do at home or at play. Even at work, you may communicate differently with your superiors than with your subordinates, coworkers or customers. No one style is right, but some are more effective for certain people, in particular circumstances, and in interactions with others who have the same or different styles. Just as you can convey different qualities through variations in your appearance, body language and voice, you can also vary your communication style to influence impression formation dramatically.

Based on more than a decade of research and thousands of interviews, communication expert Linda McAllister, author of *I Wish I'd Said That!*, has identified six different communication styles. She calls them: *Noble, Socratic, Reflective, Magistrate, Candidate* and *Senator*. No one uses one style exclusively, but everyone tends to use one more than the others. Just as Dr. McAllister has found that various styles in isolation influence the flow of communication among those who use them, we have found that each style makes a unique contribution to impression formation when mixed with the other six Colors.

Nobles are very direct, even blunt and close-minded. They're committed to their ideas, and are quick to express them. They generally don't beat around the bush or worry much about how others feel about what they have to say. Their objective is an honest and efficient exchange of information. They also expect, and even prefer, candid, no-nonsense communication. *Nobles* are perceived as trustworthy and capable. But they suffer in the caring and humility departments, particularly when they interact with those whose communication styles are less direct and are more concerned with feelings than facts. Men who use a *Noble* style tend to meet our stereotypical expectations that men are more direct and forceful. Just the opposite is true for women.

Socratics are so named because, like the Greek philosopher Socrates, they believe that lengthy discussion, negotiation and debate should precede any decision. They tend to be verbose, detail-oriented and drawn to more abstract analysis. At times, they talk incessantly about matters that don't seem particularly relevant. This tendency can be very frustrating to a *Noble,* who gets right to the point. *Socratics* tendency to verbosity and debate makes them appear less straightforward than *Nobles,* but they still appear trustworthy. Yet they appear uncaring and not very humble, since they seem to enjoy hearing themselves talk. Their penchant for detailed analysis, thorough fact-finding and discussion impresses others with their capability.

Reflectives don't like confrontation, and see communication as a way to develop good personal relationships. They tend to be equivocal, and try not to say anything that might lead to disagreement or alienation. Their friendly, soft-spoken and nonassertive manner shows that they are caring and humble. Because they seem wishy-washy, *Reflectives* are not perceived as particularly capable. They can also impress others as untrustworthy. They're not malicious liars, but they try so hard to please that they often are not candid with their true thoughts and feelings. Women who use a *Reflective* style meet our expectations, but the *Reflective* style is more sensitive and talkative than we expect from men and often creates negative impressions when preferred by them.

Magistrates combine the styles of *Nobles* and *Socratics.* They are outspoken and solution-oriented like *Nobles,* and verbose like *Socratics.* They're reluctant to change their minds, and try to persuade others to their point of view. The most significant difference between *Magistrates* and either of their derivative styles is their tendency to be headstrong, which impresses others that they think they are better, smarter and more capable. This adversely affects their impression with respect to each of the Compass Qualities.

Candidates blend the styles of *Reflectives* and *Socratics.* They are talkative like *Socratics,* and friendly and encouraging like *Reflectives.* Like the candidates after which they are named, they don't want to alienate anyone. They seek to persuade, not through forceful rhetoric like a *Socratic,* but with disarming charm and friendliness like *Reflectives.* Because *Candidates* are good listeners and are nonconfrontational, they're seen as caring and humble. However, since it is difficult to know where they really stand on any issue, like *Reflectives,* their trustworthiness and capability may be questioned.

Senators are like chameleons. They vary their communication style from *Noble* to *Reflective* depending upon the situation. When confidence, control and authority are at a premium, they have learned that the *Noble* style is most effective, and use it. When strong interpersonal relationships are a higher priority, they become agreeable communicators and excellent and supportive listeners, like *Reflectives. Senators* manage Impression Formation through this dual communication style.

The techniques of mirroring and echoing are particularly useful as you manage your communication style. Most people expect others to use a communication style similar to their own. Certain communication styles are relatively compatible. Others are not. To best manage the impression your communication style makes on others, you should be alert not only to the style that you use, but also that which is favored by others. The style that you use to get the most out of every situation should vary from interaction to interaction, as can be illustrated by two conversations any businessperson might have during the course of his or her day. As an example, we will use a typical morning in Peter's life as an accountant.

Peter's day begins with a meeting with his office manager, Nick. Nick is accountable to half a dozen different partners, all of whom are opinionated and strong-willed. His first priority is to help the partners make informed and intelligent decisions about the management of the firm. Even though he often harbors strong personal feelings about the direction the firm should take, he has learned that he is better able to influence decisions if he provides the partners with detailed information in a nonassertive way, and then keeps the dialogue flowing with positive comments and suggestions. Nick has developed a *Candidate* style of communication that incorporates the *Socratic's* tendency to discuss issues in detail, and the *Reflective's* excellent listening skills and nonconfrontational manner.

Peter, on the other hand, has a classic *Senator* style of communication. From circumstance to circumstance, he alternates between a *Noble's* blunt, direct and often intimidating style, and a *Reflective's* passive, warm and nonconfrontational approach. Peter has learned that if he communicates with Nick in his *Noble* style, Nick will defer to him so readily that Peter may not benefit from the insight of Nick's true opinions. Since Nick's opinions are important to Peter, in his meeting with Nick, Peter favors the *Reflective* style of communication that encourages Nick to express his views freely.

Peter's next meeting in the day is with Ann, the chief financial officer of a large corporate client. Ann is a very direct, no-nonsense type, who definitely communicates in the *Noble* style, as is frequently the case with hard-charging, successful businessmen and women. Ann wants a no-nonsense and direct assessment of her company's problems from Peter, and his recommendations for appropriate action. As a consequence, Peter adopts the *Noble* style of communication with Ann. *Nobles,* like Ann, don't want anything sugarcoated; and if Peter adopted a *Reflective* style, Ann would think he was indecisive. If Ann were herself a *Socratic* or *Reflective* communicator, Peter would probably talk in detail about all of her options and their advantages and disadvantages, and frequently invite Ann's input. But with Ann, he briefly identifies what he believes are undesirable options, tells Ann why he has dismissed those and then outlines the approach he believes the company should take, and why. This approach impresses Ann, since she is a *Noble*. If Ann were a *Reflective* who was more comfortable with a less direct and more chatty approach, she probably would have found Peter to have the accountant's equivalent of a bad bedside manner.

Neither style that Peter adopted for his very different conversations was phony or insincere. Just as Peter would use technical accounting jargon in a discussion with another accountant and simple English when he spoke with a typical client, he changed his communication style to communicate most effectively with his audience.

If you are sensitive to the various communication styles that you can use to make the best possible impression on different people in different circumstances, you can incorporate the other six Colors into the process to manage your impression even more effectively. Once again, we'll use Peter's conversations with Nick and Ann as illustrations.

In Peter's discussion with Nick his goal was to use a *Reflective* communication style to encourage Nick to speak freely. Let's assume he also wanted to retain the appearance of leadership and authority. He could couple the caring and humble *Reflective* communication style with authoritative traits that would leave the impression that he was a friendly and open-minded boss, not just a friendly and open-minded peer. He could keep his jacket on during the meeting, maintain more rigid body posture, speak in a more authoritative voice and even schedule the meeting in his office, rather than in Nick's. If he wanted to soften his impression, he could take his jacket off and loosen his tie, laugh and smile more, speak in a less authoritative tone and hold the meeting in Nick's office.

If Peter wanted to satisfy Ann's *Noble* need for direct, no-nonsense communication, but also develop a personal rapport with her to enhance their relationship, he could deliver the goods in a direct *Noble* fashion, but personalize the exchange with a host of traits designed to project friendliness and painted with the other six Colors. Or, if Peter was certain that

Ann wanted and expected the most businesslike approach possible, he could adopt the authoritative traits that he used with Nick when he wanted to enhance his image of leadership and professionalism.

When you select the communication style that meets your audience's needs and expectations, and augment that style with traits from the other six Colors, you can accomplish almost any objective without diminishing others' impressions of any of the Compass Qualities. If you want to soften a no-nonsense message, use the *Noble* style but temper it with caring and humble traits. If you want to project openness and friendliness without losing control of a discussion, accompany your *Reflective* communication style with more powerful and authoritarian traits. The combinations are as numerous as the interactions that fill your life.

Regardless of the style you find most effective in any particular situation, or with any one individual, each of the techniques discussed in the balance of this chapter will enhance the effectiveness of that style.

LEARN TO LISTEN

Many people are great talkers but bad listeners. When we are excited, angry, impatient, bored, in disagreement, or just because we have bad communication habits, we often interrupt, defend, attack and engage in a host of other behaviors that are toxic to good communication. Good listening skills are essential to favorable impression function because they allow you to:

- Make others feel important;
- Acquire information from which you can determine others' needs, biases and stereotypes;
- Give others confidence that you have heard and understood them;
- Make appropriate comments;
- Avoid boring others; and
- Encourage others to listen to you.

LISTENING MAKES OTHERS FEEL IMPORTANT

When you demonstrate your ability to meet others' needs, you make them feel important. Even if you can't actually do anything to satisfy their cravings, they will know they are still important to you if you just favor them with a few minutes of attention.

One morning Jo-Ellan was riding up to her office in the elevator with a woman whom she had seen in the building on several occasions. Jo-Ellan noticed she was wearing a small sequined-encrusted poodle brooch. Jo-Ellan asked her, "That's a beautiful brooch. Do you have poodles?" The woman was standing in the elevator, her mind on some distant thought and her shoulders slightly hunched as if already bearing the weight of the upcoming day. When Jo-Ellan spoke, the woman turned and smiled, surprised that anyone would have taken even a moment out of her day to have shown interest in her.

"I have two. A five-year-old male, Romeo, and a four-year-old female, Juliet. Once my kids moved out of the house they became my little babies," she giggled. "I bred them once a year ago and they had six puppies. I wanted to keep them all, but my husband said if I did. . . ." She stood in the doorway of the elevator sharing with Jo-Ellan the joy her dogs gave her until the elevator beeped that it was time to say "goodbye."

Each time that Jo-Ellan has bumped into the woman in the building since then, she has smiled and they have exchanged pleasantries. It only took a few minutes for Jo-Ellan to express interest in her and listen intently as she described something that was important to her. Yet those few moments made a lasting impression.

LISTEN TO UNDERSTAND OTHERS' NEEDS, BIASES AND STEREOTYPES

In your quest to manage stereotypical associations, you need to anticipate what associations those in your life are likely to make. Some associations are made nearly universally. Others are based on individuals' unique background and personal beliefs. Each person carries a hodgepodge of experiences with him or her that will influence his or her attitude toward you.

When you listen carefully to others, you learn about them. Often someone will make a comment that will give you a direct glimpse into his or her character and experiences, and hence how he or she will respond to you. For example, a man may comment, "I can be stubborn at times." Listen carefully: He's probably right. If he is in fact stubborn, he will probably think those who are resistant to his ideas are close-minded. You would be wise to incorporate this information in your efforts to impress him. If you tend to be direct and forceful, recognize that he is likely to be put off by that approach. If you want him to think that you are intelligent and creative, don't force your ideas on him. Present the reasons underlying them in an nonassertive way, and let him agree with you.

A woman may say, "My ex-husband always complained that I'm selfish and self-centered." Sure, this is just one man's opinion, but it's the opinion of a man who at one point in her life knew her better than anyone else. The fact that she repeats it suggests that her ex-husband may have had a point. The glimpse she gives of this perspective should alert you to the possibility that she is needy and self-centered.

If you listen carefully you will identify not only those who may be particularly needy, but also their specific needs. Listen for any hints of what is important to them. Do they talk a lot about appearance, which indicates that they need affirmation of theirs, and will likely place greater weight on yours? Is money a recurrent theme in their conversation? If so, financial success, material acquisitions, security and your ability to help them achieve these objectives may be what they want from you. Do they lace their conversation with references that they are "stuck in a rut" or "bored silly"? If they do, a relationship with a person who is fun, interesting and exciting may be what they crave most. If they explain that their former employees, spouses or associates were cheats, you should emphasize those traits that are associated with trustworthiness.

Your ability to fulfill others' needs is so important to their impression of you that you should never miss an opportunity to identify what those needs are because you weren't listening carefully.

Careful listening also establishes an early warning system that will alert you if for any reason you have failed to meet the needs of those who are important to you. Many people play "emotional hide and seek," and are reluctant to reveal what society generally perceives as negative emotions, such as jealousy, envy, anger, greed and resentment. Instead, they send messages in quick and sometimes subtle bursts that you will miss if you're busy thinking about what you want to say next, instead of listening intently. You don't want to miss that symptom of frustration that, if ignored, can lead to resentment and then anger if left untreated.

LISTENING GIVES OTHERS CONFIDENCE THAT YOU HAVE HEARD AND UNDERSTOOD THEM

It is extremely frustrating to attempt to explain something to someone who isn't listening. When you don't listen, you do more than just tell someone that what he has to say isn't important to you; he'll also naturally assume that if you don't pay attention, you are not likely to hear and understand his message and respond capably. That may or may not be the case. You may appear to be riveted to what someone says, and actually be clueless, or your attention may seem to be elsewhere even though you hear and understand everything he says. In either case, if you want to send the message that you're capable in the fullest sense, you will be much more effective if you are an intent listener.

This is particularly important if the other person is upset, agitated or angry. Resolving conflict is difficult when emotions are aroused. If you don't hear someone out under these circumstances, he will become even more convinced that his emotions are justified. Let him say his piece. Acknowledge that you have heard and understood what he has said. Then respond, and he will listen to you with a more open mind.

GOOD LISTENING SKILLS
WILL HELP YOU MAKE APPROPRIATE COMMENTS

Attentive listening is the best antidote for foot-in-mouth disease. If you suddenly look up and ask a question about something that has already been discussed, the other person will naturally question whether you were paying attention. But if you listen carefully, you will have intelligent comments to add to the conversation, or at least you will be able to ask relevant questions. The effect on Impression Management is obvious.

LISTENING PREVENTS OTHERS' BOREDOM

Most of us talk too much. What's worse, those who are the worst listeners are usually the biggest talkers, and the most tiresome bores.

Ambrose Bierce, in *The Devil's Dictionary*, defines a bore as, "A person who talks when you wish him to listen." None of us is bored by what we have to say; many of us are bored by what others have to say; but all of us are bored by what others have to say when we want to say something.

LISTENING ENCOURAGES OTHERS TO LISTEN TO YOU

Attentive listening is contagious. If you let others speak their piece they are much more inclined to let you speak yours. The process enhances not only your impression as a good listener, but also gives you the opportunity to express your thoughts without interruption when it is your turn to speak. You will be able to convey a positive image more effectively if your comments aren't cut short in a perpetual tug-of-war for the opportunity to speak.

NINE TIPS TO GOOD LISTENING

As important as good listening skills are to impression formation, they are exceedingly rare. Yet they are easy to acquire and to incorporate into your Impression Management Plan. There are nine keys to effective listening:

- Listen for, and with, emotion
- Don't interrupt
- Avoid distractions
- Be an objective listener
- Be patient
- Actively participate
- Prompt others to talk
- Be direct and responsive
- Self-disclose

LISTEN FOR, AND WITH, EMOTION

When we speak to one another, much of our communication takes place on an emotional level. The most effective listening requires that you hear and speak more than just words. You must listen for and with emotion.

As you speak with someone, watch her carefully. Hear her breathing, watch her movements, listen to the sounds she introduces into her environment. Focus not just on her words, but on how she conveys her emotions with each of her Seven Colors, and respond with each of yours. Notice her facial and body motions. Is she tense or relaxed? Does her skin become moist with perspiration? Use your sense of smell to detect alcohol, medication, perfume or sweat. If your relationship permits intimacy, when you touch her or she you, feel her warmth, anxiety or passion.

Imagine how much more you would "hear" in every conversation if you were to listen intently to what was said with each of the Seven Colors. If you listen only for words and only with your rational brain, you will hear only a fraction of what is said. But when you listen for and with emotion, you hear the language of emotion. This is the language with which we all communicate most effectively.

In today's world we recognize that you must frequently interpret words without emotional context. Even so, whenever possible, create an environment that allows you and your partner to exchange both emotional and rational signals. Fight the urge to communicate in whatever manner is easiest. You may be able to send an e-mail message to every employee in the company with the push of a button. When you do, you lose the opportunity to show them in person that you care about its contents, and their reaction to it. You can send a fax to your customers around the country, or around the world, in a few minutes. But telephone calls will provide you with a better opportunity to truly communicate. Worst of all, you could delegate the communication to someone else and deny yourself any direct contact.

Quantity, not quality, has become the watchword for communication in our electronic culture. Make more calls. Add to the mailing list. Send out more circulars. Bid more jobs. Automate. Duplicate. Expand. Henry Ford proved that automobiles can be produced most effectively on an assembly line; but relationships can't. Nor can great impressions. They take time. They take effort. They take the personal touch. They take contact. They require that you create opportunities to paint with as many of your Seven Colors as possible.

There are many times when the personal touch just isn't possible. But ask yourself honestly how often you pass up an opportunity to make personal contact simply because it's easier to push a button—*even if it's not as effective.* It would also have been easier for Michelangelo to paint the ceiling of the Sistine Chapel with only beige paint, but what impression would that have made?

Don't take the easy route if it won't lead you where you want to go. Don't rely on e-mail for critical communication. Schedule a casual lunch where you can talk and listen—*really* talk and listen. Knock on doors, and take a few moments to see and be seen, hear and be heard. Move out from behind your desk in your office, or the lectern if you speak in public. In a large group, lean forward slightly so that everyone can see you, and you them. Remove extra glasses, centerpieces or flowers from the table that might obscure direct view. Turn and face your partner. You will send and receive much more information if your bodies and faces are squared to one another rather than in profile.

When you must communicate only with the written word, personalize your correspondence as much as possible. Use the same techniques in your e-mails and letters that we've suggested in your oral exchanges. Add a personal reference or comment. Take the time to update your mailing list so that at a minimum the salutation in your form letter is "Dear Joe," not "Dear Valued Customer." This will not only add at least some emotional element to your communication, it will more likely produce a more personal response.

Don't Interrupt

If you want to make a bad impression, the formula is easy—just interrupt. It tells your partner that what you have to say is more important than what he has to say.

You may interrupt for any number of reasons, perhaps at times with the best of motives. You may be excited and eager to join in, or try to fill a pause to avoid an awkward moment, or "help someone out" as he searches for the right word or call someone's attention to something that needs immediate action. Many other causes for interruptions have no noble explanation. You may try to change topics, get attention, show disagreement or intimidate.

Regardless of your motive, studies have proven that interruptions are among the most antisocial of all behaviors. Men tend to interrupt more than women, and their interruptions are better tolerated since they are expected to be more impatient, aggressive and assertive. But frequent interruptions, by both men and women, tarnish good impressions. They don't just send the message to another that he or she is not important. They also prevent the critical flow of information. They derail the speaker's train of thought, which may never be regained. When interrupted frequently, most people increase the pace of their speech, which provides less opportunity for them to express their thoughts and emotions clearly. When that happens, their message is distorted. Even worse, they may simply stop talking out of frustration.

Interruptions occur not just when you speak over someone. There are many other ways to interrupt. Interruptions can result from something as subtle as the quick inhalation of air that signals impending speech, or as obvious as when you stand and begin to sidle toward the door. Between these extremes, you can interrupt when you turn your body away from the speaker, raise or extend your hands or arms, open your mouth, read your mail, pick up a telephone or turn on the TV.

If you interrupt frequently, invite your family and closest friends to help you modify your behavior. Ask them not to ignore your interruptions as they normally would out of courtesy. Invite them to point out each time you interrupt with a signal as subtle as a shake of the finger or as obvious as the comment, "You interrupted again."

Whatever you want to say usually can, and should, wait. Let the other person finish, and listen intently. Perhaps occasionally you will have forgotten what you wanted to say by the time the other person has finished. But it is better that you should forget what you wanted to say than what they just did.

One related technique that deserves mention is how to score points when someone else in a conversation interrupts the speaker. If another interrupts, wait until the interruption is finished, and turn to the person who was interrupted and ask her to finish her thought. Do this politely, and it won't be taken as thinly veiled chastisement of the person who has interrupted, but it will show the person who was interrupted that you were listening and want her to continue.

AVOID DISTRACTIONS

Mark once worked with a man who had the annoying habit of doing a variety of things as he spoke. He would eat his lunch, buzz his secretary, shuffle through the papers on his desk, comb his hair and sometimes even make phone calls in the middle of a meeting. Mark wondered how much of what he said made it through. With time, Mark found that the man actually was able to do many things at once, and still hear and understand what Mark said. That knowledge came with experience. Most of your contacts won't afford you that luxury, and even when others believe that you are able to understand them while you do something else, they will always question how important they are to you if it appears that you don't think they deserve a few minutes of undivided attention.

Good listening requires focus. Focus on the other person, what he has to say and how he says it. Whether the objective is to communicate your thoughts to others or to gather information about them from which you can formulate your Impression Management Plan, neither you nor the other person should be distracted. Distractions, like interruptions, don't just break the flow of the conversation that may affect the content of what is said, they also add outside stimulation that may garble emotional transmissions.

BE AN OBJECTIVE LISTENER

Attentive listening requires that you keep your personal agenda in check. If you start a conversation focused on only what you want to communicate, you won't be sensitive to everything the other person says and will miss crucial information. The more emotionally invested you are in the outcome you want, the more likely your emotional brain will tint, distort or even ignore, information that is critical to successful communication.

We all tend to see the world through tinted lenses. Of all the keys to good listening, learning to remove your emotionally tinted lenses is the most difficult. We struggle with this every day. Lawyers and witnesses are so consumed with their need to tell their side of the story that they can be oblivious to everything else. The same happens to the sales rep who is so anxious to make a sale that he doesn't see the customer's reservations or impatience, and the woman who is so in love that she doesn't notice her boyfriend's efforts to maintain distance, and the parent who is so frustrated with her child that she doesn't realize that his misbehavior is a cry for her love and attention.

For two decades we have searched for a cure for the "tinted lenses syndrome." We've tried every approach imaginable with lawyers, witnesses and others. We've reviewed the scientific and popular literature for insight. We've even considered the benefit of hypnosis, meditation and prayer. We have found no magic pill. Our emotional brains are simply too powerful for our rational brains to control completely.

But we have found that you can become a *better* listener and process information *more* reliably if you consciously practice objective listening. Objective listening is listening as if you were a third party. It helps create the emotional detachment that allows you to immediately recognize what a creep your best friend is dating when she thinks she's found Mr. Wonderful, and makes it easy for you to hear the irritation in your boss' voice as he discusses your coworker's latest project, even when your office mate whispers to you as you leave the meeting, "I think he really liked my ideas."

The first step to objective listening is to identify when your objectivity is most likely impaired. Four conditions most frequently affect your objectivity. They are red flags that should never be ignored.

- Emotional commitment
- Neediness
- Fear
- Defensiveness

Whenever you have feelings of love, friendship, contempt, anger, envy or other powerful emotions, you can't help but see those who trigger those emotions through tinted lenses. You will have difficulty recognizing good in those you dislike, or bad in those you love. In 1957, Leon Festinger coined the term "cognitive dissonance" to describe the aspect of human nature that causes us to turn a blind eye (and mind) to that which is uncomfortable or disturbing. Your emotional brain wants your world to make sense. It wants your emotional responses to parallel your rational thought. So before it allows your rational brain to process information, it distorts, manipulates or obscures impulses that don't correspond to your emotional framework. When you have an emotional commitment you don't want to acknowledge evidence that it may be misplaced.

This same cognitive dissonance distorts your objectivity when you are needy. You've been out of work for several months and are desperate to find a job. You apply for positions for which you're not qualified, but still make assurances to potential employers that you can do the job. You're lonely, and in search for someone to share your life. Your day care provider moves away without notice, and your need to replace her quickly is so overpowering that you entrust your children to someone you wouldn't trust to care for your pet schnauzer if you thought about it rationally. You're desperate, and desperate people do foolish things. In this state of neediness, you overlook others' flaws, or worse, you attempt to mold your personality to conform to theirs.

Objectivity also falls victim to what many psychologists consider our greatest motivator: fear. You fear loss, pain, death, loneliness, failure. You react—or more precisely, overreact—to your fear. Sometimes the "flight or fight" instinct, rooted deep in your emotional brain, kicks in. You look either for a place to run and hide, or you prepare for battle. Sometimes you do what animals do in the wild when they're neither swift enough to run away, nor strong enough to fight—you freeze in the hope that the threat will pass.

Defensiveness is the last of the common red flags that signal a loss of objectivity. No one likes to be attacked, criticized or condemned. When you are, your mind slams shut. You defend your emotional and intellectual turf and reject any thought or emotion that threatens it.

Whatever the reason for your loss of objectivity, the best remedy is time. Don't make decisions or expect to clearly receive and process, or effectively respond to, what others have to say while your mind is clouded by emotion. Step back and view the situation as if you were a neutral third person sitting quietly in a corner of the room, watching and listening. Disengage temporarily from the emotional upheaval.

The next time you think that your objectivity may be clouded by emotional commitment, neediness, fear or defensiveness, imagine that you have been wading in a silt-bottomed pond and have dropped your watch. The pond is already too cloudy for you to see your watch as it sinks to the bottom. If you trample around looking for the watch, you will only make the water more murky. You are more likely to find the watch if you sit on the shore and wait a while until the water clears.

Whenever possible, use this same approach as you participate in an exchange that presents strong emotional issues for you. Listen carefully to what the other person says. Let it sink in. Don't even think about responding. Think instead about what you can learn about his motivations and emotions. Once you understand them, and have given yourself sufficient time to regain your objectivity, you'll be better able to respond in a way that will further, not defeat, positive impression formation.

BE PATIENT

Modern-day Americans are an impatient lot. We like fast food, fast conversations and fast answers. But people are entirely too complex to understand quickly. Patience is not only essential to achieve objective clarity; it is also necessary to promote good listening skills and ensure the most revealing flow of information.

Patient listeners don't just let someone finish a sentence; they let him finish his thought. That usually takes more than a single breath. Even if he seems to ramble, let him go. No two people get to a point the same way. If you hear others out, you will not only avoid a rude and distracting interruption, you will learn more than if you were to interrupt and direct their thoughts. If you try to put words in someone's mouth, or ideas in his head, he may adopt them, whether they are heartfelt or not. On the other hand, if you let him talk, even if he's long-winded, you will learn what associations he makes between different subjects and he'll volunteer more information about how he thinks and feels, and why, which will allow you to understand him more and to better predict how he is likely to view you.

Impatience—or its twin, overeagerness—often prompts you to respond more quickly after someone has finished talking than you should. Neither you nor your partner may notice this consciously, but your rapid-fire responses are counterproductive in most instances.

A slight pause before you respond has two advantages. First, it gives you a moment to reflect on what someone has said and to collect your own thoughts before you speak. This increases the probability that what you say will further your efforts to make a good impression. If you frequently say to yourself, "I wish I hadn't said that," this approach is particularly warranted.

Perhaps more important, a slight delay sends both a conscious and subconscious message that you have heard, considered and understood what the other person said. The pause need not be long. Pause for a second or two before you reply and watch how much more attentive your partner is when you finally speak. By your pause you have told him, "I have heard and understood what you have said, and am about to respond directly to it." When you do, he will be eager to hear what you have to say.

Patience when initiating a conversation can be just as important as patience during one. There are times when someone just doesn't want to talk. There are other times when he is happy to talk, but just not about certain subjects. If you attempt to force a conversation when someone is unwilling, very little productive conversation usually ensues. You can't expect clear signals from someone if her heart or mind is elsewhere. If she's preoccupied, she won't focus on what you have to say, or even on what she has to say.

If you simply must have the discussion immediately, at least consider how your forced timing may affect the signals you receive. Also bear in mind that if you force a discussion on your timetable you risk being thought of as rude, uncaring or unprofessional.

ACTIVELY PARTICIPATE

Imagine talking to someone who sat perfectly still, face unflinching, eyes steadily fixed on yours, and completely emotionless. Is she hearing what you say? Does she understand it? Does she agree or disagree? Does she have a pulse? Are you motivated to keep talking?

When you actively participate in conversations, you encourage others to speak more freely and honestly. Active visual and verbal feedback stimulates trust, likability and persuasion.

Active listening begins with good eye contact. Others expect eye contact while they speak. It means you're paying attention. Eye contact tells them, "I'm listening, keep talking." If you don't look at them, they will assume you're not listening to them, even if you are.

Your facial reaction to what is said also sends strong emotional messages. Artificial, ill-timed reactions won't be effective. You will seem either insincere or unintelligent. But a genial smile in response to a humorous comment, a broad smile in reaction to a joke, a wince when a painful experience is related, or a compassionate look when someone shares her troubles, will. When your facial expressions mirror what others say, you communicate that you understand and empathize with them.

As you respond, however, make sure your facial expressions don't broadcast judgment, criticism or disbelief unless sending those messages is more important than promoting honest dialogue. People are loath to express their opinions or emotions to someone who reacts with a look that says, "What you have just said is untrue or foolish." When this happens, the speaker will either stop talking or try to persuade you that your judgment is unwarranted. Either way you will: (1) never know what he might have said if you did not offend him; and (2) be judged harshly yourself.

Exaggerated facial expressions are also undesirable. You may get away with a few before the other person's conscious or subconscious brain pulls the "phony" alarm. Even the most egotistical among us know that everything we say is not hilarious, brilliant or charming. When someone pretends that it is, we see the pretense and question his trustworthiness.

Nods and tilts of your head also send emotional signals. Research has shown that tilting the head to the side is generally interpreted as either doubt or confusion. Even if you feel doubtful or confused, don't tilt your head. Instead, wait your turn and express your concerns or ask for clarification. When you explain your doubt or confusion, you increase your partner's ability to perceive your comments in a positive light. If the only message he receives is a cocked head, he may draw the wrong conclusions.

Head nodding is consistently viewed as a sign of affirmation or agreement. It is also seen as a sign of encouragement, empathy and understanding, which says in essence, "Go on, I'm with you." This is a very positive message. That's not to say that you should bob your head up and down as someone talks. Too much head nodding is distracting, and like any exaggerated motion can easily backfire and make the speaker wonder if it represents an honest expression of agreement, a bad habit or the way you disguise your lack of understanding.

Posture and body positioning are also important. Whenever you have an important discussion, try to be close enough to a person to be able to see even the slightest flinch in his eyes or face. It will provide your and his emotional and rational brains with more input to evaluate. You will also feel more in touch if your bodies face one another squarely.

Active nonverbal listening is even more effective when it's accompanied by appropriate verbalizations. Our brains are so accustomed to hearing a quiet, "ah-hah," "yes," "okay," "I see" or "that's interesting" that we don't even record them at a conscious level. For that reason, they don't present distractions or interruptions, although they register in our emotional brains, which reinforces the same positive messages sent by good eye contact, facial expressions and head nodding.

In addition to these cues by which you can signal to others that you are interested in what they say, and understand it, you can add the technique of echoing. As we discussed earlier, echoing is not the same as mimicry. Some communications experts have suggested that people will respond favorably when you simply restate what they have said with exactly the same words.

Him: "I'm really upset about what's going on at work."
You: "I understand, you're really upset about what's going on at work."

Him: "I think my boss doesn't like me."
You: "You're upset because you think your boss doesn't like you."

A little of that goes a long way. Most people will pick up on, and be offended by, that type of mimicry in fairly short order. Effective echoing is not parroting. It's not playing back what someone said as if you were a human tape recorder. The point is not how good your memory is of what someone said, it's how well you understood it. Consider saying instead:

Him: "I'm really upset about what's going on at work."
You: "What's upsetting you?"
Him: "I think my boss doesn't like me."
You: "Why do you think he doesn't like you?"

Both styles clearly demonstrate that you have heard and understood what he has said. The second, however, doesn't simply play it back. It incorporates what has been said and asks for more information, which signals a level of interest beyond the passive parroting displayed in the first example.

A final technique that is effective to establish not only that you are listening but also that you value what someone has said is one Mark learned from his friend Steve. Steve is a great listener in every respect, but he has one practice that places a beautifully tied bow on an already exquisitely wrapped package.

After someone has finished a story, Steve often responds, "That's a great story. I'll have to remember that," or "I've got to remember to tell that story to my wife. She'll get a big kick out of it." This adds that special touch that leaves others feeling just a little bit better than they would have otherwise.

PROMPT OTHERS TO TALK

Most people's favorite topic of conversation is themselves, their interests, their opinions. Great impressions are assured when you tap into, and satisfy, others' love of themselves. Whether you start a conversation with a question about them, or acknowledge a statement they may have made during the course of the conversation, you validate them. But you do more than just stroke their ego. You stimulate great conversation. Your ability to make others talk freely about themselves creates an emotional bond that doesn't exist if they just listen to you. Think about the conversations that have drawn you closer to someone. Did she pour her heart out to you as you patiently listened, or did she listen attentively as you did? Did the most memorable conversations occur when others told you about their passions, or when they listened to you talk about yours? If you're like most people it's the latter. And it doesn't have to be some emotional upheaval or personal revelation that's discussed. It may be as simple as somebody listening to your views about current movies.

We have another test for you. Be honest with yourself. When someone tells you something about herself, how often does the next thing you say focus on *your* experiences or your feelings?

Your colleague tells you she just came back from a bike trip in New England, and you respond, "Oh, I love to cycle, I've been riding for twenty years"; or "I went to New England two years ago, and stayed at a beautiful bed and breakfast inn called the Berkshire Manor." There's nothing wrong with comments that reveal some commonality, but next time, allow the other person to have at least a moment in the sun.

First, acknowledge what she said. When she tells you she just returned from a bike trip in New England, ask, "Where did you go?" or "How long was the trip?" or "Have you been biking long?" Give her a minute to tell you about *her* experience and *her* feelings. *Then* you can add, "I've biked for twenty-five years" too; or "I love New England."

It may seem like a little thing to delay your self-directed comments, but great impressions are made of little things.

BE DIRECT AND RESPONSIVE

When we ask jurors about their impressions of witnesses, one topic that almost always is mentioned is whether the witnesses were direct and responsive in their testimony. Those who prompt comments like, "She seemed very forthright," or "He seemed to try hard to answer the questions," usually end up on the winning side. Those about whom jurors remark, "She was incapable of answering a question directly" or "I felt like he parsed his words too carefully," are usually the losers.

The suggestions we offer to witnesses when we prepare them to make great impressions at trial apply equally in any situation in which people exchange information. Your objective to establish each of the four Compass Qualities is best met if you are direct, don't change subjects, don't ramble and aren't evasive.

If you don't listen carefully, you may accidentally appear evasive, indirect or nonresponsive. There's a reason why someone raises a subject in a conversation—he wants to talk about it. He may want to discuss it because it's on his mind and he wants to express his feelings; or he may ask you about it because he wants some information from you that will help him make decisions—possibly even decisions about you. What he doesn't want is for you to avoid a direct and responsive answer. When this is what you give him, you do everything but satisfy his needs and create a good impression.

SELF-DISCLOSE

It's almost impossible for someone to warm up to you, or trust you implicitly, if he knows nothing about you; and he won't, if you don't show him a glimpse of yourself. It's also almost impossible to connect emotional brain to emotional brain with someone if all you ever exchange are facts and figures. Peoples' level of self-disclosure varies from the closed-mouthed stoic whom you can know for five years, and not know at all, to the heart-on-his-sleeve type who tells you more than you ever wanted to know about him within five minutes. Between these two extremes, the question is how much is too much or too little?

Too much self-disclosure is interpreted as neediness and insecurity, social ineptness and a lack of competence and intelligence. If disclosure seems to be intended to influence behavior, as if a salesman volunteers what a devout Christian he is, or how badly he needs the sale to keep his job, it sounds like a sales technique and adversely affects trustworthiness as well. Too little disclosure, on the other hand, also triggers stereotypical associations of untrustworthiness, as well as lower ratings in the friendliness and competence departments. Our expectation is that honest, friendly and competent people naturally open up a bit.

Appropriate self-disclosure will make you appear relaxed, confident, honest, open and friendly. It also encourages others to disclose, which allows critical bonding to take place. But too much self-disclosure makes others feel very uncomfortable.

The balance between appropriate and inappropriate self-disclosure is usually not difficult to achieve if you keep each of the following five principles in mind.

- *Familiarity.* The nature of your relationship dictates expected levels of self-disclosure. The more intimate the relationship, the more self-disclosure is expected; and the more casual or professional, the more others expect little self-disclosure of a personal nature.
- *Reciprocity.* Everyone expects, or at least wants, others to reciprocate when they show emotion. Self-disclosure is no exception. It's a psy-

chological, "I'll show you mine if you show me yours." The safest way to avoid under- or over-disclosure is to take your cue from the other person. Disclose matters of about the same level of intimacy as others disclose to you.

- *Concealment.* At times, the failure to disclose something about yourself will be perceived as dishonesty. There are occasions when you have an obligation to volunteer if you are to appear honest.
- *Voluntary or Involuntary Disclosure.* What is excessive self-disclosure if volunteered is usually perfectly appropriate if requested.
- *Special Impression Management Needs.* Self-disclosure can be an effective component of your Impression Management Plan. As you give thought to your strengths and weaknesses, think about your attributes and accomplishments that will offset the negative impression people might have if only they knew of them, and look for opportunities to disclose them naturally.

Bear in mind that those who are more reserved may never initiate more intimate discussions, but often welcome and respond to them. Test the water slowly. Raise a topic that is only slightly personal or private. If they rebuff your efforts, back off and respect their desire for privacy. If they seem to welcome a more personal dialogue, by all means pursue it— slowly. Self-disclosure builds trust that opens emotional doors. And when it does, it provides valuable listening material.

CHAPTER 11

Content of Communication

We may be able to land men on the moon and send messages around the world in a millisecond on the World Wide Web, but people today just don't turn a phrase the way they used to. Your choice of words, and how you combine them, present opportunities to communicate more than just facts and ideas. Carefully chosen words paint mental pictures from which feelings and emotions emerge. As Mark Twain wrote, "The difference between the right word and the almost right word is the difference between lightning and a lightning-bug."

You will recall our earlier discussion of Albert Mahrabian's study that found that only 7 percent of the impression listeners formed of a message was derived from content, while 38 percent was communicated by vocal qualities and 55 percent by facial and body expressions. This is true in certain situations, but the importance of content relative to the other six Colors increases dramatically when you discuss a topic of particular interest or importance to your audience; when you communicate logical and factual information rather than emotion-laden content; when the content of what you say is consistent with your nonverbal communication; and when your listener is familiar with your nonverbal communication style.

Because content generally yields to the impact of the other six Colors when there is an inconsistency among them, content alone will seldom salvage an otherwise negative impression. The opposite isn't true. A single insulting comment, rude remark or faux pas can make such a powerful negative impression that it will overpower an otherwise positive one.

WRITTEN VERSUS ORAL CONTENT

All content is not created equal. Since the written word presents an opportunity for more reflection than is possible when you speak, rational-brain-oriented expectations are higher. We don't expect others to be as articulate during extemporaneous speech as when they write. Furthermore, there are no nonverbal behaviors to add meaning to words on a page or screen. As a result, your written words frequently will be subject to more critical scrutiny than your spoken words.

When you write letters, e-mails or proposals, recognize that misspelling, typographical errors and improper punctuation all detract from a favorable image. Don't just rely on your spell check, which doesn't know the difference between "two" and "too," "here" and "hear," or "six" and "sex." Pay attention to your grammar and writing style. If you tend to write frequently to those who will form impressions of you, and you have long since forgotten what you learned in English class, check out a copy of Strunk and White's *The Elements of Style* or a similar book.

When you speak or write, bear in mind that effective written and spoken communication rely on very different foundations. Written words, transmitted without the aid of sound or sight, communicate primarily to the rational brain. But when people can hear and see us speak, we are able to communicate more directly to others' emotional brains. When we have read the written transcripts of some of the most inspiring courtroom closing arguments, we are often surprised to see that they don't read very well. On the other hand, many speeches laden with insightful content fail to inspire when delivered by a poor speaker.

If you choose your words as carefully when you speak as when you write, you will lose spontaneity. As you struggle to select the right words and string them together in perfect order, or worse yet, read from a script, you will sound like a White House press secretary who carefully parses each word as she addresses a sensitive issue. Such precision is seldom required in oral communication, and invariably delivers the death blow to any hope of communicating emotionally and enthusiastically. Don't worry that you may sacrifice some precision; you will compensate for that loss with passion and persuasiveness. Afterwards, you may think back with your rational brain and fashion a better way to have said what you did, but that will remain your secret. If you communicate spontaneously and enthusiastically orally, your audience will never know what you might have said better.

That is not to say that you should make a habit of "winging it" when you speak. Instead, you should prepare to be spontaneous. Don't write out your speech word-for-word and memorize it. If you have something important to communicate, outline it—either on paper or in your mind. Think through each point you want to make and how you intend to make it. Commit the outline to memory or jot down a few key words on a note card for each point. If you structure your presentation in your mind, you will communicate what you planned to say and give yourself the latitude to be spontaneous and improvise during your presentation.

CONTENT "DOS"

After our years of asking individuals about their impressions not only of witnesses and lawyers, but also of politicians, celebrities and other news-makers, it has become clear that certain components of the content of what people say warrant inclusion in the "dos" column of every Impression Management Plan. Other ways individuals paint a picture of themselves through the content of what they say consistently produce negative impressions, and always should be included in the "don'ts" column. What follows are those aspects of content you should always stress.

MAKE YOUR MESSAGE UNDERSTANDABLE

The first function of communication is to be understood. As Albert Einstein said, "Everything should be made as simple as possible—but no simpler." Your audience will appreciate your ability to communicate coherently, even if you use simple terms and concepts. There are two rules that you can apply effectively in every communication to achieve this goal:

- *Divide Your Communication into Digestible Bites:* Your ability to communicate complex thoughts and ideas depends on your capacity to broadcast them in short, manageable bursts with sufficient time between them for each burst to be absorbed. If you speak too quickly or run your thoughts together, you create information overload. When that happens, people become frustrated and are likely to think you are either arrogant, inconsiderate or unable to communicate clearly.

    Make it a practice to divide what you want to say into small bite-size pieces. Communicate each portion slowly and incorporate some dividing line between the bursts. The dividing line can be a pause, a short summary of what you just said, or a discussion of each burst before proceeding to the next. We have seen how effective these techniques are when lawyers or witnesses use them in trial. They can be equally effective when used in sales presentations or in casual discussions among friends. They make your communications "user friendly," which in turn makes you appear more sensitive and intelligent.

- *Match Your Language to Your Audience:* Both your vocabulary and conversation topics should match your audience. Discussing existentialist authors with a group of literature bugs might impress them, but the same conversation in most lunch rooms will make you appear arrogant or obnoxious, even if you use simple vocabulary.

  Your choice of both vocabulary and conversational topics should reflect the interests and aptitude of your audience. You might think you will impress others with your vocabulary and mastery of obscure topics, and you may in fact project intelligence when you do. But common sense is more highly regarded than intelligence, and others won't think you have very good judgment if you appear too foolish or inconsiderate to recognize when you speak over their heads.

There are occasions, however, when you can appeal to your audience if you incorporate words of art or technical jargon into your speech. When you know that someone communicates in a particular lingo, learn a little bit about it and sprinkle it throughout your conversation. As Lee Iaccoca observed: "It's important to talk to people in their own language. If you do it well, they will say, God, he said exactly what I was thinking. And when they begin to respect you, they will follow you to the death."

USE EXPRESSIVE WORDS

The average adult knows approximately 10,000 words, yet regularly uses as little as 10 to 20 percent of his vocabulary. Can you image a pianist who used only 8 to 16 of the 88 keys on his piano to try to communicate the emotion of a song? Yet that is exactly what most of us do every day.

Some of the words we use most frequently are not expressive. If someone asked you what you thought of a movie or your dinner, you might respond: "It was fine." Do you mean, "fine" as in "fine wine," or "fine art?" Or do you mean, "fine" as in "excellent, good, *fine* or poor?" "Fine" can be an endorsement or a silent indictment. There are hundreds of words that, like "fine," express very little meaning. They are fillers. Choose words that are more expressive, like "great" or "terrific" or "wonderful" if you want to express pleasure, and words like "adequate" or "satisfactory" if your intent is to communicate that the movie or meal was okay, but nothing more. These words won't be misunderstood.

Use Humor

Life is intense. Car pools, deadlines, bills, household duties—they can beat us down until we become drones who escape our daily tedium only in our sleep—that is, if we can sleep. Humor and laughter are antidotes for just about anything that ails us. The best part about humor is that you can fill the prescription yourself as often as you like, and share it freely with your friends, family and coworkers. It is a gift that you can give everyone in your life; and they will thank you for it.

Humor is valued so highly because it makes us feel good. It brings a smile to our face when we are depressed, relieves stress when we are anxious and defuses tension. It is little wonder that something so highly prized enhances any Impression Management Plan.

When you laugh, smile and exchange humor, you seem more natural and relaxed. This enhances your impression of caring, humility and capability, as one would expect. But lighthearted humor is also associated with honesty.

Laughter and good humor are not just valuable in personal relationships. They also contribute to the best business environments. Intense, humorless environments quash creativity and morale as thoroughly as a young boy stomping on a beetle. Humor stimulates us and leads naturally to supportiveness, teamwork, good morale and creativity.

Our research to identify the most effective and positive ways to express humor led us to a conclusion that parallels the observations of others who have examined the question: No one technique works for everyone. What we did find, however, is that certain characteristics of humor are consistently well received. Among them are: the ability to tell, *and take,* a joke; the ability to find humor in events that arise from everyday life; humor characterized by optimism and good cheer; and an appreciation for the humor of others.

Although it is difficult to write a prescription for any one individual for how to project humor, it is easy to identify those attempts at humor that convey consistently negative associations.

- *Cruel Humor:* Humor at someone else's expense is perceived in a negative light, not just by its victim, but by all who witness it. Humor should be used as a tool to build, not destroy, relationships. It should create bonds, not distance. It should be soft, not sharp. Caustic humor erects barriers and is toxic to comfortable and respectful relationships.
- *Buffoonery:* No one is drawn to a bufoon who constantly makes jokes that he appreciates more than anyone else in the room. Those who fall into this category are seen as egotistical dolts, whose humor is tiresome, not invigorating.

- *Self-Deprecating Humor:* Self-deprecating humor, if not overdone, effectively communicates humility and openness and tells others that if you don't take yourself too seriously, you probably won't be hypercritical of their foibles. But if you are too harsh in your self-criticism, you will be perceived as weak and insecure, not humble. Consistent self-deprecating behavior becomes tiresome and uncomfortable for those who witness it.

- *Silly Jokes or Puns:* Silly jokes or puns may not impress others with your wit, but instead give them the impression that you are goofy, insecure, immature or self-impressed. Puns may be the most intellectually complex form of humor, but they usually are not well regarded except by other punsters. More often, they are seen as irrelevant distractions forced into a conversation to display your wit.

USE POSITIVE WORDS

The importance of a "can do" attitude was driven home in an exchange Mark recently had with a travel agent. He decided at the last moment to book a family ski vacation during the Christmas holidays. He knew he would have difficulty finding appropriate accommodations. When he called a travel agent and advised her of his predicament, she asked, "Why did *you* wait so long? It would have been better if *you* started earlier." As his youngest son would say, "No, duh." After politely explaining that his reasons were rather complicated and not particularly relevant, he was met with more negativism. "I don't think *you'll* be able to find a place. Everything will be booked." Mark patiently asked her to try. With a deep sigh, she said "Oh, all right. I'll get back to you." He had to fight back the urge to say: "I'm sorry if I'm putting you out."

After he hung up, Mark thought it might be best to call another travel agent, which he did. In sharp contrast to the previous conversation he was told, "*We* may not have a lot of options, but if the ultimate location isn't critical, I'm sure *we* can find something." She sounded as if she looked forward to the challenge.

As it turned out, the first travel agent never called Mark back, and the second was able to find great accommodations.

The difference between the two travel agents highlights the two ways you can incorporate positive expression in your speech. First, the distinction between the "can do," and "can't do" attitude of the two is obvious. Somewhat more subtle, but equally important: the first travel agent made no effort to communicate that she was prepared to "partner" with Mark to find a place to stay. Her comments, "Why did *you* wait so long?" and "I don't think *you'll* be able to find a place" distanced her from him. It was clearly Mark's problem, not hers. In contrast, the second said, "*We* may not have a lot of options," and "*We* can find something." She was an advocate, a team member, someone who would fight for Mark, not place barriers in his path.

Many words that convey negativity are registered and processed by the emotional brain en route to the rational brain. The message the rational brain ultimately receives is that the person who uses negative words is predisposed to failure. On the other hand, when you use positive words, you create enthusiasm and confidence that tells others that if anyone can get the job done, it's you.

Read through the following list of words and think about the impression you would have of someone who favors them:

Can't, won't, shouldn't, wouldn't, must not, should not, fail, afraid, unavoidable, uncontrollable, impossible, overwhelming, hopeless, incapable, problem, crisis, catastrophe.

Now review these words and consider the impression that you would have of those who choose them:

Can, will, may, eager, hopeful, confident, solve, resolve, manage, feasible, succeed, accomplish, productive, achieve, alternatives, innovative, plan, opportunity, challenge, potential.

Those words we identified first send messages of failure, incapacity and defeatism, and directly influence the impression of those who use them. The words in the second group, however, reflect hope, optimism, resolve, commitment, imagination and success.

The same contrast exists between words that do or don't reflect the concept of "partnership," which is essential to let others know that they are important to you, and that you will meet their needs. This can be seen in words such as these. First the positive:

We, our, team, together, help, guide, cooperate, confer, collaborate, build, coordinate, care, loyal, united and consult.

Contrast these with words of divisiveness.

I, me, mine, my, control, blame, fault and insist.

When you use words that convey a "can do" attitude, you create an impression of capability. Words of partnership strike an even more central chord. They show that there is a bond that joins two or more people with one common purpose. Others will inherently trust and like you if you are willing to invest yourself in their endeavors.

We have sat through hundreds of meetings between lawyers and clients that are no different than those that occur between salesmen and customers, friends or spouses. We have heard lawyers who consistently refer to "the problems in *your* case," or "the biggest hurdle *you* must overcome." We also have heard those who say, "*we can* address the *challenges our* case presents," and "if *we* focus *our* efforts to overcome these obstacles, *we will* be *able* to *help* a jury come to the right conclusion." Those attorneys who focus on the negative and refuse to take any responsibility in a joint effort leave their clients doubtful and insecure. Those who project a solution and team-oriented approach invariably instill confidence and trust. A mid-level executive who presents a concept for a companywide program in a positive and team-oriented way, or a spouse who addresses parenting issues with optimism and unity, sends the same message.

BE LIBERAL WITH YOUR COMPLIMENTS

An honest compliment is a cherished prize, but compliments should not be handed out disingenuously. A forced compliment under circumstances that suggest it is contrived doesn't say "You're important." It says, "I think so little of you that I believe that I can manipulate you to do or think what I want by stroking your ego." Give compliments when they are due. If you keep your eyes open, you'll have no trouble finding opportunities. But don't force them.

To compliment someone most effectively, you need to determine first where he most wants validation. Like beauty, compliments are seen through the eyes of the beholder. The most meaningful compliments recognize not what you necessarily consider important, but what the person you compliment does. If someone takes great pride in his clothing but cares little about his computer prowess, an admiring word about his ensemble will score more points than praise of how fast he can store data on a floppy disk. A misguided male superior might think a compliment on his female subordinate's wardrobe, hairstyle or new makeup will make her feel valued. But if what she craves is to be complimented on her work product and executive potential by her boss, not her looks, the compliment may do more harm than good. Yet a sincere "You look stunning" might be just the compliment she wants from her boyfriend as she meets him at the door on their way out for the evening.

Compliments are a two-way street. The way a compliment is received also sends a message about the esteem with which you hold the one who offers the compliment. We have been socialized to consider it immodest to acknowledge compliments with much more than a bashful "Thank you." Yet when you brush off a compliment with an awkward, "It was nothing," as you glance away or continue whatever task is at hand, you deny the person who gave you the compliment the opportunity to feel good about extending it. It can be demoralizing to try to show someone you value him only to be met with a response that tells you that it makes little difference how you feel.

When you receive a compliment, stop what you are doing and allow yourself and the person who has extended the compliment to savor the moment. Give her positive reinforcement by telling her, "That is most gracious of you," or "You are very kind." Better yet, let her know the esteem with which you hold her by saying, "It means a lot to me to have you say that."

APOLOGIZE WHEN WARRANTED

In the 1949 screenplay *She Wore a Yellow Ribbon*, John Wayne said, "Never apologize and never explain—it's a sign of weakness." We couldn't disagree more. A sincere apology enhances others' impressions of each of the four Compass Qualities. Those who openly, candidly and unequivocally apologize are more often forgiven than those who don't. There is something about human nature that makes us want to extend forgiveness to those who sincerely ask for it, and to exact some level of vengeance on those who refuse to apologize even when they should.

When you have done or said something that warrants an apology, apologize and mean it. A halfhearted or insincere apology can be worse than none at all. An equivocal "I'm sorry," said without conviction and humility, doesn't work like a "Get Out of Jail Free Card." Don't lay blame elsewhere, don't qualify your apology and, whatever you do, don't gut an otherwise effective apology by immediately following it with the word, "But." An "I'm sorry, but . . ." will be perceived as an excuse, not an apology.

If you are late for a meeting, don't say, "I'm sorry, but the traffic was bad." Say, "I'm sorry, I didn't anticipate how heavy traffic would be." If you say something hurtful to someone, don't expect it to be forgiven if you say, "I'm sorry, but I think you are overreacting." If an apology is warranted, come right out and apologize. Say, "I'm sorry I hurt your feelings. I hope you can forgive me." Chances are, he or she will.

CONTENT DON'TS

Profanity, slang, sarcasm, gossip, biting humor and offensive remarks are so potent that they can single-handedly destroy the impression you make on others. But there are many other toxic traits that will seriously diminish your impression, or in combination deal it a deathblow.

Many of these traits have been mentioned frequently in our surveys and interviews as a basis to discredit someone's trustworthiness, caring, humility or capability. Most of them have no redeeming value. In those rare cases when the traits can be both beneficial and harmful, we will suggest ways to manage them effectively.

Avoid Assurances of Honesty

Don't start sentences with "Frankly," "To be perfectly candid" or "To be honest." Many people react to such introductory remarks with suspicion. Comments such as, "Every time he started a sentence 'to be frank,' I wondered how frank he really was," are common.

Don't Guess as if You Knew

If you don't know something, admit that you don't. If you try to "wing it" and profess actual knowledge that others later discover you didn't have, they will assume that you either knew you misstated the facts when you made your statement, have little regard for the truth or are too lazy to make the effort to be accurate.

Don't Exaggerate or Engage in Hyperbole

No one always knows the best restaurant, has the perfect plan or is the most knowledgeable person about a particular subject. How many times can you say that you saw "the lousiest movie I've ever seen in my life," encountered "the most dishonest person on the planet" or have had "the worst experience with a dentist, doctor, lawyer or mechanic" of anyone in the room? If you consistently speak in extremes, you lose credibility.

Avoid the Canned Presentation

Preparation is essential to a good impression. But it can be overdone. When a presentation appears to be "canned," it raises suspicion, whether in a business setting, or across the table at dinner with a friend. If you sound as if you are reading from a prepared speech, particularly about a topic that is emotional, rather than factual, people will tend to question your sincerity. They want to hear you speak from your heart, not from a script.

Don't Be Too Defensive

There are times when people will expect you to defend yourself. Your failure to deny or explain incriminating facts or inferences often will be interpreted as an admission of wrongdoing. As Chris Matthews said in *Hardball,* "Most people believe that if any shot goes unanswered it must be true." On the other hand, the type of blatant defensiveness that led Shakespeare to write, "Methinks the lady doth protest too much," also is seen as a sign of dishonesty.

Defensiveness can take the form of withdrawal, aggression or overselling. If you fall silent when you feel attacked, your action may be interpreted as a reflection that you have no defense or justification for your behavior. Yet, if you try to deflect criticism or defend yourself too vigorously, others may assume you have adopted a "best defense is a good offense" posture, particularly if you attack your accuser.

The best way to manage a situation in which you feel defensive because you have been unfairly attacked, criticized or questioned is usually to acknowledge and discuss your emotional response openly. This will allow others to understand why you feel defensive, and in most cases will produce the many benefits that arise when you communicate openly and honestly.

If you are caught in a lie, half-truth or concealment, don't become defensive and try to justify your actions. Apologize, and ask for forgiveness. Don't try to laugh it off, or you will project a casual attitude toward the truth. Others need to know that you appreciate that what you did was wrong, and serious.

Avoid Ingratiating Behavior

The formal word for someone who engages in extreme ingratiating behavior is "sycophant." The disdain with which the average person holds such behavior is reflected in the much more common terms: "kiss up," "suck up," and "brown-noser," to cite but three of the tamest. It's great to agree with others, compliment them and show them that you are eager to please. But if you appear to be too solicitous, you will seem insecure, or worse, dishonest.

Overtly ingratiating behavior is a form of manipulation, which is seen as a form of deceit. It is an effort to induce others to think or act toward you in certain ways by appealing to their egos. The direct subject of your ingratiating behavior may be so swept away by her own ego that she will perceive your conduct as nothing more than justified adoration. But others who witness such behavior will usually see it in a very different light.

NEVER MAKE PROMISES YOU CAN'T KEEP

If you consistently make promises you don't fulfill, others may think you just want to keep everyone happy and tell them what they want to hear. Or they may conclude that you just don't think things through before you speak. Or worst of all, they may think you have very little regard for the need to fulfill your promises. In any event, you will damage your credibility. If you regularly fail to fulfill your commitments, even relatively insignificant commitments, jot a note down in the "don'ts" column of your Impression Management Plan to make an effort to think through your ability to perform before you promise performance.

AVOID WEASEL WORDS

"Weasel words" are words and phrases that are equivocal and evasive, and offer plenty of room for interpretation or misinterpretation. There is nothing inherently wrong with words like, "I don't remember," "I don't recall," "maybe" and "possibly." But they are fatal when they are used in circumstances in which others expect a commitment or an absolute statement upon which they can rely.

DON'T QUESTION EVERYONE ELSE'S HONESTY

If you constantly question others' trustworthiness, you will be suspected of "projecting." Think about someone you believe is naively trusting. Do you ever doubt her trustworthiness? Now reflect on someone you consider highly suspicious of others. Do you have the same confidence in his trustworthiness? Those who are trusting demonstrate a mental framework in which dishonesty is foreign. They don't consider the possibility that others deceive them, because they themselves are not deceitful. Those who constantly question others' trustworthiness suggest that they think dishonesty is a prominent component in every interaction.

USE KIND, NOT HARSH, WORDS

Some words are so powerfully charged that using them, even in isolation, can have a lingering effect. Others are more subtle, but when used frequently have an additive effect that can be just as negative. On the other hand, as Mother Teresa said, "Kind words can be short and easy to speak, but their echoes are truly endless."

Others' perception of your caring nature is derived both from what you say to them, and what you say about others. Harsh remarks directly toward the person who forms an impression of you will be taken more personally, and given greater weight in the impression formation process. But don't assume that you can speak harshly of those who aren't participants in a conversation without repercussions.

On those rare occasions when an unflattering description of someone is necessary, choose your words carefully. You don't need to call someone "stupid." You can say, "She's not very bright." The meaning is the same, but the impact is very different. You can say someone is "ugly" or "not very attractive"; an "incompetent typist" or "not very proficient"; "a damn liar" or "untruthful"; "a bum" or "homeless"; "a loudmouth" or "too talkative"; "a slut" or "promiscuous." In each of these cases, and in virtually every other situation, the same meaning can be communicated with a sharp, acidic term or an equally descriptive but kinder word.

You also can convey either caring or harshness on a broader scale. If you choose, you can notice and mention only the bad in others. Or you can adopt a more charitable view. You can hear someone else's ideas and immediately point out any flaws or inconsistencies, or you can first recognize whatever kernels of wisdom might exist and then address any concerns you might have.

Each of us has known a handful of people who never speak ill of others. We hold them in high regard. We admire them, trust them, feel comfortable around them. They not only don't criticize us, they also don't speak harshly of anyone. If you admire those traits in others, emulate them. Keep your negative thoughts to yourself unless you truly need to express them; and if you do, choose your words carefully to show compassion.

AVOID FIGHTIN' WORDS

In John Grisham's *The Rainmaker,* the insurance adjuster who denies the claim of a woman whose son is dying of cancer points out that her claim had been denied on many prior occasions and that she must be "stupid, stupid, stupid" to have resubmitted it. We wish such exchanges took place only in fiction. Unfortunately, they occur frequently. Words like "stupid," "ridiculous," "ugly" and "bumbling," and phrases like, "That's the dumbest idea I've ever heard," and "This report is a piece of junk" have the same effect as pouring gasoline on a fire. They trigger violent emotional reactions and invite confrontation. They are not simply unkind and harsh, they provoke retaliation, which quickly escalates into the worst kind of unproductive communication. Such hostile words can't be justified as just "telling it like it is," because there are too many other ways to express yourself to justify the resort to fightin' words.

DON'T SHOW DISRESPECT FOR OTHERS

We cringe every time we hear a lawyer examine a homemaker during jury selection and ask, "Are you *just* a housewife?" or men refer to the "office girls" or whites refer to minorities as "them." Anytime you begin a description of someone as "just a . . ." or describe a person or group as "them," you suggest not only that they are different from you, but also that they are less worthwhile. These are demeaning, hurtful, uncaring terms. Excise them from your vocabulary.

DON'T BE JUDGMENTAL

If you want to halt open communication, just pass judgment on what someone has said or done. Let her know that you think she is evil, foolish, uncaring, immoral or unethical. If she doesn't clam up altogether, she will become defensive.

Don't just resist the temptation to judge what people have done or said; fight the urge to tell them how they should, must or ought to think or behave. If invited, make suggestions and talk about how they might approach a problem. Propose alternatives and discuss their advantages and disadvantages. If you feel compelled to give your opinion even when it hasn't been requested, ask for permission. Say, "Can I make a suggestion?" or "Maybe I can help you work through your options." Let others know you care about them, but don't force your views upon them unless you have a relationship in which your intervention is expected whether or not it is invited, such as a parent and child, employer and employee or teacher and student.

AVOID UNNECESSARY SELF-PROMOTION

Research indicates that self-promoters are often thought to be more competent. If their self-promotion includes cocky body language and vocal qualities, they are also considered less likable. Self-promotion, accompanied by arrogant or self-centered nonverbal behavior, also tends to raise doubts about an individual's truthfulness. Those who tout themselves verbally but communicate humility through their nonverbal behavior are often able to overcome the disdain held toward cocky self-promoters.

The two keys to managing self-promotion effectively are: first, always accompany your statements with humble nonverbal behavior; and second, don't insert self-promotion when it's not called for.

In the workplace, where you sometimes need to promote yourself, your expressions of confidence will not be perceived as arrogance if you demonstrate your lack of self-absorption in other ways. If you pour coffee for others in the staff room, volunteer to help secretaries with copy projects, or carry packages to the customers' cars, others will be predisposed to believe that you are humble. When you assume a leadership role in a meeting and express your merits firmly and confidently but with relaxed and open body language and a soothing voice, others will see you as a leader to be admired and followed, not as an arrogant dictator against whom to rebel.

Excessive self-criticism can be as damaging to your image as overt self-promotion. It violates others' expectations, which tends to draw attention to your self-effacing comments. As with other traits that violate expectations, self-effacing behavior frequently results in low likability ratings and almost always causes the listener to believe the speaker is not socially adept. Self-deprecating comments also detract from the impression of capability, since even if made in jest, others often assume there is some truth to them.

There are a few simple techniques that will help temper your self-promotion when you find it is truly necessary.

- *Recognize Your Accomplishments and Abilities, but Give Credit Elsewhere.* Acknowledge: "I'm very proud of what I've accomplished," but where appropriate add, "but I recognize that I have benefited immensely from the support and assistance of so many others without whom I could never have achieved any measure of success."

- *Express Gratitude for Your Good Fortune.* Thankfulness for your abilities shows both pride and humility. Preface your self-praise with words like, "I was blessed with a good memory," or "I'm lucky to have been in the right place at the right time."
- *Embrace the Word "We."* Consider the difference between a manager who says, "I have the most successful sales department in the entire company," and the one who says "Our sales department is the most successful in the entire company." To include yourself within a group worthy of praise, even a group as small as two, or even one that you lead, does not dilute your worth, but helps remove the toxin of arrogance.
- *Don't Take Yourself Too Seriously.* Any intense focus on yourself, either critical or adoring, reflects self-centeredness.

USE GOOD GRAMMAR

In one poll, 83 percent of those surveyed said bad grammar "annoyed" them. In another survey of 2,000 people, more than 86 percent said that good grammar creates positive impressions. Those who speak grammatically are assumed to be more intelligent, competent and professional than those who don't.

We cannot overemphasize how important it is for you to objectively assess whether your speech is grammatical. If it is not, you should make an effort to improve it. Listen to tapes of your own speech, and you will identify most of your grammatical lapses. Pay attention to those who use good grammar and learn from them. Go to the bookstore or library and find some basic grammar texts. Play grammar games with your children at the dinner table, so not only you, but they, will learn better grammar.

Remember that good grammar is particularly important when you communicate in writing; when content, and to a lesser extent, communication style, are the only two Colors that paint the image of you. Take a few extra minutes to draft your correspondence, and proofread it carefully. A grammatical slip that might not be noticed in an oral conversation is often obvious when reduced to writing.

PRONOUNCE WORDS PROPERLY

Everything we've said about good grammar is true of good pronunciation. Don't think it doesn't matter if you pronounce a word incorrectly—it does. A mispronounced word registers in the listener's mind as a misused word, even though it may be perfectly appropriate in context.

People often continue to mispronounce words that they have heard pronounced correctly many times. Don't fall into that trap. If you pronounce a word differently than others, or if you don't know how to pronounce a word, look it up in the dictionary and see how it should be pronounced. If on the spur of the moment you consider using a word you don't know how to pronounce, opt for a synonym.

AVOID HIGHBROW VOCABULARY
AND SNOBBISH WORDS

We have a simple guideline we give witnesses to govern their choice of words: "Don't use fancy words when plain words will do." We don't limit this just to use of words that may not be understood. We also include words that sound formal or snooty. There are occasions when only the million-dollar word fits perfectly. But they are few.

Any increase in the capability ratings of those who use more formal and sophisticated vocabulary is usually more than offset by lower ratings in other categories. For example, in one study speakers used either vocabulary based on Latin roots such as "inundation," "domicile" and "facade," or their less formal synonyms, "flood," "house" and "face." Those who used the Latinate forms were considered more difficult to understand and harder to listen to and their audience was more easily distracted. They were also considered pompous and less friendly. Those who used simpler terms were considered more flexible, helpful, sociable and accommodating.

There are also certain words that convey an air of arrogance. Someone who describes her dinner as "divine," the shrimp "to die for" and the theater production "glorious" will seem to have adopted an air of sophistication. If you think others will be impressed, think again. The chances are much better that they'll consider you snobbish and pompous.

SKIP THE FANFARE

Good deeds may occasionally go unnoticed, but usually those who are the beneficiary of your kindness will recognize and appreciate it. When you accompany every good deed with fanfare, you don't enhance the impression of your generosity. Instead, you suggest that you expect something in return. You did not give freely and charitably. You gave, so that you would get—recognition, appreciation, adulation, payback of one kind or another. Generosity, favors, good deeds of all types, are bricks from which wonderful impressions are built. Don't allow fanfare to undermine them.

DON'T SOUND LIKE
A BROKEN RECORD

Someone tells a joke, and no one laughs. In fact, no one even acknowledges the jokester. He tells the joke again with no greater response. Everyone heard the joke the first time, and definitely the second. They just ignored it. But the jokester wants attention. He wants recognition. He thinks he said something funny and wants everyone to appreciate his wit.

The conversation winds its way from topic to topic. Everyone goes with the flow, except one person. She constantly pulls the conversation back to her favorite topic, which is usually one of her special interests. Each time she brings the conversation back to her topic of choice, someone else redirects it. She pulls it back again.

If you tell a joke, make a pun or what you believe to be a witty observation, chances are others heard it. They just don't care about it, or feel awkward responding to it. Maybe they didn't find it all that funny, and neither want to pretend to enjoy your humor, nor to offend you. Perhaps the subject that you found so enthralling holds no interest to them. They want to talk about something else.

Play your favorite tune once. If no one asks to hear it again, move on.

DON'T PREACH

Sometimes your urge to express your opinions is so irrepressible that you become like an evangelical preacher intent on converting the nonbelievers. You don't just express your opinions. You tell others that they "should," "must" or "need to" think and act as you do, as if the world will come to an end if they don't. They need to dump their girlfriend because she's no good, or be more strict with their children, network their computers at work or eat bran. In most cases you firmly believe that you have the answer, and that you will make others' lives better if you can just convince them. But no one likes to be preached to. It's the ultimate form of opinionated communication—and highly offensive to most.

ELIMINATE "FILLER" WORDS

Many "filler words" can creep into your speech—"you know," "like," "okay," "well," "sorta," "um," "er," "uhh." Some people who use filler words have one or two favorites. Others have quite a repertoire.

Most people are irritated by filler words. Even those who aren't annoyed typically think those who lace their conversation with filler words are less intelligent, confident and competent. Filler words can raise questions about trustworthiness as well, since people identify the frequent use of filler words as a technique to buy time while the speaker plans what to say, or as a trait indicating nervousness, which in turn is often associated with dishonesty.

Even if you have used the same filler word or words for years, you can rid yourself of this habit remarkably quickly if you follow this simple four-step process:

1. Tape your speech frequently enough that you forget about the tape recorder, and resume your normal speech patterns.
2. Play back the tape and notice how frequently you use filler words, and what filler words you tend to favor.
3. Each time you use a filler word later in conversation pause for a second and take a shallow breath while you think to yourself, "stop that." The pause won't be as distracting to others as you might fear. In any event, it can't be any worse than filling the void with a protracted "uh."
4. Ask your closest friends and family members to repeat any filler words you use to help you recognize when you use them.

If you work with this program for a week or two, you will find that filler words will disappear.

AVOID EUPHEMISMS

Cats use the "sand box," toddlers the "potty" and young girls the "little girls room." Mature, intelligent, capable adults use the "bathroom," "restroom" or "lavatory." Most euphemisms create much the same impression as when someone speaks with a childlike voice—immaturity, and a lack of social sophistication, intelligence, competence and professionalism. Men use euphemisms less frequently than women, but when they do, the response is even more dramatic since their use of euphemisms is even further beyond common expectations.

Don't Use "Cutesy" Language

Like euphemisms, cute sayings may sound friendly and unpretentious, but they detract from your image. If you say, "yellow" or "howdy doody" instead of "hello," or you say "okey-dokey" instead of "okay," it will show informality and a lack of pretension. It will also seem immature, unsophisticated and will not enhance your image as an intelligent, capable individual. It's not worth the trade-off. Let someone know you are pleased to hear from him with an enthusiastic tone of voice and a friendly smile, but keep the "howdy doodies" to yourself.

Don't Overuse Clichés

Most composition books will tell you to avoid clichés like grizzly bears—stay as far away from them as possible. We disagree. Many clichés, like maxims and proverbs, are popular because they express complex thoughts in relatively few words. Because of their frequent usage, they have developed a clear meaning and serve as shorthand to communicate complex messages.

"You can lead a horse to water, but you can't make him drink," for example, is a very descriptive phrase, the meaning of which everyone understands instantly. Just try to write out the concept it embodies in enough detail to deliver the same message and you will see just how efficiently and effectively clichés can communicate.

With that said, we'll again caution, if you'll pardon the cliché, "You can have too much of a good thing." If clichés dominate your speech, you will appear unimaginative and less intelligent. If you use more than one or two clichés in any conversation, you probably overuse them. Clichés should be used even more sparingly when you write, particularly in professional correspondence where they appear uncreative.

AVOID TRENDY WORDS AND SLANG

Those who favor slang and hip words are often considered shallow, unconfident and less competent. Trendy vocabulary carries much the same associations as trendy clothing styles. They will make you appear less credible and capable. Save such terminology for your teenagers. Most others won't be impressed.

DON'T USE INAPPROPRIATELY CASUAL WORDS

"Yup," "yeah" and "yes" have identical meaning. Yet each carries different associations. "Yup" connotes less sophistication and education. "Yeah" is more casual and less professional than "yes," which is the most formal.

It is usually good to inject a certain degree of informality into your conversations. It enhances the appearance of a caring and humble nature. But choose another method. Very casual words, phrases or guttural utterances are too consistently interpreted negatively. Instead, consider relaxing your image with more casual clothes and body language, a warmer conversational tone of voice and a comfortable environment.

CHAPTER 12

Actions

One morning a member of St. Francis of Assisi's Order learned that St. Francis was to travel into town to preach that day. He asked to join him. They walked through town for hours tending to the poor and ill. At the end of the day St. Francis told his young follower it was time to return to the monastery. The young monk asked, "I thought we were going into town to preach." St. Francis replied, "My son, we did preach. We were preaching while we were walking. We were watched by many and our behavior was closely observed. It is no use to walk anywhere to preach unless we preach everywhere as we walk!"

That is the essence of the sixth of the seven Colors—actions. You are judged by everything you do and don't do. Early in relationships others will rely on those characteristics they can most readily see or hear. Others will assume that your actions will be consistent with your other traits, but, in time, those initial impressions either will be reinforced or dispelled, depending upon how consistent they are with your actions.

Certain actions almost always produce a positive or a negative response regardless of the circumstances, such as rude or aggressive behavior on the one hand and considerate actions on the other. Others will inevitably lead to favorable impressions, such as kindness and generosity. But most actions can have varying effect depending upon the circumstances, the people involved and how the actions are managed.

You shouldn't take Emily Post's admonition, "To do exactly what your neighbors do is the only sensible rule," too literally, but a good rule of thumb as you question how your actions will be interpreted is to mirror the actions of those who will judge you. If you are at a business dinner and your client orders iced tea, you would be well advised not to order a double bourbon. Dancing on a table with a lampshade over your head is never a good idea at an office party, but you can feel free to loosen up somewhat if everyone else does. If the same formal decorum that is typical in the office also pervades the annual holiday party, you should maintain it there as well.

261

Practicing the Golden Rule is another universally effective Impression Management technique. No single concept has been expressed more consistently in more diverse cultures. It is a fundamental rule of interpersonal relationships, not just a religious tenet. Ask yourself who in your life you most admire, trust or love, and we'll bet they are people who live their lives by the Golden Rule. They are kind, fair, honest—not selfish, manipulative or cruel. There is a reason why the Golden Rule has so predominated human thought from the time existence first meant more than clubbing a wild beast to death and dragging it home for dinner. The Golden Rule, when followed, assures that you will meet others' needs, and it promotes reciprocal behavior.

The impact of the Golden Rule on others' behavior and attitude toward you results from their sense of obligation to repay you in kind. As French anthropologist Marcel Mauss noted, "There is an obligation to give, an obligation to receive, and an obligation to repay."

Dr. Robert Cialdini, one of the nation's leading experts on persuasion and social influence, calls this phenomenon "reciprocation." In his insightful book *Influence, the Psychology of Persuasion,* Dr. Cialdini tells of a university professor who tested our instinctual tendency to reciprocate by sending Christmas cards at random to complete strangers. He was curious to learn how many of those strangers would reciprocate. Return cards were sent in droves.

A study conducted by Professor Dennis Regan of Cornell University further illustrates the power of the natural human tendency to reciprocate. In the experiment, Dr. Regan's assistant was paired with unsuspecting subjects who were asked as part of an experiment in art appreciation to rate a number of paintings. During the middle of the experiment Dr. Regan's assistant excused himself and, after a few minutes, returned. Half of the time the research assistant returned empty-handed. The other half of the time, he returned with two bottles of Coca-Cola and told his research partner, "I asked if I could get myself a Coke, and he said it was okay, so I bought one for you, too."

After the "art appreciation" exercise was complete, the research assistant asked each of his partners if he or she would buy some twenty-five-cent raffle tickets he was selling. Twice as many of the "partners" for whom the assistant bought what was then a ten-cent Coke bought raffle tickets from the assistant when compared to those "partners" for whom the assistant had not extended this simple "favor." The average partner who had received the ten-cent Coke spent fifty cents on raffle tickets.

The experiment became even more interesting when the research assistant's "partners" were asked if they liked the assistant. Those for whom the assistant bought a Coke purchased more raffle tickets than those who had not been extended this favor, *whether or not they liked the assistant.* As Dr. Cialdini notes in his discussion of this study: "For those who owed him a favor, it made no difference whether they liked him or not; they felt a sense of obligation to repay him, and they did."

For students of influence and persuasion, the implications of reciprocation are immense. Religious sects like the Hare Krishna discovered that they substantially increase "donations" from strangers when they first present them with an inexpensive gift like a flower or booklet. This same phenomenon is what prompts many businesses to send calendars, holiday gifts or other presents to their clients, and motivates retailers to give "free" samples.

The tendency to feel obliged to repay a gift or favor is prominent in every human society, according to sociologist Alvin Gouldner. As Dr. Cialdini notes, it applies to unsolicited kindness and gratuitous gifts, as well as those made based upon some expectation or preexisting relationship. For example, Dr. Cialdini reports that the Disabled American Veterans receive donations from approximately 18 percent of those who receive a typical mail solicitation. However, when the Disabled American Veterans include a free gift of mailing labels with the recipient's name and address, the response rate almost doubles to 35 percent.

The principle of reciprocation also has profound implications on Impression Management. There is truth to the adage "What goes around comes around." If you act trusting, people will in turn trust you more. If you show your concern for others, they will be more caring toward you. If you're humble, others will be less selfish. If you perform your obligations capably, others will do their best to do likewise.

Keep in mind the rule of reciprocity as you respond to the kindness and consideration others show you, since others will form expectations about the likelihood that you will reciprocate based upon how you respond to their gestures. Even though we have learned social graces almost exclusively in the context of conventional gift-giving, the psychological dance that takes place is the same when other "favors" are exchanged. You should give and accept any gift—praise, favors, candor, caring—in the same manner that you give and accept material presents. When you receive a gift, you should acknowledge its importance. When you do, you will reassure the gift giver that you will meet his natural expectation of reciprocity. Also give freely. Don't make a production of every penny you spend, favor you confer, or compliment you bestow. When you encourage the ebb and flow of the gift-giving ritual to occur naturally, you will allow others to feel good about the exchange, and about you.

ACTIONS
FOR ALL OCCASIONS

There are many actions that enhance the impression of each of the four Compass Qualities because they satisfy people's cravings to feel important and to have their needs met. They establish an emotional comfort level, build commonality, break down barriers and instill trust. They accomplish the objective through different mechanisms, but all arrive at the same end result.

PERSONALIZE EVERY RELATIONSHIP

The lawyers and businesspeople with whom we work frequently complain about the lack of loyalty in today's business environment. There was a time in the not too distant past when lawyers and other professionals represented the same clients for decades, and suppliers' relationships with customers survived the ups and downs of their respective businesses. Today, price points, discounts, promotional support and other bottom line factors, not personal relationships, have become paramount to most consumers of goods and services. It's not just the consumer who shows no loyalty to the provider of goods and services; the providers of goods and services also often show no loyalty to their consumers. This is due in part to the highly competitive marketplace. However, it can also be attributed to our failure to develop personal relationships that instill loyalty.

In our conversations with businesspeople about what creates lasting loyalties one theme dominates: personal relationships. Personal relationships are what keep employees from jumping ship when a competitor offers them a few more dollars. They make patients return to dentists and doctors who might be a bit more expensive than others. They motivate bankers to extend their business customers' lines of credit, and suppliers agree to payment schedules to accommodate their customers' short-term cash flow problems.

Every relationship is strengthened when it is personalized, from that between the CEO of a huge company and his investment banker to that between the owner of a small business and the handful of men and women who work to make it a success, to the relationship between you and the man at the dry cleaners or your tax preparer.

A study conducted on a New York City beach proved how influential even minimal personal contact can be. One researcher sat down on a blanket a few feet from complete strangers and listened to his radio for a few minutes. He then stood up and walked away. Once he left, a second researcher picked up his radio and walked away with it. Only four out of twenty of the strangers observed in the study did anything to try to stop him.

The researchers then duplicated the experiment, but as the first researcher stood up, he asked the strangers to "watch my things." When his accomplice took the radio under these circumstances, nineteen of twenty people intervened to stop him.

This study demonstrates how even brief contact and committment personalized the radio thief's victim. With this added personal touch, those on the beach were no longer "strangers" in the fullest sense, and were willing to fulfill the commitment they made to watch the victim's things, even if it meant chasing the thief down the beach.

Personalize every encounter. Make an effort to meet frequently with those whose loyalty you hope to build on. Don't walk into a meeting and immediately get down to business. Say "hello" and chat even if for just a few seconds. Ask those you meet how they are in a way that shows you really care. When they answer, follow up. Show that your inquiry wasn't just a social courtesy, but a sincere effort to get to know them. They will feel that you care about them, and they will reciprocate by caring about you.

MAKE EVERYONE FEEL SPECIAL

There are hundreds of ways you can make others feel special, and hundreds more that will make them feel unimportant. If you meet a potentially important customer, you try to draw her into conversation, ask about her, listen carefully when she talks and wouldn't dream of whispering to someone else in front of her, turning your body away from her or ignoring her. Yet frequently that is precisely how many of us treat others we encounter, and it does not go unnoticed.

Early in a relationship, both people dress carefully for one another and are punctual. The man opens the car door for the woman. The woman thanks the man at the end of each meal. They show one another that they are important in many small ways. There is no reason why the same attention, courtesies and kindness can't be shown to everyone in your life, not just at the inception of a relationship, but also as it matures. Your impression will be enhanced in every relationship if you keep Confucius's words in mind: "Behave to everyone as if you were receiving a great guest."

SHOW CLASS

You don't need to be rich to be classy; and just because you are wealthy doesn't mean you are. Class springs from dignity. A loud cackling laugh isn't classy, whether favored by a millionaire or his chauffeur. Good table manners, a bottle of wine or a bouquet of flowers for someone who has invited you to dinner; sympathy, get-well and birthday cards; handwritten thank-you notes and dozens of other small gestures show class and sophistication.

Classy and dignified individuals are thought to be more trustworthy, caring, humble and capable. A lack of class detracts from each of the Compass Qualities. Yet the class that most enhances your impression isn't blatant or pretentious. It arises from subtle courtesies and manners that don't set you apart from others, but bring you closer to them.

IF YOU CAN'T DO IT RIGHT,
DON'T DO IT AT ALL

Your actions always send messages. If you offer to take a friend to lunch for her birthday, the impression she forms of you, and of the importance of your relationship with her, will depend upon whether you take her to a restaurant you know she will enjoy or one you selected either because of your personal preference or its cost. That's not to say that you need to take her to the most expensive gourmet restaurant in town. She may love that little hole in the wall around the corner. If so, that would be a great choice.

If you are unwilling or unable to do something that reflects favorably upon the Compass Qualities, it's usually better to do nothing. If nothing is expected of you, no one will notice if you don't do anything, but they will notice if you do something cheesy. When you are expected to act, don't take the gesture lightly. If something is worth doing, it is worth doing right.

DON'T ASK OF OTHERS
WHAT THEY CANNOT DO

No one likes to be a failure, and no one likes those who make them feel they have failed. If you have unrealistic expectations or do not recognize others' limitations, you doom them to failure. Resentment is inevitable.

If in doubt about others' capabilities, ask them if they feel comfortable with your expectations. If they say "yes," and fail, they won't blame you. If they say "no," find out what they are comfortable with, and encourage them to achieve that goal. When they reach that first target, you can prod them on to the next step, and the next. But don't push too hard, too fast.

DON'T SET DOUBLE STANDARDS

We worked with a law firm a few years ago that brought home this point. The firm was extremely busy, with several lengthy trials under way at the same time. As we worked late into the evening, the halls of the law firm were like Southern California freeways. Young lawyers, paralegals, secretaries and other support staff rushed about as they prepared for the next court day. What amazed us was not a law firm where people worked late, and worked hard; that scene is very familiar. Rather, what was truly extraordinary was that at ten o'clock at night you could hear the laughter, upbeat conversation, and positive hum throughout the office. The firm's employees easily could have been depressed, belligerent or resentful, but they weren't. They weren't because the senior attorneys in the office never asked anything of their staff that they weren't willing to do themselves.

The partners were in the office even before the other employees arrived in the morning, and worked just as late every night. At about six-thirty in the evening someone would pass through the hall collecting dinner orders. Everyone ordered from one of three or four local restaurants that delivered. For many of the staff this was almost like eating out. As food arrived at about seven-thirty, most of the people took a short break and talked about their cases or simply engaged in social conversation. No distinction was made between the most junior file clerk and the most senior trial lawyer. They were all treated the same. It was clear: They were a team. They had a partnership.

ACT WHEN IT WILL DO
THE MOST GOOD

When a crisis strikes, a line of well-wishers always forms. Where were they all when the crisis could have been avoided? Don't wait for a crisis to show that you care. Those who are most revered are the ones who step to the plate in time to actually do something productive, not just commiserate after the fact.

If your friend seems upset, offer a friendly ear or a shoulder to cry on. Ask if there is anything you can do to help. Don't wait to join the ranks of well-wishers after your friend announces that he is getting divorced. Before your wife is overwhelmed by the burdens of working, shuttling the children to and fro and trying to maintain the house, chip in before she becomes ill from stress and fatigue. Be proactive. Don't be offensive or aggressive. Respect others' privacy, but step up to the plate before the game is over.

GET YOUR HANDS DIRTY

Whether you're George Patton or the supervisor on the loading dock, nothing will cause your troops to follow you as loyally into your everyday battles more than if you are there, side by side with them. People resent those who spend time in an ivory tower, and admire and follow those who climb into the trenches with the infantry. There is something inspiring about a boss who gets his hands dirty, literally and figuratively.

This was dramatically demonstrated in a successful mid-sized real estate development company run by Roger. Roger made a point to chip in when possible to help the staff—from large copy jobs to cleaning up the staff room after companywide meetings. Like most busy executives, Roger had priorities that kept him behind his desk most of the time, but he wanted to demonstrate to his employees that he was not above the most menial chores in the office when time and circumstances permitted.

At the annual holiday party, Roger set up the Christmas tree and helped decorate it. At the company picnic, Roger toiled over the barbecue, cooking for all of his employees. It was important to him that his staff understood that while they each had their different professional responsibilities and talents, he did not believe he was more important than they were. As Roger flipped burgers for them and hollered out, "Who wants them bloody or burned?" he communicated a powerful message. The boss, a wealthy highly respected businessman, served them. There was no "we" or "they," no "labor" or "management."

BACK UP YOUR KIND WORDS WITH ACTION

Every management book and expert we have consulted has touted the importance of kind, supportive and encouraging words. Some have even said that words of encouragement, praise and gratitude contribute more than anything else to positive morale. While our research and experience indicate that there is a large measure of truth to this notion, like so many prevalent concepts, it's not that simple.

Supportive, encouraging bosses and friends are well-liked and well-respected, but their friends' and employees' positive responses can't be chalked up to occasional kind words. They more often depend upon the quality of their actions. Most people who speak positive, supportive and encouraging words also engage in behavior that reinforces those words.

When a crisis strikes, step in to help out; don't simply offer condolences or gratuitous advice. If a coworker is hopelessly behind schedule, don't just suggest ways he could organize his day; ask if there is something you can take off his plate. If a friend has had a death in the family, sympathy cards and condolences are great, but a trip to the grocery store to do his shopping, volunteering to take his kids to school or running errands for him will speak much more loudly of your sincere concern and compassion.

Don't expect others to respect you just because you talk a good story of hard work, support and team play if you're always the first one to leave work "exhausted," or never seem available to pick up extra duty because you have a doctor's appointment, haircut or Little League game to attend. Most others also get exhausted, have doctor's appointments, get their hair cut and attend their kids' activities.

What people really want to see is personal sacrifice. They want to see actions. If you want someone to take a bullet for you, let her know that you'll take one for her. If you're always quick to run for cover when the going gets tough, don't expect your troops to stand up and take so much as a Nerf ball on your behalf.

That doesn't mean you shouldn't take a moment to write a nice card, extend a compliment or say "hello" in the morning. All of those things are essential to a good impression. But they are not enough, at least not in the long run. Without action to support your kind words, you eventually will be perceived as insincere, hypocritical and selfish.

BE FAIR

Everyone continually struggles with issues of fairness. And their assessment of your fairness directly affects their impression of you. Plato expressed the belief of many when he said: "Of all the things of a man's soul which he has within him, justice is the greatest good and injustice the greatest evil."

If you are thought to act unfairly, you will be considered untrustworthy, uncaring and even egotistical and less capable. Most people assume that those who act unfairly are either so self-centered or foolish that they don't see the error of their ways, so callous that they don't care or so dishonest that they are willing to act unfairly to achieve their personal objectives. The lesson is clear—never act unfairly.

People's perception of what is fair varies. If the company's policy forbids smoking at work, and an otherwise excellent employee with a spotless record is caught smoking, is it fair to fire him? If a customer is a day late with payment, is it fair to sell his order to someone else? If your friend promised to meet you at your house at six A.M. to head up to the mountains for a hike, is it fair to leave at six-fifteen if she hasn't arrived?

After listening to thousands of people describe what actions were thought to be fair or unfair, and why, we have seen them focus repeatedly on the same three issues.

- *Notice:* The first question they ask is whether the person who was punished had advance notice of the consequences of his actions. For example, did the employee know that a single violation of the company's no-smoking policy was grounds for immediate termination? If someone acts with full awareness of the consequences, most of us believe that he should take responsibility for his own actions.
- *Knowledge:* The next question people ask is whether the decision maker did a thorough investigation before she took action. Did the employer ask the employee if in fact he smoked on the job, and why? Did the employer give the employee an opportunity to be heard? Even if your assumptions prove to be correct, you will find that you will be questioned more about a decision if you didn't conduct a reasonable investigation before you acted. If you didn't verify the facts first, others may assume you were just looking for an excuse.
- *Compassion:* In court we call it "jury nullification." It occurs when the facts and law justify a particular verdict, but the jury believes there are circumstances that compel compassion and forgiveness. We would hate to defend an employer who is sued by an employee who was fired one month short of his thirty-year retirement because he smoked a cigarette in an area within the company that posed no safety threat to others. Even if the policy was clear, and a thorough investigation was conducted, the jury would expect a little mercy.

In your relationships with business associates, friends and family, make your expectations and requirements clear. If harsh consequences will flow from an action, be sure that those consequences are communicated to those who may suffer them. Make important decisions only after you talk to everyone who is impacted by them. When others assess your fairness, the process by which you make a decision can be as important as the decision itself. If the process is flawed, your actions will be suspect. Most important, remember that just because you have the right to take harsh action doesn't mean that you should.

BE FORGIVING

People who hold grudges are scary. They're intimidating. They cause anxiety. No one wants to live in fear that if she makes a mistake, she will pay for all eternity.

Forgiveness is the purest form of compassion. When someone has wronged you, she has no reason to expect your forgiveness, which makes it that much sweeter. As with all good deeds, forgiving others creates a feeling of obligation to be equally charitable toward you.

Better yet, don't condemn or judge others in the first place, and you will have nothing to forgive—only something to understand, and that's a lot easier. Almost any slight or disappointment can be seen from different perspectives. On the one hand, it can be viewed as an assault on you that arouses your most basic survival instincts are aroused. You become defensive, angry and often lash back. In this state of mind, it's hard to find forgiveness.

Instead, you can tell yourself that the wrong that was done to you was not motivated by a desire to hurt you, which is seldom the case. Rather, it was prompted by the other person's insecurity, selfishness or other needs. Don't view it as a personal attack that will incite your emotions, and you will find forgiveness much more readily.

NEVER HOG THE CREDIT

The benefits of sharing credit seem so obvious that the logical question is, "Why doesn't everyone do it?" The answer lies in our failure to balance on the one hand our desire to show trustworthiness, caring and humility, and on the other to demonstrate our competence. Most people act as if their success is diminished if they share credit. This is wrong. Leaders achieve accolades as much for their ability to motivate others to great achievements as for their individual accomplishments. They also demonstrate that they are team players, which makes their superiors feel less threatened. No boss wants to promote a subordinate who always takes credit for others' achievement into a position where he or she may now compete for credit with the boss. The words, "I think she may be gunning for your job" are the kiss of death if they apply to you. This should be taken into consideration as much in social environments as in professional ones. No one will want to work with you on a committee, or host a party with you or organize a trip with you, if he believes you will hog all the credit if the venture is successful.

TRUSTWORTHY ACTIONS

Remember, trustworthiness requires both honesty and reliability. Actions that are inconsistent with either quality erode your trustworthiness. Our survey results identified three general categories of actions that people most frequently consider as they determine whether or not you are trustworthy.

- Do you do what you say you will do?
- Are you consistent?
- Are you driven to do the right thing?

DO WHAT YOU SAY YOU WILL DO

A thirtyish single man who attended one of our seminars told us a story that illustrates how trustworthiness can be eroded when you don't back up your words with action. Sid had dated Gail for several weeks when she invited him to her house for a home-cooked gourmet meal. In her effort to impress Sid, Gail touted her culinary expertise. Sid's taste buds were tingling in anticipation.

Gail decided on a pasta with pesto sauce for the entrée, to be accompanied by a green salad, asparagus and garlic bread. When Sid arrived, the ingredients were carefully positioned on the kitchen countertop as if in preparation for a Julia Child cooking class—a great start. The meal went downhill from there. It quickly became obvious to Sid that Gail did not know her way around the kitchen. The end result was sticky pasta, clumpy pesto, wilted asparagus and even burned garlic toast.

Sid told us that his interest in the relationship plummeted as a result of that evening, not because he particularly valued culinary skills in a lover, but because he valued honesty. If Gail would so blatantly misrepresent that aspect of herself, how much of what she said was reliable?

When you make promises you can't or don't fulfill, some people will assume that you are dishonest, others that you are well intended but unreliable. In either case, you will prove you are untrustworthy. Take your commitments seriously. Others will.

CONSISTENT HONESTY

Paula engaged a loan broker to help her refinance her home to take advantage of lower interest rates. To get the best rate, the broker wanted to present the most favorable financial picture to prospective lenders. He could achieve this objective if he showed as much income and as few expenses as possible, and valued the property that was to be the collateral for the loan as high as possible.

Paula gave the broker all of the information that he needed to prepare the loan application. When he returned it for her signature, she saw that her income and the value of the property were overstated significantly, and her monthly expenses were understated. Sure, this would present the best possible picture to prospective lenders, and probably result in a lower interest rate since the loan would present less risk. But Paula's first reaction wasn't to applaud the loan broker for his creativity. She was appalled that he cavalierly asked her to sign a fraudulent loan application. The fact that this seemed of no concern to him immediately caused her to draw the conclusion that he was not honest. This in turn made her wonder whether he was any more candid with her than he was with prospective lenders. She insisted that he change the documentation to reflect accurate information, and went forward with the refinancing because she was concerned that interest rates might go up if she started the process over with a new broker. But she still wonders whether the broker got her the best deal, or if he chose the lender that paid him the biggest fee.

People expect and assume consistent behavior. They may not react as violently when your dishonest acts are directed toward others as when they are the victims. However, your dishonesty toward others also will ultimately erode your trustworthiness in their eyes.

DO THE RIGHT THING

The first two criteria that others apply to evaluate whether your actions reflect trustworthiness—whether you do what you say you'll do, and whether your actions are consistently honest—are more obvious than the third. Earlier we described the three-step process by which trust is developed: observation of behavior, inference of character and faith. No one will trust you completely until they have concluded from a consistent pattern of behavior that your acts are dictated by a fundamentally trustworthy character. Before they have faith in you, they need to conclude that you're not the kind of person who acts dishonestly or unreliably.

Any fundamental weakness of character—trustworthiness, caring or humility—will impact others' assessment of your basic nature. If you are to be perceived as trustworthy, you must also be seen as caring and humble.

CARING ACTIONS

If you do nothing and say nothing, others may still assume you are humble, trustworthy and capable. But passive sympathy, empathy, concern, compassion and sorrow are invisible. Caring is an active trait. It must be affirmatively shown, or its opposite will be assumed.

Men, more than women, have been socialized not to reveal their caring and compassion for others. They have been taught to be tough and stoic, and are often afraid that if they show emotion they will be perceived as weak. Yet there is little support for that bias in today's culture. Sensitivity and caring by both men and women are viewed in a positive light.

There are as many ways to show you care about others as there are moments in the day. We can't possibly catalog them all, but in our research we identified several common themes that should be included in everyone's Impression Management Plan.

BE THOUGHTFUL

Not surprising, the first trait participants in our studies say exemplifies caring is thoughtful actions—the little things. Cards and notes sent to recognize birthdays, holidays and special achievements, gifts for appropriate occasions or no occasion at all, flowers and a box of candy—all say "I care." Such niceties usually take very little time and aren't prohibitively expensive. Yet they make an impression.

The most precious gifts and gestures of thoughtfulness aren't purchased at a store, and can't be gift wrapped. In intimate relationships they may be hugs, kisses and "I love you"s. At work they may be "thank you"s, or an inquiry about someone's weekend, vacation, health or dreams. In every relationship, they're expressions of emotional support in times of sorrow, encouragement in moments of doubt and joy on occasions for celebration.

FOCUS ON OTHER'S NEEDS, ·
NOT YOUR OWN

Mary is a romantic. Candlelight dinners, flowers and thoughtful gifts represent love and affection to her. She loved Francis, and could think of no better way to show her affection than to send him flowers and buy him gifts. She spent hours shopping for him, and could not understand why he doubted her love.

The problem was that Francis was so overwhelmed with his new business that he did not have the time or energy to focus on Mary's flowers and gifts. They weren't important to *him*. What *he* really needed and wanted from Mary was for her to help him handle some of the demands of his business. He would ask her to run an errand or make a phone call, and she would "forget," or say "I thought it could wait" or "I just didn't get to it." As the days, weeks and months passed, Francis became more and more direct about his needs. The more he complained about Mary's lack of attention, the more flowers and gifts he received.

If Mary had just listened to what Francis equated with caring and concern, and had spent a fraction of the time helping relieve his work-related stress that she did shopping for flowers and gifts, Francis would have been overwhelmed by her thoughtfulness. Mary never did tune into the messages that Francis broadcast; and never appreciated that her view of how to show compassion and attentiveness, no matter how well intended, was not shared by him. Eventually Francis became convinced that Mary didn't really care about him, and never would, and ended the relationship.

If you want to be perceived as caring by someone who is overwhelmed by a pressing deadline at work, bring her dinner to eat at her desk. Don't tell her what *she* really needs is to take a break and go out to dinner with you. That's not what *she* wants. It's what *you* want. If you force her to go along with your program, chances are she won't see you as caring at all, but rather as insensitive and unsympathetic. Your effort to be perceived as a kind and compassionate person will fail because that is really *not* how you have behaved. Kind, compassionate and sensitive people learn to detect what *others* value, and to deliver it.

This requires attention to others' needs, and disregard for what you believe will make you appear caring. Ask questions. Listen carefully. Provide others what they want. When you show someone that you listen, and respond, your caring actions will carry twice the weight.

SHOW CONSIDERATION FOR OTHERS

In our surveys and interviews we have found that caring people are usually described with reference to their positive traits. But many people, when asked what makes a person "caring," also identify the *absence* of certain negative traits. For example, we frequently hear comments, such as: "They don't waste my time"; "They don't infringe on my privacy"; and "they don't ignore me." What follows are the three most frequently mentioned ways you can avoid to appear uncaring.

Respect Others' Schedules

One of our pet peeves, and one that many others have expressed to us, is the tendency of some people to walk into our offices and insist that we talk with them when it is obvious that we're busy and distracted. If someone glances down at the papers on her desk, looks at her watch, and repeatedly comments, "I really have to get back to this," don't ignore her. You may win the battle—she'll hear you out rather than be rude—but you'll lose the war.

Don't be so focused on what you have to say that you ignore the other person's body language, voice and what she says. If you're in doubt about whether you are interrupting, ask her, "Is this a good time?" If it's not, reschedule.

We also hear frequent complaints about people who are habitually late. How better to tell someone, "My time is more valuable than yours," than to keep him waiting. If you think all is forgotten and forgiven just because the other person is gracious enough not to chastise you for your thoughtlessness, think again. This practice is high on almost everyone's list of pet peeves.

Respect Others' Privacy

Insensitivity comes in many flavors; but one almost everyone finds particularly distasteful is an invasion of privacy. The invasion may take many forms. The most obvious occurs when you pry into personal and confidential matters. Your curiosity, even if well intended, will be offensive to those who neither wish to share their intimacies with you, nor be placed in a position where they must rudely rebuff you. If you believe someone may benefit by talking about something personal, ask him if he would like to talk. If he says, "No," respect his wishes. Don't force *your* desire to share his intimacies upon him.

Another commonly offensive intrusion into others' privacy occurs when you express anger or discuss sensitive topics in public. Most of us don't want to air our dirty laundry or reveal our innermost secrets in front of strangers. You may be thick-skinned and not care what others think, but most people don't share that temperament. Pick the time and place for sensitive conversations carefully. Start with the assumption that they should be held in private.

The revelation of others' secrets is also a violation of their privacy. Secrets are inherently private information. Any violation of another's confidence not only makes you untrustworthy, it shows you are uncaring. Secrets are not meant to be shared; yet many people can't seem to resist the temptation.

Be Responsive

Remember, what people crave most is to feel important. A phone call not returned after three days, a letter or e-mail to which there is no reply, an invitation that requests an RSVP that goes unanswered—these don't make someone feel important. And if you don't make someone feel important, you won't impress them.

We try to impress upon everyone in our offices just how important it is to return phone calls promptly by recounting a conversation Mark had with a client early in his career. The client called while Mark was on the phone, and left a request for a return call. As soon as Mark hung up, he returned the call. The first words out of the prospective client's mouth were, "I'm impressed. I was first referred to someone else. When he didn't return my phone call after a day and a half, I figured it was time to get another recommendation. If I'm not important enough to warrant a return phone call before he signs me up as a client, I have to believe things will get even worse later on."

There will be occasions when you simply cannot be responsive. In these situations, when you do follow up, make sure to explain the reason for your delay. Research, primarily in the customer relations area, has shown that people who are dissatisfied with the service they receive are quite forgiving if the culprit quickly makes amends.

A study by the Research Institute of America commissioned by the White House Office of Consumer Affairs found that 96 percent of the customers who believed they were treated discourteously do not complain; but 90 percent of those who are unhappy with the service also do not return. The study also found that the unhappy customers complain to a minimum of nine others, and 13 percent will complain to more than *twenty* others. However, between 54 and 74 percent of those who complain about the service they receive become repeat customers if their complaint is addressed; and as many as 95 percent will return if they receive prompt satisfaction.

These statistics are just as applicable outside the customer relations arena. Consider their broad implications. Anyone you shun, abuse or mistreat is likely to tell anyone who cares to listen, and many who don't, all about it. That's how reputations are destroyed. On the other hand, if you provide an explanation, and address their concerns, the vast majority will forgive and forget.

HUMBLE ACTIONS

When we ask others to identify the traits that reveal humility or arrogance, they frequently refer to "actions." But the "actions" to which they refer usually more precisely fall within one of the other six Colors. "He acts like he's God's gift to the world," for example, really means that he dominates every conversation, swaggers or speaks in a snooty tone of voice. However, there is one exception to the rule that humility, or its absence, is normally not conveyed by actions. Selfishness is typically revealed most directly by actions.

Selfish actions are not difficult to identify, and their impact on impression formation is equally obvious. If you are always the first one in line when goodies are handed out, and the last one to volunteer; or the first one out of the door at the end of the day, and the last one to show up for work in the morning; or someone who always seems to ask for help, but never gives it, your selfishness will be lost on no one. If you find any of our comments strike a bit too close to home, don't fail to note this characteristic in the "don'ts" column of your Impression Management Plan. As we have mentioned earlier, a lack of humility is not easily overlooked. It guts the very core of effective Impression Management—*others'* importance, and your ability to meet *their* needs.

ACTIONS THAT DEMONSTRATE CAPABILITY

One of the most challenging aspects of our job as impression managers is to distill the essence of what forms impressions from the many comments we receive from those we interview and survey. In our most recent survey, we received more than five hundred responses to questions that asked what traits demonstrate the four components of capability—intelligence, competence, confidence and professionalism. As we reviewed them along with the thousands of similar comments we have heard in interviews, we identified four traits that were mentioned most frequently. The respondents did not necessarily use the same terminology we use here, but their words embodied the same concepts. The four traits were:

- Decisiveness
- Enthusiasm
- Creativity
- Practical Intelligence

We have found that each of these traits must be managed to convey capability effectively. Of the four Compass Qualities, capability presents the greatest challenge to Impression Management because each trait that establishes capability potentially diminishes one or more of the other three Compass Qualities. In the balance of this chapter, we will discuss how decisiveness, enthusiasm, creativity and practical intelligence can be communicated effectively, without diminishing the other Compass Qualities.

DECISIVENESS

Capable people, like all leaders, are doers. They don't just talk a good story. They take charge. They act. They make decisions, and implement them decisively.

If you want to be considered capable, you can't be an indecisive handwringer. You can't wait for others to take control or shirk responsibility in the hope that others will fill the void. You must be a problem solver.

But it's not that simple. Decisive action is essential to an impression of capability, but so are caution, preparation and consensus building. If you're too quick to act, others will think you are a loose cannon. If you act alone, you won't be seen as a team player. This may seem an impossible dilemma to avoid, but it's not. It simply requires that you recognize that decisive action does not require that you abandon careful preparation and input from others.

Careful Preparation

Decisive action is not the same as *hasty* or *imprudent* action. Actions taken precipitously and without due thought and circumspection raise doubts, not confidence. Human experience has created the expectation that action is more likely to produce the desired result if it is carefully considered, and preceded by appropriate preparation.

The conflict between decisive action and careful preparation is easily reconciled. Decisive action does not mean that you proceed from the conception of an idea to the end result without careful planning and preparation. It requires only that you initiate planning and preparation decisively and move steadily toward a resolution. We'll illustrate with an example of how the vice president in charge of expansion for a national chain of clothing stores might address the question whether or not to expand into a new region.

When presented with the question, the manager could wring his hands and take a wait-and-see attitude, or he could establish a committee to investigate the advantages and disadvantages of expansion, and allow the issue to linger indefinitely. Both of these approached would be seen as indecisive; and wouldn't project capability.

On the other hand, he could quickly consider the proposed expansion and make a firm and decisive decision on the spot to either expand or not to expand. This would clearly be decisive, but would not reflect careful preparation if he had not yet obtained adequate information to make an informed decision. Such foolhardy decisiveness would diminish others' confidence in his capabilities as much as the indecisiveness in the first example.

Third, the manager could consider the proposal, identify what further information was required to make a fully informed decision, establish the procedures by which that information would be obtained, set a deadline to obtain it and schedule a meeting at which the information necessary to make the decision would be considered. If, at the subsequent meeting, he still was not satisfied that sufficient information had been accumulated to make the best possible decision, he could repeat the process. His actions would be carefully considered and his preparation thorough, but he also would act decisively. Obviously, if this process dragged on indefinitely while the manager searched for divine inspiration, he would no longer be considered decisive.

If properly managed, there is no inconsistency between decisive action and careful preparation. They can be merged to project capability in both personal and social contexts. You simply need to quickly and steadily advance the ball at a pace that is not so fast that you may overlook something, but not so slow that you seem to suffer from analysis paralysis. What you don't need to do is make the ultimate decision imprudently.

Consensus Building

Another common misconception is that decisiveness requires independent action by a lone wolf, as reflected in a memo written by a marketing executive that was published in a magazine that ran a contest for real life "Dilbert" quotes. The memo read: "Teamwork is a lot of people doing what I say." Nothing could be further from the truth. To the contrary, you reap the greatest benefit from decisive action when you welcome the input, support and participation of all of those who might be affected.

ENTHUSIASM

Enthusiasm was listed among the "Magic Pills" in Chapter 5 because of its universally positive contribution to impression formation. Enthusiasm shows commitment, excitement and interest, and touches others' emotional brains in ways that can't be replicated. In the extreme, however, it runs afoul of another trait that our surveys reveal is expected from those who are capable. People associate capability with a calm, quiet control, not unbridled energy. When you act cool, calm and collected, you convey assurance and self-confidence. The challenge is to show the essential trait of enthusiasm, while also reassuring others with your calmness and control.

The first step is to recognize that there are many ways to display enthusiasm without impassioned speeches or overly animated motions. When you propose a new project, you can show your enthusiasm for your proposal with follow-up contacts, memos, phone calls, scheduling another meeting or perhaps a celebration to honor the program's launch. Your energy, enthusiasm and commitment to the project are displayed by these actions, even without impassioned words or gestures. In the process, you also demonstrate that you are in control of the process, and have the capability to move it forward. These actions convey all of the positive aspects of enthusiasm, without risking that you will tarnish your impression by appearing too emotionally committed to it.

CREATIVITY

"I'm more the creative type," sounds more like an admission rather than a recommendation. In many cases it is. It means, "I'm not very analytical, organized or disciplined," which, in turn, translates to "I'm not that capable."

The next challenge to managing the best possible impression of your capability is to exhibit creativity, imagination and innovation on the one hand, and focus, discipline, organization and concentration on the other. Those who are merely creative are thought to have tremendous potential, if only they could focus. Those who lack creativity are thought to be drones who spit out carbon copy ideas. The secret to dealing with this apparent Impression Management dilemma is to recognize what traits give rise to the negative connotations associated with undisciplined action on the one hand, and unimaginatively thinking on the other, and to eliminate them.

True creativity is not dependent upon many of those traits that "creative people" often adopt. Creative people can be organized, keep their desks clean, prepare for meetings and give attention to detail. Nowhere in the credo of the creative is it written, "thou shalt be a flake." Nonetheless, many creative people either fall victim to the mystique that creative minds are also disorganized minds, or use that explanation as an excuse in the hope that others will accept it. Couple your creativity with traits that reflect organization and focus and you can project the best of both tendencies.

If you are a creative soul, you are one of the lucky ones. You can easily have it all. You can be imaginative and also display organization, focus, discipline and concentration. It's much more difficult for the organized, focused, disciplined person, who doesn't have a creative bone in his body, to project an impression of creativity. But it is possible. Of course that will take you only so far. But if you actually listen to and incorporate the thoughts of those who by nature are more creative, you will find your own creativity will improve.

PRACTICAL INTELLIGENCE

What we call "practical intelligence" is the combination of the intellectual horsepower of your rational brain and your ability to control and direct your emotional brain with what Daniel Goleman calls "emotional intelligence" in his 1995 best-seller of the same name. These two "brains within a brain" combine to convey what others perceive as your level of intelligence.

Eminent Yale psychologist Robert Sternberg conducted a survey in which he asked what makes someone an "intelligent person." Practical people skills were again mentioned frequently. Good judgment and common sense also were high on the list in our survey in which we asked what traits reflect intelligence.

Such research answers the question, "Why do some people who don't have particularly high IQs impress us with their intelligence?" The answer provides you with a road map, which, if followed, will lead to a consistently favorable impression of your intelligence, even if you have never performed well on standardized tests.

The Importance of Demonstrating Traditional Signs of Intelligence

No matter how "emotionally intelligent" you may be, if your knowledge, vocabulary and grammar are poor, you will not be viewed as remarkably intelligent. Long before anyone can assess your good judgment, common sense and people skills, they will have heard you speak. To benefit from the positive impression your emotional intelligence conveys you must first meet others' minimum expectations of raw intelligence by displaying knowledge, vocabulary and acceptable grammar. As we discuss the significant contribution other traits make to your overall impression of intelligence, don't minimize these. If you don't first get over these hurdles, you'll seldom have a chance to finish the race.

How to Develop Practical Intelligence

In a study published in the *Harvard Business Review* in 1993, researchers Robert Kelley and Janet Kaplan examined what makes brilliant individuals stand out in an environment inhabited entirely by the intellectually gifted. They chose what was then the Bell Laboratories' "think tank" as the setting for their study. The scientists at the Bell Laboratories were all stand-out graduates from the best schools in the United States and from across the world. They develop technology that is beyond the capacity of most of us to comprehend, let alone create. If ever there was an environment in which success would be expected to be tied to intellectual brilliance, it was there.

Kelley and Kaplan asked members of the Bell Lab team to identify the 10 to 15 percent of the scientists and engineers who stood out as the brightest stars. These were the men and women who distinguished themselves as the most effective performers in teams of between five and one hundred fifty that work together on large and complicated projects.

The first observation Kelly and Kaplan made was that those who distinguished themselves were not more academically successful, nor did they possess higher IQs than the others. What was it then that made these few more successful than their peers?

The answer came after extensive interviews that focused not just on academic and intellectual prowess, but on interpersonal skills. From the results of their study, read in conjunction with many others, we can identify three traits that create a level of practical intelligence that exceeds what can be achieved by raw intellectual power alone.

- Personal motivation and drive
- Recognizing, monitoring and controlling emotions
- Interpersonal skills

Personal Motivation and Drive

Over the past ten years the media have repeatedly reported the disproportionate numbers of Asian Americans at both the undergraduate level and in advanced degree programs in American colleges and universities. At some colleges and universities the percentage of Asian Americans is many times greater than the percentage of Asian Americans within the population at large. Are Asian Americans that much smarter than other ethnic groups? They certainly outperform other ethnic group on achievement tests by which college applicants are measured.

In fact, studies have shown that Asian Americans' IQs are on average only two to three points higher than the average American's IQ. Yet many perform as if their IQs were ten to twenty points higher on standard achievement tests. The explanation for this dramatic disparity is simple. Asian American children, on average, spend 40 percent more time than other children doing homework. They simply put forth more time and effort cultivating their intellectual abilities.

Time and effort are not the only predictors of increased academic and professional success. Discipline and the willingness to delay gratification to achieve long-term objectives have proven equally important. In another study reported by Daniel Goleman in *Emotional Intelligence,* researchers at Stanford University in the 1960s conducted a simple test of four-year-olds enrolled at preschools on the Stanford campus, and elsewhere. This study has been dubbed the "marshmallow study," because the children were given a marshmallow and were told that they could eat it whenever they wanted. However, if they waited for fifteen to twenty minutes, until the experimenter returned after running an errand, they would receive two marshmallows. Approximately one-third of the preschoolers pounced upon the single marshmallow almost immediately. The rest managed to avoid temptation, at least for a while, through a wide assortment of techniques ranging from covering their eyes, talking to themselves, sleeping, singing and playing solitary games.

Twelve to fourteen years later the researchers tracked down the test children as they were about to graduate from high school. Those who at four years old had the discipline to delay gratification in order to increase the ultimate reward were found to be better adjusted and more successful by virtually any measure. They were more trustworthy, reliable, self-confident, socially adept, persistent, organized, self-assertive and effective. Those who as preschoolers showed less self-control were found to be more socially reserved, indecisive, easily frustrated, stress ridden, doubtful, resentful, jealous, irritable, argumentative and had lower self-esteem.

The distinction between the one- and two-marshmallow children extended to academic performance as well. The one-third who quickly consumed the single marshmallow obtained average SAT scores of 524 (verbal) and 528 (math), while the one-third who waited the longest before yielding to temptation averaged SAT scores of 610 (verbal) and 652 (math). The combined differential in SAT scores, 210 points, is staggering.

The importance of effort and discipline for enhancing practical intelligence cannot be ignored. It is no magic pill that will result in immediate transformation, but hard work and committment to acquiring knowledge and skill will pay off with time.

Recognizing, Monitoring and Controlling Emotions

A substantial body of research supports the premise that we can consciously influence the extent that our emotional responses influence our behavior. Studies have shown, for example, that those who dwell on their unjust treatment by others tend to perpetuate, or even increase, their anger; and those who ruminate over events that make them sad or depressed sink further into the abyss. Yet those who concentrate on positive thoughts and consciously choose to forgive those who have wronged them are able to lessen their anger; and those who think of happy moments in their life or engage in pleasurable activities are able to improve their mood, and their cognitive function.

If you don't think you can consciously control your emotions, consider this. Have you ever become sexually excited by the thought of a particularly beautiful or sexy individual, or a passionate or romantic moment? In fact, right now, you could probably visualize the most sexually stimulating experience you can remember and consciously generate a physical and emotional tingle. That is your rational brain controlling your emotional brain.

Anger management can be used as an illustration of how you can enhance your practical intelligence, and others' perception of it, by recognizing, monitoring and controling your emotions. Anger is one of mankind's most primal and powerful emotions. Anger is a reaction to threat. The threat need not be physical. It can be psychological. Rude behavior, insults, unfair treatment, frustration, confrontation, accusations, embarrassment, indifference or any other behavior that is a threat to your self-esteem, confidence and self-worth will do.

When threatened, chemicals are released by the instinctive programming embedded in your brain. They make you flush, sweat, tense or shake as you are literally "fired up" like a steam boiler stoked with coal.

The initial surge of chemicals lasts no more than a few minutes, after which you feel the tingle, burning sensation and tension drain from your body. But the chemicals produced by anger can linger for hours or even days. They make you edgy, quick to lapse into emotional outbursts, or mutter obscenities under your breath to an inattentive motorist. If you've ever wondered how you could have "lost it," only to be embarrassed or ashamed at your inappropriate behavior a few hours later, this is the answer. You were on drugs—albeit natural ones.

When you are agitated, the signals sent by your emotional brain to your rational brain are so garbled and distorted that your rational brain doesn't work properly. A common misconception is that if you vent your anger, you will resume your normal state more quickly. In fact, when you express anger by venting, you prolong these chemical surges and your irrational behavior. Instead, cool down. Take a walk. Distance yourself. Don't dwell on your anger. Try to understand and sympathize with the person who induced your anger. That motorist who cut you off may have been preoccupied with an ill child or problems at work. He wasn't out to get you. His behavior was a function of his own problems. It had nothing to do with you. Let it go.

Most important, address your anger early, and always before you act upon it. Don't allow it to simmer. If you have produced an angry response in someone else, attempt to neutralize it as quickly as possible. Apply the techniques that will reduce your own anger in reverse. Apologize. Suggest you both cool off. Don't insist that you resolve the problem when one or both of you are emotionally agitated.

The effectiveness of this process was illustrated in an experiment in which a researcher deliberately provoked subjects with sarcastic remarks. Later, the subjects were given the opportunity to retaliate when they were asked to evaluate the researcher; and retaliate they did—except when another researcher intervened while the sarcastic member of the team was out of the room and explained to the subjects that the first researcher was under intense pressure because he was preparing for his graduate oral exams. When the second researcher intervened and explained to the subjects that the first researcher's behavior had nothing to do with them, and therefore was not a threat, most of them were charitable in their reviews of the first researcher. Some, however, were still highly critical. These were the subjects who were so outraged by the first experimenter's conduct that their emotional brains had taken control and kept their rational brains from accepting the explanation.

You can manage all of your emotions to some degree by conscious thought, just as you can recognize, monitor and control anger. When you do, you can lessen emotional reactions that interfere with the perceptions by others of your practical intelligence.

When you are under the influence of a powerful emotion, try some or all of these techniques. They're bound to help.

- Engage in pleasant distractions. Go to a movie, listen to music, plan your next vacation.
- Pamper yourself. Buy that dress or golf club you covet.
- Do something at which you excel. Give yourself the surge of confidence and security that comes from success.
- Exercise. Aerobic exercise can counteract many of the chemicals released in the body during emotional surges.
- Make someone else happy. It makes almost everyone feel better about himself or herself.
- Pray. For those with strong religious beliefs, prayer brings comfort and solace.
- Most important, give yourself time to cool off before you speak or act.

Interpersonal Skills

The stars at Bell Laboratories had many distinct attributes; but they all shared one—well-developed interpersonal skills. They were relationship builders. They were able to establish rapport, friendship and trust, which others with only raw intelligence couldn't.

Think about it. The think tank at Bell Laboratories was an environment that required more intellectual horsepower than almost anywhere else on earth. Yet even in that environment where you would expect the "best and the brightest" to be those with the highest IQs, they were actually the ones who were most able to build relationships. Just imagine how valuable that skill is for the rest of us who work in environments where we don't have to be a genius to succeed?

In America, from the time you entered school until you moved into the workforce, your capability has been measured almost entirely by a single standard: your ability to perform well on examinations. But once you have entered the real world, where your performance can't be measured by a computerized grading system, your intelligence, like the other elements of capability, will be measured as much by your ability to communicate with others, emotional brain to emotional brain, as by your ability to connect rational brain to rational brain.

What all of us need to stand out is the ability to build consensus, motivate others, promote teamwork, avoid conflicts and instill trust. When we do, we become successful, and others attribute our success to our intelligence, whether or not we have triple-digit IQs.

Throughout this book we have described techniques to convey the four Compass Qualities. At first blush, many of these may not have appeared even remotely relevant to the impression others have of your intelligence. Yet traits like sensitivity, empathy, communication and listening skills, cooperation, affection and honesty are essential to convey what counts most to convey intelligence—practical intelligence. Keep this in mind as you formulate your Impression Management Plan. Don't neglect traits that display trustworthiness, caring and humility in favor of those that appear, in isolation, to better enhance your image of capability alone.

CHAPTER 13

The Environment

Environment is as critical to the formation of your impression as it is for development of the characters in a successful movie. Everything and everyone—from your neighborhood to the people who come and go in your life—contribute to your image. Your environment not only reveals clues about your job, education, hobbies, religion, culture, family, politics, friends and financial status, it also reflects personality characteristics, such as ego, efficiency, friendliness, intelligence, professionalism, confidence, responsibility, ambition and work ethic.

In our surveys, environment is always the least frequently mentioned of the Seven Colors. But don't be fooled. Environment has a much greater impact on impression formation than most people think. Because there has been much more discussion in the media and literature about the other ways that we convey impressions of ourselves—appearance and body language in particular—environmental factors don't come to mind as quickly to people as other factors when they fill out survey questionnaires. However, in individual interviews, and when we poll audiences at seminars, we find that very strong impressions are formed from a person's environment.

Many of the associations made from our environment parallel those made from our clothing and other aspects of our personal appearance. Your choice of trendy or classic, cheap or expensive, gaudy or conservative, severe or warm triggers the same stereotypical associations in both contexts. Environmental stereotypes also arise from the neighborhood and style of your office or home, as well as its decor, furnishings, layout and other characteristics. Even the car you drive says much. Beyond this, however, lies one of the most often overlooked aspects of your environment: your human environment. The lovers, friends and colleagues you choose to include in your life, like your physical environment, contribute to the impression of who you are, or who you want to be.

Environment has a unique effect on impression formation. In psychological terms, your environment serves as a "non-conscious effective prime," or what is more commonly called a "subliminal suggestion." The effect is much the same as when images of popcorn are flashed on movie screens at a rate too fast to be perceived by the rational brain, but slow enough to be recorded at a subconscious level. No one in the theater notices the images, but they buy more popcorn. Whenever and wherever someone encounters you, a similar subliminal association is made between you and your environment. Once that association is made, the receiver's rational brain seeks to reinforce that association. A beautiful home makes its occupants seem more attractive, an organized office makes its inhabitant appear more organized, a clean and functional garage makes a mechanic appear more efficient and a warm, friendly day care facility makes the day care provider seem caring.

Some of these conclusions are reached at a rational level, but many aren't, as demonstrated by the relative infrequency in which environment is mentioned by the respondents in our and others' studies. Yet the associations are made. Don't ignore them.

THE NEIGHBORHOOD

Every city has its upscale residential neighborhoods and business districts, its middle-class housing developments and small office and industrial areas and its homes and businesses that lie, literally or figuratively, on the other side of the tracks. Logically we assume that those who own businesses or live in trendier neighborhoods are more wealthy, but beyond that logical assumption, there aren't many purely rational conclusions drawn from the neighborhood in which we encounter someone. However, studies have shown that there are many associations that are made at an emotional level.

People will tend to suspect your trustworthiness if you live or work in an environment that falls at either end of the extreme. As we have mentioned before, people are suspicious of the honesty of those who are wealthy. But they are also suspicious of the honesty of those who are very poor. Just ask yourself if you would feel more nervous if you left your car unlocked in a wealthy or poor neighborhood. Upscale and low-class neighborhoods, however, tend to send opposite messages with regard to each of the other three Compass Qualities. Upscale neighborhoods project a lower degree of caring and humility, but a much higher degree of capability. Lower-class neighborhoods project a more caring and humble nature, but a less capable one.

The choice of neighborhood as an aspect of your Impression Management Plan is simple in most respects. If you want to appear more successful and capable, establish your business in a downtown high-rise or a trendy office building, not the neighborhood mall or the old section of town, and buy a house in an upscale community if you can afford one. If you want to temper that upper-class image, move down a notch or two within the neighborhood. If you choose a fancy office building, don't take the penthouse suite. If you live in a fancy neighborhood, don't buy the biggest house. Likewise, if you live or work in a less expensive neighborhood, you can minimize the negative associations and help maintain the positive ones if your home or business is well maintained.

For most of us, decisions about the neighborhood in which we live or work are driven largely by our finances: We tend to live and work in neighborhoods that we can afford. However, before you make that decision, give some thought to what the neighborhood, the building in which you live and work, and even the location within that building say about you, and whether whatever financial resources are available to you have been allocated in a way that best projects the image you want.

DECOR

Office or home decor can be efficient, functional and practical, or it can be artistic, fun and frivolous. It can be inexpensive or opulent, thrown together or well decorated, trendy or conventional, casual or formal, dark or airy, sterile or warm, dirty or clean, cluttered or organized. The style, fabrics, colors, cost and cleanliness of your decor sends many of the same messages a person receives from your hair, pants or jewelry.

There is generally no "right" decor. But a thrown-together look, or an office or home environment that is dirty, cluttered or disorganized, are truly toxic environments that have no redeeming qualities. You are fooling yourself if you think that you won't be judged critically by those who walk into a dirty, cluttered office or home with stacks of magazines and papers pouring out of the trash can and dirty cups and dishes strewn here and there. If your environment is cluttered, disorganized, dusty, dirty or smells bad, your image will suffer.

As long as your environment is free of these toxins, your choice of decor will depend upon which Compass Quality is valued most highly by those you want to impress. A public relations firm will want to emphasize creativity, expressiveness, success and trendiness, while the marriage, family and child counselor will want to create a caring and nurturing environment, which could be artistic and expressive, but not at the expense of warmth and comfort. So it is with each person and each profession. A balance should be reached based upon your objectives, with application of the same principles by which you select your clothing.

One aspect of your home and office environment, which should always be considered, is whether it is open and airy, or dark. Light has a tremendous psychological influence. It invigorates and exhilarates. Darkness is sedating and tends to be depressing, though it also can be more relaxing. When you are seen in a light environment you will appear more energetic. If you maintain a dark environment, you will seem more sedate and reserved.

Some may prefer the calming influence of darkness to help project a more passive, nonthreatening impression. In most instances, your impression will be enhanced when the psychological association is made between you and the light that fills your environment. Light walls, large windows, no heavy curtains or pulled blinds and good lighting literally and figuratively place you in a better light.

Color will also influence others' response to your environment. Many of the impressions we described as we discussed the color of clothing also apply to colors in your environment. More subdued hues will appear more friendly and professional, bright colors flamboyant and energetic and dark colors sophisticated. But color should be used more sparingly in your environment. A bright blue dress won't send a message as dramatically as a bright blue wall; and a bright red scarf won't accent your wardrobe to the same degree that bright red furniture will influence the impression made by your decor.

As you choose the decor in your home or workplace, also keep in mind the Magic Pill of enthusiasm. You can project energy and enthusiasm if your photographs show smiling people and your artwork and posters convey action or display bright colors. An airy, clean, uncluttered office will also help, as will plants and flowers.

THE LAYOUT

Just as body language can convey openness, friendliness and approachability, or distance and coldness, the layout of a home or office sends distinct messages that encourage or stifle communication. People tend to communicate more in interactive settings. They engage in better eye contact and display other more open and friendly nonverbal communication when they face each other without physical barriers or significant space between them. They make more contact. When you create an environment in which you make greater contact with others, you open the door to more favorable impressions.

In your work environment, make yourself accessible. Keep your door open and face your desk toward the door. If someone glances into your office and sees just the back of your head as you lean over your desk, he won't feel welcome, and you won't have the opportunity to see him as he passes by and initiate interaction with a "hello" or a smile. If your office will accommodate a conversation nook with two chairs and a small table where you can sit and talk, it will encourage better communication. If you sit behind a desk in a large executive chair and relegate your guests to small, stiff chairs, you will create an environment in which you are in greater control and you will appear more powerful and authoritative. In some situations this may be desirable; but in most, it will create a distance that will enhance your status, while making others feel less important and cared for.

Consider the layout of your home and office to be an extension of your body language. Make it open, relaxed and not controlling. Position chairs and couches close enough so that you aren't more than four to six feet away from someone as you speak to him or her. Better communication occurs if you stay closer to the "personal zone" discussed earlier. On the other hand, don't force someone to sit so close to you that you invade her personal space. Arrange the furniture so that you look directly at one another, rather than sideways. Position flowers or other decorative items where they won't interfere with your sight.

PROPS

Like a set designer, you have an almost infinite choice of props with which to portray a particular image. If you are like most of us, you have included many of the items in your home or workplace without much thought to what they say about you. If you want to make the best possible impression, rethink your choices. As you review the following list of props that can be added to either your home or workplace, think about those that you have included or excluded in yours and what that says about you.

Alcohol	Candles
Artwork	Children's toys and furniture
Ashtrays	Clocks
Books, magazines and other reading material	Coffee/tea service
Bookshelves	Collectibles
Business card/holders	Computers
Calendars	Diplomas
	Display case and contents

Exercise equipment/sports gear	Musical instruments
Flowers and green plants	Paperweights
Food	Pharmaceuticals
Fax machine	Pen sets
Furniture	Photographs
Garden equipment	Plaques
Guns or gun racks	Posters
Hat stand	Radio
Holiday decorations	Religious pictures, books or
Items on the refrigerator	sayings
Items reflecting physical disability	Rugs
(cane, wheelchair, oxygen tank)	Stereo system
Knickknacks	Television
Lamps	Tools
Mirrors	Trophies
Mugs (especially with logos or	Vitamins
quotes printed on them)	Umbrellas

Each of these items reflects upon the four Compass Qualities. Some tend to be particularly noticeable and significant, for example:

- Books, magazines and other reading material
- Artwork
- Collectibles and knickknacks
- Flowers and plants
- Furniture
- Professional or recreational items
- Signs and plaques

We highlight these seven items from among the many props at your disposal because they tend to be what others notice first when they enter your home or work environment. As such, they can be used to help project a favorable impression of your trustworthiness, caring, humility and capability.

We don't suggest that you place a Bible on the corner of your desk, or that you create a religious shrine in the entry hall of your home in an attempt to display your honest or caring nature. Such blatant demonstrations may be perceived as disingenuous by all but those who already know you well. But you should give attention to how you convey positive or negative qualities by the props that you include in your environment, and use them to further your Impression Management Plan.

A plaque or poster reading "Excuse me, but I think you mistook me for someone who cares" is cute, but it reflects poorly on your caring and professional nature. Replace it with a friendly and inspirational saying. On the other hand, flowers, plants, throw pillows, coffee, water and snacks for your guests are a psychological welcome mat. They create a warm and inviting environment, which in turn sends the message that you are warm and inviting.

Photographs with celebrities, an overabundance of plaques, trophies or other signs of your accomplishments and success will show that you are professional and competent, but they also make you appear arrogant and self-centered. Exceedingly expensive or pretentious knickknacks demonstrate success, but send the message that it's important to you that everyone who enters your lair be aware of it. More understated but attractive alternatives usually will strike a better balance.

What are we to think of the employee whose computer manuals are buried under a stack of recreational reading. Why does an employee who is paid to tend to business during work hours have a dog-eared copy of a suspense novel on the top of his pile of unread interoffice memos? What of the mid-level manager whose golf clubs and putting machine enjoy a position of prominence in his office, or the truck driver whose cab is filled with litter, or the computer technician whose desk at work is stacked with computer games?

Walk through your house and your workplace and think about each of the props we have listed and any others that you have included or failed to include in your environment, and ask yourself whether they send the messages you want others to receive. Remove those that send the wrong message. Replace them with props that send the right message. Think of yourself as a movie set designer and leave nothing to chance.

ODORS, SOUNDS AND TEXTURES

Our senses of smell, hearing and touch once played a vital role in our survival. They signaled to us what was threatening or inviting, even what was safe to eat. Today, our survival is seldom dependent upon these senses, but they remain hard-wired to our emotional brain and still trigger potent reactions.

ODORS

Some odors, like cigarette smoke, dirty clothing or diapers, animals, alcohol and medication, never enhance your impression. Stuffy, smoky, dirty environments convey the same consistently negative associations made with poor personal hygiene. The antiseptic smell of cleaning products, like the smell of medication, often triggers an unpleasant association with doctors' offices and hospitals. The smell of food can be inviting, repulsive or inappropriate, depending upon the specific odor and where it is found. The aroma of fresh baked bread wafting through a home helps create a warm and inviting atmosphere; but the smell of microwaved pizza or popcorn in an office is beyond our expectations and is likely to strike visitors as unprofessional. At home, as in the workplace, your environment should always smell fresh and clean.

Each time you enter your workplace or home, take a moment to smell the message it sends to your guests. Shampoo the couches if they smell like a wet dog. Move the cat box into a back bedroom or bathroom. Open the windows and let the rooms air out. Add the pleasant scents of flowers, potpourri or room odorizers. Don't underestimate the impact of smell. The olfactory system is our most primitive scent and remains a direct channel to our emotional brains.

SOUNDS

Manage sound as you manage all traits. Eliminate those that never contribute to good impressions, like arguments, loud or annoying noises and any other distracting sounds. Use inviting sounds to create desired moods; calm background music to relax others; louder or more lively music to energize them; and quiet to allow concentration and focus.

TEXTURES

Like styles and colors, many of the textures you incorporate into your environment will convey the same messages as the textures of your clothing. Warm, soft fabrics are more friendly and inviting, but generally less professional. Smooth, colder fabrics, as well as leather, glass and metallic finishes, may be chic and professional, but are less warm. Many woods can have either a slick, high-gloss finish or a softer satin finish. Even wall coverings range from soft fabric to high-gloss enamel.

A single piece of furniture or other accent feature of your environment will seldom define the overall "feel" of the room. But in combination, the texture of furnishings can create a dramatic difference, especially when combined with colors and styles. Plush carpeting, overstuffed soft fabric couches and low gloss furniture, especially if in dark or autumn hues and traditional styles, project a calm but relatively low-energy effect. High-gloss hardwood, tile or stone flooring with contemporary, brightly colored furniture show energy and flair, and when well done will be equally professional, but less warm and relaxing.

YOUR TRANSPORTATION

The Lexus ad read simply, "It also functions like a resume;" yet what it really said was, "If you buy this high-priced, luxury automobile, others will think that you are more successful, intelligent, high-class and attractive."

Like every material possession, the cost, style and even color of your automobile sends a message. For the last century, automobiles have enjoyed a unique role as status symbols. With so many different makes and models from which to select, your choice of wheels will be noticed.

The impression of power and authority conveyed by an expensive automobile was demonstrated in a study in which researchers drove either an expensive new car or an older economy model. They stopped at traffic lights and did not move when the lights turned green. The researchers then catalogued the responses by the drivers of the cars behind them. They found that people honked less frequently at the drivers of the expensive new cars, and when they did honk, they waited longer, showing additional deference and respect to those whose cars reflect higher status.

Cost is not the only significant factor. Style is at least as important. A flashy red sports car, a four-wheel-drive pickup truck, a four-door American-made sedan, a classic Thunderbird—each instantly conveys an image of the person behind the wheel. One successful couple we know, both attorneys, owns a Mercedes sedan and a more practical Ford minivan with which to transport their twin sons and their son's friends around town. Their choice of which vehicle each would drive reflected their sensitivity to the impact it would have on the image they hoped to project. He drove the van. She drove the Mercedes. Their sense, with which we agree, was that a male professional's image would not be affected as much if he drove the van. He wouldn't be viewed as a "soccer dad," and even if he were, very few people would assume that his commitment to his professional life was less because of it. However, it is more probable that this assumption would be made if the roles were reversed and she drove the minivan. If you think they were just paranoid, consider how seldom men have been asked if their role as a father would prevent them from discharging their duties at work. Almost never. But before discrimination laws made this an illegal question, women fielded it frequently. Today, people just ask the question quietly to themselves.

Your automobile, like your home, office and even your body, can include a wide variety of ornamentation that will affect the impression it makes as much as the cost, style or color. Bumper stickers, customized license plates, license plate holders and any other writing on your vehicle that contains a message should be selected with discretion. They speak directly of your interests and character, much as do the posters on your wall, or emblems on your T-shirt.

Regardless of the cost, style or adornment of your automobile, its maintenance is always important. A dirt-streaked, cluttered car won't reflect well on you. A clean vehicle, however, will show you to be attentive to detail, organized, successful and professional.

SOCIAL ENVIRONMENTS

Environments have character. Pool halls are seedy, churches are caring and spiritual, parks are wholesome, libraries are academic, swank hotel bars are chic, ballparks are active and a mountain glade is tranquil and calm. Studies have shown that the qualities of any environment rub off on those who are encountered in them, particularly when they have had a choice in the matter and consistently chose one environment over any other.

When you invite a friend, coworker, customer or romantic interest to get together after work, you have an almost infinite variety of locations from which to choose. Each carries with it certain associations. If you choose the symphony, you might be perceived as more sophisticated, successful and intelligent, but perhaps a bit pretentious. An evening at the fights would show an aggressive, and perhaps uncaring side, but would be associated with vigor and strength. Your companion will make an association with trustworthiness, caring and humility if you invite her to a church social. The gym, a Sierra Club meeting, a walk in the park or a charity ball would each convey its own image. Even choices within different categories can carry entirely different meanings. When you invite someone out for a drink, you can take him to an upscale hotel bar, the local pub, or a topless joint. A dinner invitation could mean a meal at a fast-food restaurant, a diner or a chic restaurant. Even your choice of movies has meaning. *Rambo VIII* is a lot like a night at the fights; and a foreign documentary is comparable to the symphony.

The environment you choose should depend significantly upon your guest, and the circumstances. If you take your best client to dinner, or surprise your girlfriend on your six-month anniversary with a night out, he or she will expect a more upscale choice of restaurants. That choice will show that you care about the relationship and are savvy enough to understand what is expected of you. If you were to take them to the local diner, your client would probably question your judgment and the sincerity of your assurances that you value his patronage, and your girlfriend would probably interpret your gesture as an indication of how little you really care for her. On the other hand, a quick bite at the local coffee shop might be just the ticket, and well within the expectations of your coworker, with whom you just want to chat.

Whatever associations are made with an environment in general will attach even more rigorously when your choice of social environments becomes a clear pattern. If you spend every free minute at the gym or the ballpark, the qualities attributed to the average "jock" naturally will be associated with you. If your free time is spent in church activities, or for the benefit of charitable, philanthropic or service organizations, others' assumptions that you are caring and giving will be reinforced. If every outing ends up at the local bar, you're likely to trigger the associations common to those who are thought to drink heavily.

When you plan any encounter, remember the importance of the setting to impression formation. Think of yourself as the movie director who considers the character and thematic development when she selects the set in which a scene takes place. Remember, the character of any set you choose will tend to merge with your own.

OTHER ENVIRONMENTAL FACTORS

A quick trip to the office late at night to pick up a report to study before your breakfast meeting leads you to the elevator bank. You're dressed in old jeans and a T-shirt, your hair isn't combed and you haven't shaved. The elevator door opens and inside is a lone young woman.

It's ten o'clock on Monday morning. When you step into the elevator in your freshly pressed suit you're alone with a young woman who works two floors above you.

If you're concerned about impressions, do you behave the same on both occasions? No.

If you are a man and enter an elevator with a lone woman late at night, you have created an uncomfortable environment for her. A friendly but reserved "hello," little eye contact and as much physical distance as can be achieved within the confines of the elevator will make you appear more caring and sensitive to her needs. Yet if you encountered the same woman in the elevator during the workday, an enthusiastic "hello," big smile, warm eye contact and a moderate distance would be more appropriate. Whenever you encounter someone in what might be an uncomfortable or hostile environment for him or her, take that into consideration as you implement your Impression Management Plan.

Other environmental factors such as the time of the day, week and year also should influence your behavior. If someone stops by your house early in the morning to pick up a file on her way to the airport for an early flight, she won't expect you to be bright-eyed, scrubbed, dressed and ready for the day. If you aren't you won't be judged harshly. But if she drops by in the afternoon and you meet her at the door in your bathrobe, disheveled and blurry-eyed, she will wonder why.

A man who sports a George Hamilton tan in the summer in southern California will appear healthy, outgoing and successful. If you take the time and effort to maintain that same tan during the winter months, those who encounter you may think you are vain.

No one will doubt an employee's dedication to her job if she stays up until the wee hours of the morning on the weekend. But if she habitually drags herself into work after a late night on the town, suspicions of her professionalism will arise. Her performance will be scrutinized more closely by her boss, who would expect her competence to be impaired. Deficiencies that otherwise may have gone unnoticed wouldn't escape detection.

YOUR HUMAN ENVIRONMENT

The 1999 massacre at Columbine High School in Littleton, Colorado, horrified us all. How could such a thing have happened? Why didn't teachers, school administrators, other students and most of all the killers' parents see the signs of resentment, hostility and hatred that led two students to turn their anger and weapons upon their classmates? As America struggled to answer these questions, a renewed awareness arose that, as Euripides wrote twenty-five hundred years ago, "A man is known by the company he keeps." Parents everywhere took a renewed interest in their children's friends.

The troubled teenagers at Columbine High were members of what was known at the school as the "Trenchcoat Mafia." Their friends, like they, espoused hatred and violence, saluted their friends like Nazis and frequently spoke German to one another. They were dissident, dissatisfied, disenfranchised, outcast, angry and ultimately violent. Friends and families of the murderers who claimed afterward that they seemed to be normal, well adjusted young men overlooked what was so obvious to the rest of the country.

Others will assume that you surround yourself with friends, lovers, business associates, employees and coworkers who fulfill your needs, and you theirs. They also will assume that your needs won't be met by those whose behavior and values are antithetical to yours.

We have seen many who have mismanaged their impression by including within their social or professional sphere those who by association discredit them: The businessman who wants to project an image of professionalism and competence, but retains a receptionist who can't seem to pick up the phone before the twelfth ring, and then directs the call to the wrong extension; the man who wants to impress his new girlfriend with his commitment to a monogamous relationship but spends his free time bar-hopping with his womanizing friends; or the clerk at work who hopes to project the image of someone who should be promoted to higher levels of responsibility within the company, but gossips at every break with known malcontents.

In one of our surveys in which we asked respondents to identify the traits with which they associate leadership, one man responded, "By who follows them." His observation was astute, and might well have continued, "and by whom he follows." You will be damned or exalted by association. As Confucius said, "Have no friends not equal to yourself."

CHAPTER 14

Success

"Knowledge—Zzzzzp!—Money—Zzzzzp!—Power! That's the cycle democracy is built on," Tennessee Williams wrote in *The Glass Menagerie*. It's also the standard by which most of us have come to measure success.

By this measure if you were to walk into a room full of strangers, you probably would be able to identify those who were successful, and those who weren't. Your tip-offs might be their clothing, their grooming, their bearing, their voice or their vocabulary. Most probably, it would be a combination of all their characteristics. A perfectly tailored suit accompanied by a bad haircut or scuffed shoes, vulgar language or an inarticulate way of expressing ideas won't carry the day. But in combination, you'll know if they have it—"Knowledge—Zzzzzp!—Money—Zzzzzp!—Power!"

Success today is measured quantitatively, not qualitatively. Parents don't boast that their son is the most "successful" person they know because he works as a park ranger and lives the life he chooses, in a way that makes him happy and satisfied that he contributes to society, or that their daughter is a "success" because she has raised three healthy, happy children. Instead those whose children have become doctors, lawyers or wealthy businesspeople are the ones who boast of their children's "successes."

In one of our surveys we asked the respondents to identify those traits that led them to believe people were "successful." The big winner was their appearance, and in particular how well they dressed, followed by their possessions and occupational status. Trailing in fourth place was their intelligence. Only four out of one hundred and twenty-five identified happiness as an indication of success. A single, and perhaps the most enlightened soul of the lot, said success, like beauty, "is in the eye of the beholder."

As we reviewed our survey results, the picture of success that emerged was one of Donald Trump, Madonna or George Steinbrenner. Clothing, cars, homes and jewelry were the watchwords. The qualities possessed by Gandhi or Mother Teresa weren't mentioned.

SUCCESS DOESN'T MEAN
SELLING YOUR SOUL

Even the Devil in his eternal search for the souls of man cannot force mortals to join his legions. But he can tempt them to voluntarily conscript. In the legend of *Faust,* memorialized by the German writer Goethe, the Devil wanted Faust's soul desperately and made Faust an offer he couldn't refuse. Faust would be blessed with what he most desired—youth. But in exchange, Faust had to agree that when he died he would relinquish his soul to the Devil. Faust made the deal and for years enjoyed the fruits of his shortsightedness. As his life drew to an end, Faust realized he had made a horrendous bargain.

While less dramatic than the choice Faust foolishly made, each of us makes a choice about how we live our lives—what we will sacrifice and what we will cherish.

Ultimately, your definition of "success" will depend upon your own value system. How you weigh the relative importance of the quality of your relationships, your status, possessions, achievement, spirituality, physical health and well-being and other factors is uniquely personal. It is not our purpose to cast judgment upon your individual definition of success, but only to urge you to examine your personal values, goals and objectives as you incorporate in your daily life the Impression Management skills and techniques we have described. Only you can assess who you want to be and how you want to live your life. The extent to which your actions blend seamlessly with your answers to these questions will define your personal success.

Dr. Albert Schweitzer was not "successful" by the definition of doctors whose objective is a thriving medical practice, and the wealth and material possessions it brings. He rejected a traditional medical career and chose instead to bring the benefits of modern medicine to the most remote regions of Africa. When he died at age ninety he had obtained a level of incomparable success when measured by his objectives, but not necessarily by others'.

Mother Teresa lived a life of abstinence and material simplicity. She devoted her entire life to improving the quality of the human condition throughout the world, and became one of the modern world's greatest symbols of love, compassion, charity and selflessness. Was she "successful?" Undeniably.

John D. Rockefeller personified the need to find "success" consistent with one's own values. He died when he was ninety-eight years old, satisfied that he had lived at least half of his life successfully. But even though he accumulated unsurpassed wealth for the first half of his existence in this world, his material "success" brought him little happiness. It was not until he discovered the personal joy and satisfaction of his remarkable philanthropy that he became "successful" in his own mind, and enjoyed the happiness that had eluded him for his first fifty years.

Before you set out to convey an image of "success," define it consistent with your own values. For some, Ferraris, multi-million-dollar estates and lavish vacations are the ultimate goal. Others' introspection will lead them to the conclusion that the term "material success" is an oxymoron.

We have given you the tools with which to forge an impression on others of who you are. But before you set out to convince the world that you possess certain qualities, be clear in your own mind not only where you begin, but where you hope to arrive. Before you turn your attention to "how," ask "why?"

We hope that the blend of our personal experience and research, and the wisdom of the greatest writers and thinkers of the ages upon whom we have relied, inspires you to find your way. And though we recognize that for each the path will be different, we know that your ultimate success will depend upon what qualities you display to others.

Throughout this book, we have urged you to be guided by the four points of the Compass—trustworthiness, caring, humility and capability. In every relationship, convey a deep-felt commitment to trustworthiness. Don't just be true to others; be true to yourself. Show others not just that they can believe you, but that they can believe *in* you. Let everyone in your life see that you care about them, that their needs, dreams and successes are as important to you as your own. Don't live life backwards: Love people, and use things, not the other way around. Live your life with humility—not a self-deprecating subservience, but a dignified recognition that you are an essential, but only *one,* spoke in the wheel that is your family, workplace and community—and not its hub. Resolve to be not just adequate at what you do at work, at home and in your community, but the best you can be.

Invariably, you will wander from the course you set in your efforts to show others the best you have to offer. In your moments of doubt, confusion and even failure, call upon the four points of the Compass as your guide. They will not fail you. You may stray, but you will never be lost if you know your way back.

Changing
from the Outside-In

K'ung-Fu-tzu, known as Confucius to the modern world, and Lao-Tzu, Confucius's legendary teacher and the founder of Taoism, lived in China approximately five hundred years before Christ, at about the same time that Buddha lived in Nepal and Socrates dominated the philosophical landscape of Greece. Confucius's sayings, which promoted specific desirable behaviors, reflect his emphasis on the value of *doing* the right thing. He believed: "By nature, men are nearly alike; by practice they get to be wide apart." The Taoist philosophy of Lao-Tzu emphasized instead how we should *be* internally in order to become a virtuous or "superior" person. Lao-Tzu taught: "The Master ... doesn't think about his actions; they flow from the core of his being."

As Alphonse Karr wrote 150 years ago, "The more things change the more they stay the same." Twenty-five hundred years after Confucius and Lao-Tzu debated whether the keys to a "superior" existence are found in inner qualities or outward actions, the debate rages on.

During the last half-century we have been encouraged to think positively, dress for success, invest in no-load mutual funds, eat garlic. We have been assured that we can effect change in our lives through the sheer power of our will, or by just altering the way we dress, talk and act.

Recently, however, the concept of putting positive thinking and behavioral modification to work to achieve positive change in our lives has been maligned as simply a way to trick the Fates—to achieve results without paying our moral and ethical dues, and without abiding by that ever-powerful governor, our conscience. For many, the ends have come to justify the means.

We agree that those who slap a coat of paint over a rotten foundation will find their successes are short-lived: Eventually the paint wears away. For years we have preached that anyone who believes that a person can fool ordinary folks into thinking he is someone he is not, if he just dresses, talks or acts in a carefully orchestrated manner, is dreadfully wrong.

But we also disagree with those who criticize those who strive to enhance the impression they make on others through their appearance, speech and actions. This may seem inconsistent; but it's not.

The criticism directed at efforts to modify appearance, speech and behavior to influence the impressions we make on others is based on the belief that people adapt or modify their "persona" solely to effect mere quick fixes, to manipulate or to deceive and to morph themselves, presumably only temporarily, into something they are not, in order to get something, do something or be something that brings them a measure of immediate gain. But the assumption that people seek external change without any real desire for internal improvement and growth has not been borne out either by our research or by our professional experience. After twenty years of constant interaction with people from every walk of life, some fighting for noble causes, and others on trial for unimaginably heinous crimes, we have found that it is only the rare psychopath who doesn't yearn to be a better human being.

Test our hypothesis by asking yourself why you bought this book. Was your objective to learn to manipulate, deceive or bully? Was it to learn a trick or two just to help you make it through that important sales presentation next week, or to get a date for Friday night? We doubt it. We believe your motivation was to learn to better project the positive characteristics you already possess, and to cultivate within yourself those traits that you most admire in others.

THE GENESIS OF CHANGE

German philosopher Immanuel Kant once posed the question: If a tree falls in the forest and no one is there, does it make a sound? The falling tree certainly sends sound waves through the air. But unless they impact an eardrum, which in turn vibrates and transmits impulses to a brain, which recognizes them as noise, did the falling tree really make a sound?

Kant's philosophical question illustrates that who we are, how we feel and what we believe exist only in the context of our relationships with others. Can a man who lives an isolated life in the middle of the desert be compassionate if he never has an opportunity to share another's concerns? Is he a leader if there is no one to lead? Can he be physically attractive if there's no one to attract?

Undeniably, those thoughts, values and beliefs that reside deep within us influence our actions. They are the inspiration for the images we paint on the canvas of our daily existence. But who we are, how we feel and what we believe are ultimately defined, not in the abstract, but by how we communicate our inner essence to others, and how they in turn respond. Qualities like love, compassion and friendship do not and cannot exist until they are shared; and they are shared only through our actions.

Just as inner change is ineffective without outward manifestation, it is folly to think your outward actions will lead to real change unless you view them as a vehicle for lasting inner change. No one can be happy if the way he lives his life conflicts with his true values. If his feelings and actions are not in sync, it will be just a matter of time before an intolerable conflict erupts.

How Can We Best Implement Change?

Almost everyone who has ever addressed the subject agrees that inner change is required for greater long-term success and happiness. Yet that begs the question. The question is, how do you effect inner change? William James laid out the road map almost a hundred years ago.

Action seems to follow feeling, but really action and feeling go together, and by regulating the action, which is under the more direct control of the will, we can regulate the feeling, which is not.

The cycle of change can begin with input from any of three different sources, as represented in this diagram.

Think of the cycle of change as a psychological waterwheel that will begin to turn if input is received from any of three separate ports: your feelings, the actions of others or your actions. Assume, for example, that you wanted to become more friendly.

1. You could change the way you feel, by resolving to *be* friendly. If you are able to make yourself *feel* friendly, you will naturally begin to *act* more friendly, which in turn will make people *respond* more *positively* toward you, which will make you *feel* friendlier toward them, which will make you *act* more friendly . . . and the cycle accelerates; or

2. Others could *act* more friendly toward you, which will make you *feel* more friendly, which will make you *act* more friendly toward them, . . . and the cycle will be repeated; or

3. You could change the way you *act* by showing friendly behavior, which will make people *respond* more positively, which will make you *feel* more friendly, which naturally will make you continue to *act* friendly . . . and off you go.

If any of these three ports is opened, the cycle will begin. But as William James noted, only one of the three alternative ways to initiate the cycle—*your actions*—is under your direct and conscious control.

You could wake up one morning and resolve, "Today, I'm going to *be* a friendlier person." That's certainly a start; but how many of us can turn our inner feelings on and off at will?

You also could wake up one morning and say, "Today, everyone I meet will smile and say, "Hello" to me." If they do, you will feel friendlier and act friendlier. But if you wait for others to initiate the process, you may wait indefinitely.

Finally, you could wake up one morning and say, "Today, I'm going to *act* friendlier by smiling and saying, "Hello," to everyone I meet." You can do that. It will take some effort and discipline at first, but at least it is within your direct and conscious control. That is why it is easier to change from the outside-in.

Outward Change Will Lead to Inner Change

Your emphasis on your external behavior should not turn your focus away from inner change, but act as a means to achieve it. As William James said, "Real action and feeling go together." The formula for change is simple:

POSITIVE ATTITUDE + OUTWARD ACTIONS + POSITIVE REINFORCEMENT = INNER CHANGE

Positive Attitude

The first step to effective change is a positive attitude. If you believe you can succeed, you become confident. With confidence, you enhance your abilities and the willingness of others to allow you to prove yourself. With the success that follows, you become even more confident, and even more capable.

The cycle can spiral either upward or downward. A defeatist attitude results in tentative actions and negative responses, which invite failure and a downward spiral. A positive attitude spawns positive actions and responses, and an upward spiral. Your attitude will create a self-fulfilling prophecy of either success or failure. As Henry Ford said, "Whether you think you can, or think you can't, you're probably right."

Positive thought is not the same as irrational confidence or delusional fantasy. Positive thought is the ability to see past that four-letter word "can't" and the fear of failure, and to visualize and be committed to success.

Don't Fear Failure

Psychological studies have found that when we attempt anything—from sports, to speaking, to learning, to relationship building—we succeed far more often than we fail. Nonetheless, most people avoid more opportunities for success than they pursue because they fear failure. The sad part is that when you do not make the attempt, you not only deny yourself the pleasure and enhanced confidence that comes from success, but your emotional brain records your nonattempt much the same as if you had attempted and failed. When you don't try, you don't avoid feeling like a failure; you assure those feelings. Don't dwell on the possibility of failure or you will damn yourself to it.

Focus on Your Potential,
Not Your Limitations

Most people focus on who or how they are at the moment, and not on who or how they could be in the future, and on their failures not their successes. As a result, 80 to 90 percent of adults have low self-esteem. It is their low self-esteem that causes their potential to lie dormant. Instead of celebrating who they are and what they can accomplish, they dwell on who they aren't and their limitations.

It is incredible how much you can wring out of each of the gifts with that you have been blessed with motivation and effort. Whatever the starting point, you can improve. Don't focus on your limitations. Concentrate on your potential—and you will not only reach it, you will expand it.

Visualize Success

Positive visualization techniques have been used effectively for years by sports psychologists to enhance athletes' performance. In one study, for example, students were divided into three groups. Each group shot basketball free throws on the first day. The first group then practiced shooting free throws for twenty minutes each day during the test period. The second group did nothing. The third group spent twenty minutes each day visualizing that they were shooting free throws successfully. When they were retested, the group that did nothing made no improvement. The group that physically practiced shooting free throws twenty minutes each day improved by 24 percent. The group that shot free throws for twenty minutes a day only in their minds improved by 23 percent.

As Doctor Maxwell Meltz noted in *Psycho-Cybernetics,* "The mind cannot tell the difference between an actual experience and one vividly imagined." Both imprint the same subconscious experience in our memories. Such imagined success creates the same positive reinforcement as real success.

It is easy to apply visualization techniques. If you're nervous before you make a presentation for the first time, your nervousness will show, and will hinder your performance. If you had actually made the presentation to receptive audiences on many occasions, you would be more relaxed and confident, and more effective. You can simulate previous success if you visualize walking into the room, smiling comfortably and speaking persuasively. In your mind's eye you can experience the audience reacting with pleasure and enthusiasm, and savor the sensation of success. If you play that image again and again, your emotional brain will believe that you have actually tried and succeeded many times before. When the curtain rises for real, your emotional brain, instead of cringing in fear, will tell you, "No problem, you've done this a hundred times before." You will not just *act* confident, you will have *become* confident.

Turn Positive Attitude into Positive Action

With a "can do" attitude, it is easy to move to the next step on the path to inner change: action. Even if you don't feel confident, friendly or in control, incorporate the looks, sounds and actions that project confidence, friendliness and control.

You can force yourself by conscious resolve to display the traits that reflect these and any other qualities, even at moments when you don't feel them. You can listen attentively even when you are impatient, smile even when you don't feel particularly outgoing, stand tall when you are insecure and show enthusiasm when you are bored. When you do, you will touch others in positive ways and influence their actions toward you.

Positive Reinforcement

A great attitude and positive actions can take you only so far. If you consistently bump up against a brick wall it won't be long before you retreat to the comfort and safety of your old habits, no matter how unproductive they may have been. Yet if your new approach brings rewards, it will carry you on. It's human nature. We stick with what works.

Psychologists don't agree on many things. However, one topic on which there is consensus is the power of positive reinforcement. Study after study has shown that everyone responds well to positive reinforcement. It may take longer in some instances and for some people, but eventually what works—brings us glory, money, affection—is replicated.

The positive reinforcement that results when you display traits that enhance others' attitudes toward you originates from two distinct, though related, reactions. First, when you show others more positive qualities they *directly* respond to you. You show them respect; they respect you. You show them friendship; they respond with kindness. You display honesty; they trust you. In the process they come to feel better about you, and you feel better about yourself. This reinforces your behavior because you receive a direct benefit.

But the return on your investment can be more indirect. You influence everyone in your life by your actions. Your employees, coworkers, bosses, spouses, children, friends and even casual acquaintances blossom with positive interaction. They become more productive and trustworthy employees, loving and sincere friends, cooperative and responsive mechanics, clerks or carpet cleaners. As they do, you benefit from their positive growth, which further reinforces your behavior.

CHANGE IN ACTION

Tim, a lawyer friend of ours, with whom we discussed our thoughts on the subject of inner change from outward action and positive reinforcement, told us about a neighbor he had known years earlier, and how his neighbor forever changed his life.

The neighbor, Bob, was a middle-aged man. He was good-looking, but not strikingly so; intelligent, but not brilliant; articulate, but not the most eloquent. Yet he became a successful businessman, had a wonderful family life and was liked and respected by everyone in the community. Why? While not unique in his appearance, intellect or gift of gab, he had the ability to make everyone he met feel special. He greeted everyone with a warm and engaging smile. His eyes twinkled with pleasure when he spoke. He called people by name, shook their hands warmly and asked about their jobs, hobbies and families, and truly listened when they spoke. Little wonder, he attracted friends and business colleagues.

Tim was by nature reserved. He had never been particularly friendly or outgoing. At social and business gatherings he frequently settled in at the periphery, an observer, not a participant. He rationalized his aloof behavior with the belief that it would be hypocritical for him to pretend to be "someone he wasn't" to lure potential clients, and even more offensive to bait new friends with unnatural behavior.

As he watched Bob in different situations, Tim marveled at how Bob's conversations always became animated, and were filled with smiles and laughter, well-meaning nods of the head and warmth. Tim resolved to mimic Bob, as an experiment if nothing else. After all, how could it hurt to be nice to everyone?

Within days Tim tested his new persona at a cocktail party during a legal conference. As Tim entered the room he drew a deep breath, stood up straight and walked up to the first person he saw, a young man who stood awkwardly alone by the hors d'oeuvres table. Tim reached out his hand, smiled, just as Bob smiled, and said, "Hi, I'm Tim Richards." The younger lawyer shook his hand and smiled back as he responded, "Hi, I'm Gary Sands."

"Where are you from?" Tim asked, and they were off. As the conversation continued, Tim saw his new friend relax and begin to enjoy himself. Before long, a passerby or two was drawn into their lively conversation— and so the evening passed.

As Tim told us the story, he smiled often and shook his head in amazement. "I met more people that night, and more of them have stayed in touch over the years than in the previous ten cocktail parties I attended.

The best part of it is, I never had such a great time. It took me about ten minutes to realize what I had missed—both personally and professionally."

With such positive reinforcement, Tim's behavior was forever modified. What was at first a conscious, even calculating, effort to force outward change evolved into the foundation of Tim's new, and *real,* character.

TRAVEL TIPS
FOR SUCCESSFUL CHANGE

Experience tells us that a person's ability to effect change successfully depends more on his attitude, motivation and approach than his knowledge or skill. Your ability to effect real, lasting change begins with a commitment to the fundamentals that great achievers in every field have discovered and utilized. These are basics that make the good better, and allow the great to reach unparalleled heights.

As you read on, don't just say, "Yeah, yeah, yeah. I know all this," unless you don't just *know* it, but you also *live* it. If you're one of the few who do, great. If you're like the rest of us, read these pages carefully; and stop at the end of each section and don't just say, "Yeah, I know that." Say, "Yeah, I know that; but this time, I really will do it!"

CHANGE MUST START TODAY,
OR IT NEVER WILL

How many smokers have you known who said, "I'll quit as soon as I finish this pack," or overweight people who said, "I'll start my diet after the dinner party on Saturday," or slobs who said, "I'll clean up this mess as soon as things slow down a bit." How many of them did? The ones who changed are the ones who snuffed out their cigarettes in disgust and threw away the rest of the pack, or pushed back their plates mid-meal, or stopped everything and cleaned up their home or office.

Start to make a better impression this instant. Smile at the next person you meet. Find something about him or her to admire, and express your admiration in a sincere compliment. Read a newspaper. Go for a walk or a jog. Throw out those tattered T-shirts. Resolve to incorporate our suggestions into your daily routine, starting now. Follow the wisdom of a Swahili proverb: "The prayer of the chicken hawk does not get the chicken." Convert your good intentions into action.

START FRESH

In business school they teach a concept known as "zero-sum management." It's an approach to management decisions that is designed to overcome our natural tendency to cling to the familiar, whether or not it works. If an executive wants to examine a company policy, she first puts aside whatever has been done historically, and focuses instead on what the policy should be.

Follow the same approach as you examine how you should look, speak and act to best achieve your objectives. Don't assume that there is some inherent value to the way you have always done things. Keep focused on becoming the best you can be, not how you have always been. The more this approach suggests the need for a major overhaul, the more critical it is that you follow it.

SET YOUR GOALS HIGH

Optimism must be tempered with realism. But defeatism, pessimism and limited vision are too often mistaken for realism. Sure, you may never have the rhetorical mastery of Martin Luther King, the beauty of Marilyn Monroe or the intellect of Einstein. If you are willing to settle for nothing less, you will throw up your hands and quit. But if you settle for only modest improvement or, even worse, the status quo, that's all you will experience. Stretch for greatness. Even if you don't reach your goal, you will travel much farther.

ACHIEVE YOUR GOALS
ONE STEP AT A TIME

Our obsession with immediate gratification is among the many changes in the American psyche over the past century. Only a few generations ago an agrarian American couple was content to spend their lifetimes carving out a homestead for themselves and future generations. Food was not acquired by a quick trip to the grocery store, let alone their favorite fast-food drive-through. Instead, it resulted from tilling, planting, nourishing and harvesting from season to season and year to year.

It is difficult for us to change too much, too quickly, without giving short shrift to the details that create a solid foundation for lasting change. We have only so much capacity to learn, and even less ability to incorporate what we have learned into natural, habitual behaviors.

As Buddha said, "Dripping water can fill a pitcher one drop at a time." Start with one or two goals that are particularly easy to achieve and will cause you no anxiety, such as improving your wardrobe, or getting a haircut. Tackle a new item on your Impression Management Plan every few days as you become comfortable with those you have already addressed. Keep at it until you have made every "do" a habit, and each "don't" a distant memory. Don't try to go from "A" to "Z" without attention to each of the twenty-six stops along the way.

EXPECT AND WELCOME HARD WORK

News Flash! If you think a few dollars and several hours spent reading this book is all you have to do to change your life, we have some bad news. *Success requires hard work and perseverance.* We know it's a shock, but as your kids would say, "Adjust."

Those of you who invest the time and energy over several months to manage your impressions will see incredible changes in your behavior and that of others toward you. Like anything else, what you get out of this process will depend upon how much of yourself you invest in it.

MAKE IT A HABIT

Old habits die hard. Everyone who has ever started an exercise routine knows how difficult it is at first to find the discipline to rise early in the morning or to break from a busy schedule midday and go to the gym or for a walk or a run. Yet as the routine becomes a habit, it becomes easier to sustain.

To implement your Impression Management Plan effectively, you must incorporate it into your regular routine. Don't just smile at some people, smile at them all, unless it obviously would be inappropriate. Always shake hands, dress better and talk with more assurance. As you do, these actions will become habitual. Once behaviors have become habits, you will experience three transformations: first, the behaviors will become easier; second, you won't have to "remember" to do them anymore; and third, they will appear more natural to others.

NEVER QUIT

Rome wasn't built in a day. It took time, and no doubt there were a few snafus along the way. The same is true of your new image. It will take time. You will have failures. Learn from them, adjust and move on.

Remember Mark Twain's words: "We should be careful to get out of an experience only the wisdom that is in it—and stop there, lest we be like the cat that sits down on a hot stove-lid. She will never sit down on a hot stove-lid again—and that is well; but also she will never sit down on a cold one anymore." Don't give up just because you fail on your first attempt, or even on your first few efforts. Learn from your failures as much as from your successes. When you fail, retool and try again; but never quit.

PUT *YOUR* BEST FOOT FORWARD

A few years ago Jo-Ellan found an old photograph of her college gradua-tion in a drawer. It had lain unnoticed for almost twenty-five years. The colors were faded and indistinct. It was blurry and lifeless. Yet she remem-bered that photograph well. It was one of her favorites.

She had just worked on a case in which computer enhancement was used to restore the vibrancy and clarity of some old photographs, and decided to see if she could bring that old photograph back to life. She left it with a photography lab, encouraged by the technician that, like Lazarus, it could be brought back from the dead. She hoped so, but couldn't have imagined the results. When she picked up the photograph, it was as if she had been magically transported back in time twenty-five years. Each detail was as clear as it had been the day it was printed. The colors had come alive. The images were striking, almost three-dimensional. It seemed a miracle.

Jo-Ellan didn't ask the lab technician to touch up the photograph. She wanted the photograph to be the most accurate reflection of that moment of her life—nothing more and nothing less. This is all that Impression Management demands of you—not that you pretend to have qualities you don't have and never will, but that you bring to light the unfulfilled potential that lies dormant within you.

About the Authors

JO-ELLAN DIMITRIUS, PH.D., coauthor of the best-seller *Reading People,* is the nation's leading expert on the meaning of appearance and behavior. She has been a consultant in more than 600 jury trials, including the Rodney King, John DuPont, McMartin Preschool, and O.J. Simpson cases. She has served as a consultant for many Fortune 100 companies, and has appeared on *Oprah,* the *Today* show, and *60 Minutes,* among many others, and has consulted and lectured internationally. She lives in the Los Angeles area.

MARK MAZZARELLA, also coauthor of the best-seller *Reading People,* has written and lectured extensively throughout the United States and abroad about impression formation and impression management. He also has been a practicing trial lawyer in San Diego for more than twenty years and is past chairman of the litigation section of the California State Bar.